Praise for *Heart Radical*

D0460448

"A lovely evocative book about travel and c. ...u iove. And language and teaching and dancing. And intimacy. If you have never been to China and Tibet—or if you have been many times—you'll enjoy this fresh and honest perspective."

—Sharman Apt Russell, author of *Within Our Grasp: Childhood Malnutrition Worldwide and the Revolution Taking Place to End It* and *Standing in the Light: My Life as a Pantheist*

"Anne Liu Kellor's memoir shows us how far we must go to approach understanding. Traversing two countries across two decades, *Heart Radical* gets at the multiple meanings of the heart in word, in practice, in physical and emotional use and evolution. Vivid with sensory experiences, this book offers us the chance to travel with Kellor, but also within our own interior landscapes to arrive at new and deeper ways of connecting to our hearts' most fervent and secret wishes. Kellor's nuanced, elegant, and poetic prose depicts the toughness of love, of language, how both can hurt and heal us, how we can use them against one another, or to uplift each other. The choice is ours."

—Khadijah Queen, author of *Anodyne* and *I'm So Fine*

"In *Heart Radical,* language becomes a rich metaphor for our own complicated and changing identities. 'To be radical,' Anne Liu Kellor tells us, 'is to be rooted in your essential nature.' In this soulful memoir, Kellor looks to the many ways language is a means of communication, yes, but can also be a barrier to a full understanding of ourselves and of each other. In following Kellor's journey to China and back again, we find ourselves searching for what is most radical—most essential—in our own hearts."

—Brenda Miller, author of *A Braided Heart: Essays on Writing and Form* and *An Earlier Life*

"Through personal and historical recollection and the language of wounding, *Heart Radical* speaks to land and culture, selfhood and belonging. To live within and without language, to ignore or embrace silence. This memoir is a refuge, a legacy, a heart breathing in one continuous motion."

—E. J. Koh, author of *The Magical Language of Others* and *A Lesser Love*

"*Heart Radical* is a richly absorbing, deeply moving book about one woman's search for identity, enlightenment, and connection. It's also a tender travel memoir that takes the reader on an unforgettable and intimate journey with the author as she grapples with being a twentysomething American in China—the country from which her mother immigrated. I loved this book. It's vulnerable, searching, insightful, riveting and beautifully written."

—Cheryl Strayed, author of *Wild* and *Tiny Beautiful Things*

Heart Radical

HEART RADICAL

A Search for Language, Love, and Belonging

Anne Liu Kellor

SHE WRITES PRESS

Copyright © 2021 Anne Liu Kellor

All rights reserved. No part of this publication may be reproduced, distributed, or transmitted in any form or by any means, including photocopying, recording, digital scanning, or other electronic or mechanical methods, without the prior written permission of the publisher, except in the case of brief quotations embodied in critical reviews and certain other noncommercial uses permitted by copyright law. For permission requests, please address She Writes Press.

Published 2021
Printed in the United States of America
Print ISBN: 978-1-64742-173-1
E-ISBN: 978-1-64742-174-8
Library of Congress Control Number: 2021908294

For information, address:
She Writes Press
1569 Solano Ave #546
Berkeley, CA 94707

She Writes Press is a division of SparkPoint Studio, LLC.

All company and/or product names may be trade names, logos, trademarks, and/or registered trademarks and are the property of their respective owners.

Names and identifying characteristics have been changed to protect the privacy of certain individuals.

for my ancestors

Contents

PART THREE: PILGRIM'S PATH

Author's Note

In writing this book, I relied extensively on detailed journals, research, and memory. While I did my best to represent my past as truthfully as possible, it is also a given that memory can be subjective. I changed most people's names out of respect for their privacy. This is my version of my story.

Introduction
On Language, Love, and Belonging

My entire life I've craved more words. Words nourished me when I was little, gave me refuge when I was lonely or confused. And words guided me in my twenties, when I set off from my home in the Pacific Northwest for Western China and often felt even more alone, but increasingly witnessed by myself on the written page. When I had few companions to speak to in English, and still too few words in Chinese. When I wanted close friendships and romantic love, but it felt more tangible to reach for ideas of spiritual union. All I knew was—I was filled with an intense longing and sorrow. Sorrow for the magnitude of suffering in the world, in China and Tibet, and within myself. Sorrow which I felt so clearly, but couldn't understand why I felt so deep. And as much as I wanted to be patient and not need to know or control exactly where my journey would take me, a huge part of me also wanted it all to make sense right away—a logical rational explanation of "why this is meant to be." Karma. Fate. My Path with a capital P. The People you are meant to meet. The Person you are meant to become. The ways in which you will be better loved once you do your Part to save the world.

Twenty-plus years later, I can't say I've eliminated that kind of ego-driven desire. But I can say that I've lived long enough to come back to my core of love and self-acceptance many times, in cycles.

Looking outward, looking inward. Outward. Inward. Over and over. Reaching for a sense of being settled in my skin.

Throughout these cycles, words have been my constant. My steady awareness: noticing, documenting, remembering. Making meaning. Writing. Yes, writing has saved me. Writing has filled me. Writing has emptied me. Writing has showered necessary, nourishing words, helping me to understand and reckon with my choices. And writing has brought me back to myself—again and again and again. A steady eye/I: witness. Lover. Guide. Friend.

Heart Radical is a record of a younger me, during a time when the trajectory of my life was still barely known, when I was just setting out on my Path with a capital P.

Now, there is still so much I do not know, but I do know that we each have an essential nature. And that it is our job to listen to that nature and figure out how to work with it, not how to become someone we are not.

Now, twenty-some years later, I am still the same person. And: I am vastly different. And so, I return to look at my past to discover what I may have forgotten in my middle age. For while I may no longer have the desire or ability to take off alone and forge a life in another country, I *am* able to see, name, and accept all of my layers with ever-sharpening clarity. To see how my story keeps changing, even if my essential longing—to love and be loved—remains the same.

PART ONE

MIRROR FACE

1

Searching for the Heart Radical

I am collecting heart words. Words in Chinese that are connected to the heart.

傷心 *Shang xin*: wounded heart; to be sad.

耐心 *Nai xin*: enduring heart; to be patient.

醉心 *Zui xin*: drunk heart; to be fascinated or enchanted.

I am fascinated by these words; my heart is drunk with this language.

I look in the dictionary under *xin*: 心. In Chinese, mind and heart are not held at a distance: *Xin*, 心, the word for heart, also means mind, feeling, or intention, as well as center, middle, or core. Remember this as I speak of the heart.

心潮 *Xin chao*: heart tide; a surge of emotion.

心病 *Xin bing*: heart ill; to be anxious or worry.

心虛 *Xin xu*: heart empty, false or weak; to feel guilty. Empty, like the loss you feel when you do not follow what you know. False, like the shame you feel when you do not speak your mind. Or weak, like the hot surge of regret when you hide yourself from yourself.

When I walked away from love, inside I knew, my heart knew it was bruised with sorrow. *Shang xin,* 傷心, wounded heart, I worked through each day, pushed babies in strollers and sang them sad songs, bided time until I could lie down in the shadows. Return to the darkness, be with the pain. Breathe deeply and rub slowly in circles.

If you do not give yourself love, then who will? If you cannot soothe your own wounds, then who will? The heart is a muscle. If you do not stretch and breathe into its tendons and suddenly find your core pushed, pulled, or strained—you will wake tender and sore. I'm not speaking in abstractions. I mean: a burn in your chest, a burn you press and massage gently with the palm of your hand to acknowledge.

小心 *Xiao xin:* small heart; to be careful.

開心 *Kai xin:* open heart; to be happy.

心血 *Xin xue:* heart blood; painstaking effort.

What is the blood of the heart? Can we afford to give it away? Must we feel pain before opening?

Four strokes of a brush form the shape of a heart. In Chinese, heart is a word that can join with other words to make new words, but sometimes the heart is hidden deeper. Sometimes, the heart is a "radical"—the part of a character that hints at its root meaning. *Water radical, hand radical, knife radical, heart radical . . .* I don't know which radical is present until I can see the character, examine each component, search for the meaning inside.

Once upon a time, the heart radical lived inside *ai,* 愛, the word for love. But now, they've simplified; a committee changed the characters and the heart radical is missing. In the middle of the character, instead of the four curved strokes of the heart, there is only a single straight line.

For now, both versions still live in my dictionary: the older one follows the new, shadowed between parentheses, like an afterthought, or a reminder.

2
Sky Burial

I know long bus rides in China. I know that the roads will be rough and filled with craters. I know not to grow alarmed if we break down, if we are delayed for hours before a pile of rocks that have fallen in the middle of a one-lane mountain road, or even if the passengers are asked to get out and push. I know how to squat and pee exposed on the side of the road or in a filthy shack over a hole of shit in the ground, if I must. I know I can wear my headphones and listen to cassette tapes while we ride. I know to get a window seat. I know how to sit back and watch the landscape pass by, relieved as it slowly grows more empty, mountainous and green, even though we will always be reminded of the presence of people, the Chinese who have worked this land for thousands of years.

I am good at being passive and patient.

Maybe I learned this from my childhood. Maybe I learned this from my people.

This time, the bus ride takes eleven hours, with no major breakdowns or delays. I have come to the town of Markam, in northern Sichuan, to escape Chengdu—the city where I've been waiting for the last month to hear if I will be offered a job teaching English in the fall. Chengdu's dense sticky heat, the pollution, the noise, the mosquitoes that attack me at night in my dorm room, and the stares from people on the streets—all of this has worn me down. So on a whim I decide to leave town early one morning, heading north to return to a remote Tibetan region in Sichuan province for the weekend, to the area that captured my heart on my first trip to China, three years ago, in 1996.

Now, when I finally arrive in Markam, I walk to find a pay phone and call the parents of a Tibetan monk I'd befriended in the States. But after I dial, I discover that the number does not match the area code for the region. Wrong town? Maybe I misunderstood my friend. Now what? I figure I can just look around and go back to Chengdu tomorrow. But first things first, I need to eat.

Crossing the street, I step into the first noodle shop I see, then order the local mainstay of beef noodle soup. Not long after I sit down, a young Chinese woman about my age walks in. She wears a dark blue sun hat with white flowers, a yellow windbreaker, jeans, Reeboks, and a giant black camera bag slung across her shoulder. "How much for a bowl of beef noodle soup?" she asks the young Tibetan woman behind the counter in Chinese, getting right to the point. "And for how big of a bowl? What about the *baozi*, are they fresh?"

I am the only other customer in this place, yet somehow it doesn't seem strange when the woman sits down next to me at my small wooden table. Short and slim, her dark hair pulled back in a ponytail, she introduces herself, "*Wo jiao Zhang Jie.*" Within a few minutes I learn that she is from Guangzhou, has just finished studying at the university, and now has a month free before her graduation ceremony. I am surprised she is traveling alone, especially here in these Tibetan regions, which many Chinese consider uncivilized and dangerous. Since my Chinese is far from fluent and she can speak a little English, we switch back and forth between languages. I tell her I am from America and have just graduated college myself. "I came to China for the first time three years ago and traveled then for six months," I say. This time, however, I plan to do more than just wander. This time I plan to become a teacher of English, once I finally secure a job.

As we talk, a monk comes into the restaurant, begging. I dig in my bag for small change, but the shopkeeper and Zhang Jie shoot him scornful looks.

"Don't give him money," she whispers in English.

"Why not?"

"They don't do anything. All they do is beg."

I withdraw my hand from my purse and slurp my noodle soup.

Before long the shopkeeper brings out Zhang Jie's bowl and a steamed meat bun. After a few bites she turns to me. "Are you going to Seda?"

"Where?"

"Seda," she repeats, then tells me of a monastery a day's journey from Markam. *Seda*. I didn't plan on seeking out any Tibetan monasteries this weekend, but I am intrigued.

"I tried to go to Seda today," Zhang Jie continues, "but there were no buses. There's a bus tomorrow morning at six. I just sat in my room and watched TV all day—there's nothing to see here. Why else would you come all this way?"

She seems to be suggesting I come with her. I'm not sure we are the best match in traveling partners, but why not? I'd feel disappointed if I just turned around and headed the eleven hours back to Chengdu, winding over potholed roads, forced to listen the whole way to blaring techno from the videos playing on a small TV at the front of the bus.

"Okay." I nod. "I'll go."

ঙ

The next morning I pack quickly inside my guesthouse and slip outside. The sky is still dark as I make my way to the bus station, gravel crunching beneath my feet. When I approach the minibus, the driver is hoisting sacks and boxes that belong to the other passengers up onto the roof. Zhang Jie sits near the front. *Zaoshang hao.* "Good morning," she says as I take a seat behind her next to the window. Here I'll be less squished by those who will no doubt sit on stools or bags in the aisles. Chinese buses must fill to capacity before they'll budge, ensuring a maximum return for the drivers. Even when you think that another person could not possibly squeeze in, another pair of old ladies with giant sacks slung over their shoulders will board.

Sipping on my thermos of hot tea as we wait for the bus to fill, I watch the first hint of pale light creep over the horizon. Soon the aisles grow piled with people's belongings, including a burlap sack of live chickens that blindly squawk, assaulted by unseen threats on all sides. The passengers are mostly Khampas, Tibetans from Kham, the southeastern region of Tibet, who are known for their fierce brazenness, horse-riding skills, and guerilla resistance to the Chinese government's attempts to seize their land in the late 1950s. I recognize the bright strands of red cloth that Khampas braid into their hair and then twist atop their heads, men and women alike. That, and their cowboy hats. Everything about them seems to symbolize the wild outback of this region. Their complexion is dark, their cheeks rosy pink, and their eyes stare at me with a mixture of amusement and curiosity.

I smile when I catch their gaze, but with Zhang Jie near me I feel less outgoing than I might on my own. I wonder how she sees the Tibetans, these people who are a part of her "one unified China," but who obviously live in a different world than her bustling capitalistic coastal city of Guangzhou. And I wonder how the Tibetans see us. As a mixed-race Chinese American backpacker with a white dad and Chinese mom, I never felt on my last trip like the Tibetans saw me as Chinese, even if we communicated in the language of their oppressor. While traveling through Tibetan parts of Sichuan, Gansu, and Qinghai provinces, I was often invited into their homes, where we communicated with gestures or a few words of Mandarin. Some of these areas were officially open to foreigners, but some were not.

On this trip, my plan is to travel this summer to the "real" Tibet, now deemed the "Tibetan Autonomous Region" by the Chinese, once I secure a job for the fall. I have a promising lead at a university in Chengdu's suburbs; an acquaintance back home put me in touch with his friend who is vacating his post, and the school agreed to interview me—even though I have little teaching experience (I've tutored writing at my college and ESL to immigrants, but that's about it). But I'm not worried; I love writing and I hope to transmit my love to my students, do more than just travel this time, find a community, and give back. And since Chengdu is the only place where a connection emerged, it felt like the right place to land. I want to be in an urban center, and in Chengdu, a city of nine million, I imagine I can meet other young artists and writers, "intellectuals" as they call them here. Chengdu also happens to be close to Chongqing, the city where my mom was born, though her family fled for Hong Kong when she was seven, and then to Taiwan.

But beyond all this, I like the fact that Chengdu is the take-off point for flights to Lhasa. Three years ago, I vowed I would return to China and to Tibet and learn more about their relationship. Back in the States I immersed myself in reading about Tibetan Buddhism and history and joined a month-long peace march to raise awareness for Tibet. Along the way, I befriended many Tibetan exiles, including Ani-la, a thirty-year-old nun. So many moments of synchronicity during that period told me I was on the right path, but I was also so confused about my role in it all—what did the story of China and Tibet's suffering have to do with me? How was this tied to my own purpose? I need to find out.

Now, traveling with Zhang Jie, I wonder if the Tibetans think I am Chinese, like her. Why wouldn't they? My clothing, my features, not to mention my lifestyle back home are all closer to Zhang Jie's than to theirs. How would they possibly guess that I have cried for their history, weeped for the cultural genocide of their people at the hands of the Chinese army? Their culture feels dear to me, and yet, this last year, I've stepped away from any activism. The question of whether Tibet can be saved from China's control feels too huge and idealistic. And the question of whether or not I am a true Buddhist feels like a riddle. I no longer want to tell others what they should think or do. I just know I needed to come back here. To see where my heart will lead me.

Now, I stare out the window listening to the mixtape I made before I left the States—*Flight of the Inner Winged Creature*—an eclectic mix of American rock and hip-hop, as well as Irish, African, and Indian music. The bus rattles over rocky dirt roads, winding higher across the plateau, passing grasslands devoid of human signs except for the occasional lone black or white tent, a tuft of smoke rising from within. Nomads. The people have to be somewhere, up in the hills tending their goats or fetching water from a distant stream. I think of how surprised they were each time they saw me on my last trip, wandering through their land. And yet how natural it was for them to smile and laugh with curiosity, then beckon me inside to drink yak butter tea.

Now, I watch as herds of dark brown and white yaks graze and romp about, their thick bushy tails swishing behind them. The Tibetans in the back of the bus give a little cry each time we hurtle over a particularly large hole, sending them bouncing up in their seats. All the Tibetans sit in the back of the bus . . . somehow this can not be a coincidence. What kind of wary co-existence is being played out here between the Tibetans and the Chinese passengers? What would they think of the variety show I watched on the TV on the minibus from Chengdu, showcasing "all 46" (the officially sanctioned number) of China's ethnic minority groups with three-minute dance numbers in traditional costumes? Smiling happy minorities. I want the Tibetans behind me to know that I am not like the Chinese, that I do not see them as barbaric or inferior, but I am not so eager to share my views with Zhang Jie, for I don't have the vocabulary to talk about politics or religion in Chinese. The pictures of the Dalai Lama that I brought as clandestine gifts and the photos of my Tibetan friends in the US will have to stay hidden in my bag for now. My smile will have to do.

After several hours on the road we stop for lunch at a little no-name shack whose sole business is probably buses like ours, the driver receiving a free lunch and commission. I sit at a table with a few Tibetan men, offering them some of my loose green tea as we each fill our thermoses with hot water. When Zhang Jie walks over with her plate of rice, meat, and vegetables, she looks at them uncomfortably. "Let's go sit at another table," she suggests. I oblige. After lunch, when I give our remaining food to a beggar who approaches, she looks at me strangely but doesn't say anything.

Back on the bus, we return to our old seats. At my side, a woman ceaselessly cracks sunflower seeds, spitting shells on the floor. The men smoke one cigarette after another. I let the two monks sitting behind me listen to my Walkman—they like the high soaring voice of Loreena McKennitt, but are perplexed by the electric guitar and soulful crooning of Ben Harper. As the bus winds higher, a few of the Tibetan women grow ill, leaning out the window to vomit or holding their heads low between their knees. Zhang Jie's head tilts to one side and I can tell she's fallen asleep, as have a few other passengers, their heads jarred upright every so often by a sudden bump, then slowly sinking back down toward their shoulders.

The bus grows silent as the afternoon wears on. I stare out the dusty window at the miles of endless yellow-green grasslands, framed by mountains on all sides. *I am back.* Back in this place that I've dreamed of for so long, back without having fully imagined I would be here so soon, back on a bus, watching the Tibetan landscape pass by. For three years I've longed to return to this region, yet nearly forgotten what it was that I missed.

Finally, as the sun sinks low into the sky, I see my first sign of the monastery: a lone monk walking at the edge of the road in a long burgundy robe. He glances up ands meets my eyes. Up ahead, I spot a row of white *chotens* or *stupas* marking the edge of a path that winds out of sight into a valley. *Seda*. Passengers begin to stir; we are here. The bus stops and a few people get off, the driver helping them retrieve their bags from the rooftop.

Zhang Jie turns to me. "We'll stay in the town tonight and go to the monastery in the morning." I nod.

After another mile or so we arrive in town, one dusty street with a few shops and restaurants that reminds me again of the Wild West, a few men even riding on horseback. At the guesthouse, I let Zhang Jie do the talking. She gives the Chinese woman proprietor her *shenfenzheng*, the identity card all Chinese must show before registering.

"What about her *shenfenzheng*?" The stodgy, gruff woman gestures to me suspiciously.

"One *shenfenzheng* is enough, isn't it? You don't need both of ours." The woman shakes her head. "I need both of your *shenfenzheng*."

Zhang Jie sighs as if this is an unusual request. "She's a *Huaren*," she explains. "She doesn't have a *shenfenzheng*." *Huaren*. Overseas Chinese. Zhang Jie didn't say *Meiguoren*, American. Blood affinity is established. *She's one of us*.

The woman seems to be relenting, but still shakes her head. "Must have *shenfenzheng*. Foreigners can't stay here."

Zhang Jie sighs again. "Come on," she pleads with exasperated aloofness, "it's only for a few nights. Anyway, her mother is Chinese." I stand to Zhang Jie's side trying to appear pleasant and non-threatening. Suddenly grateful to be traveling with her, I admire her feisty, not easily daunted character, a quality which reminds me of my mother. The guesthouse owner finally gives in. *Hao le, hao le.*

"Fine, fine, write down your name." She thrusts out a form, takes our money, grabs a ring of keys from a nail near the door, and leads us to our room.

Inside, an old rusty stove sits between two hard twin beds on a bare wooden floor. I set down my backpack, then step outside to take in our surroundings. In front of our room is a small field with a few grazing yaks. The sun sets behind silhouetted peaks, and I breathe in the familiar smell of burning coal and yak dung, overcome with a sense of elation. Here I am, out under the open sky, out of the oppressive city, and beyond any place that has yet been claimed by my guidebook. Just like some of the areas I stumbled upon during my last trip, Seda is not open to foreigners. But this time, traveling with Zhang Jie, I will not get kicked out. Instead, I've been allowed to slip inside and stay, a renegade visitor on a stealth mission, protected by my Chinese decoy friend.

I wander off to find the toilets, or rather the holes in the ground to squat over, and when I return Zhang Jie sits talking in our room with a tall young man in his late twenties, dressed in a sporty red and black windbreaker and matching pants. "This is Xiao Mao." He rises to shake my hand limply, meeting my eyes briefly from behind wire-rimmed glasses. "He's from Tianjin," Zhang Jie says, and I nod. I know that Tianjin is a big city near Beijing where a distant uncle of mine lives—an uncle whom my mother has not heard from in many years. Sitting on my bed, I listen as they talk, picking up bits and pieces of Xiao Mao's story. He tells Zhang Jie how he first came to Seda two years ago and stayed for a whole year, building a little wooden cabin and studying Tibetan Buddhism. Last year, he went home to save up money, and now he is back for a short visit. He speaks quietly, his expressions restrained. I've never met a Chinese person who studies Tibetan Buddhism, and I want to ask Xiao Mao what led him to Buddhism and to Seda, but I'm not even sure how to say Buddhism in Chinese, for I understand so much more than I can say. Zhang Jie seems animated, speaking faster and with more complicated words than she uses with me. Not wanting to interrupt the flow of their conversation, I sort through my backpack and listen. After Xiao Mao leaves, Zhang Jie volunteers to make a fire. I stretch out on the bed and watch as she intently arranges a few strips of wood on top of a small pile of coal in the stove. It occurs to me that this is the first time that I've shared a room with a Chinese traveler, for it is rare to meet Chinese backpackers and usually hotels place them in separate dorm rooms, apart from us foreigners. Zhang Jie crumples a ball of newspaper, then lights a match and carefully blows on the small flame.

Huddling under filthy bed quilts and several layers of clothes, we talk about college. She was a business major; I studied writing, art, and dance. I try to explain how we were allowed to create independent contracts and then travel or study subjects of our own choosing. "Did you do that?" she asks, but I shake my head. How could I tell her about the peace march? About the way we gave presentations on Tibetan human rights and the Chinese government's invasion? How could I tell her about the spark of connection I felt with Tibetans, without somehow drawing comparisons to the "less-open" or "less-friendly" Chinese? And how could I begin to express how much I mourned for China's history, too. For the thousands of students killed ten years ago at Tiananmen Square, or for the 30 to 40 *million* killed during Mao's Great Leap Forward—numbers I can barely comprehend with my mind, but can attempt to grasp with my heart. I fear that without the vocabulary to get into my views in depth, my stories would only confirm that Americans are always chastising the Chinese or acting as the "world's policemen," especially now after the US recently bombed the Chinese embassy in Belgrade, supposedly by "accident." I've already noticed how the people on the streets of Chengdu have felt colder to me on this trip, the stares a little more incessant. Whereas a couple years ago their stares felt friendlier, especially once I smiled and broke the ice, this time many glare at me as I walk by—my presence clearly foreign, even if my mixed-race features and fluent-sounding tones confuse them. So for now, it feels easier to just stay silent and observe, to let Zhang Jie believe that she invited me to a place where I have no prior connection.

The next morning we rise early and board a black jeep with Xiao Mao, a Tibetan monk, and the driver. The sky a clear blue, the hills blanketed with green, we ride back to the *chotens* we passed the day before, then turn to head up the dirt road to the monastery. "They call the monastery the heart of a lotus flower," I think Xiao Mao says, explaining how it is nestled on four sides by rounded peaks. Our jeep winds up the bumpy path, leaving thick plumes of dust behind. After about five minutes, we turn a corner and suddenly the hillside is covered with small wooden structures—what must be the quarters of the monks and nuns. Long draping cloths with Tibetan symbols hang in place of doors. I think Xiao Mao says that there are almost 10,000 monks and nuns studying here at Seda, but I can't believe these numbers. Did I understand him right? No, can't be. Maybe he said 1,000; still impressive for a faith that is only cautiously tolerated. Either way, I know there has been a resurgence of religious activity in the last ten or fifteen years, and that the government is more relaxed in these Tibetan areas of China's Western provinces than it is in the official Tibet.

A few monks stare curiously as we step out of the dusty jeep. The air is cool and fresh, tinged with the scent of burning coal and juniper. Xiao Mao leads us through a complex of temples, cabins, and shack-like wooden stores that sell pictures of the monastery's lama, books of scriptures, bowls of instant noodles, and bottles of Pepsi. If it wasn't for such reminders of the modern world, we could be in a medieval monastic village. Many of the temples are newly built or being repaired by monks who busily hammer, saw, and paint Tibetan symbols on wooden beams in bright red, yellow, green, blue, fuchsia, and white. At the top of a hill, a small group of pilgrims circle an unfinished temple, its roof partially covered with a shining plate of gold.

After we tour the area, Xiao Mao leads us to a tiny dark restaurant to eat some *baozi*, steamed meat dumplings, known as *momos* in Tibetan. We sit on little stools before a low wooden table, the only customers in the place. A monk comes out of the kitchen with a few small glasses of hot water. As my eyes adjust to the dimness, Zhang Jie asks Xiao Mao more questions about the monastery. I can never be sure I am getting the details right. I understand him to say that the monastery was bombed during the Cultural Revolution, which does not surprise me; most religious structures were destroyed back then, one way or another. Yet now, apparently the government is allowing Seda's recent growth to unfold under a watchful eye.

"How many Han Chinese did you say are studying here?" I finally ask. Han is the ethnic Chinese majority.

"Over three hundred maybe," he replies.

"And it's okay for them to come here?"

"Yes. There is a special temple for the Han students where the instructions are given in Mandarin."

I had no idea so many Chinese were interested in Tibetan Buddhism, but it makes sense; after all, they are a lot closer to Tibet than those of us who come from the West, and Buddhism itself is deeply ingrained in Chinese culture.

"So the government allows this? They don't care?"

"Yes, they know. Sometimes they come around and make them tear down some of the cabins. They say it's for health reasons. But then they go away."

"Health reasons?"

"Yes. The stream that comes from the mountains is becoming polluted."

I nod, thinking of the piles of plastic bags, bottles, and waste I saw.

Xiao Mao looks at me closely. "Why are you so interested? Are you Buddhist?"

"No." I shake my head, my cheeks growing hot. "I'm just curious."

"I can take you both to visit the lama here if you'd like," Xiao Mao says.

Zhang Jie quickly shakes her head. I feel a tug of longing to meet the holy man that presides over this place—what would it feel like to stand before him? Might I feel a flash of recognition, like our meeting was meant to be? But then I, too, shake my head no. I don't want to be an opportunistic Westerner of dubious faith, coveting an interesting encounter with a "real Tibetan lama." And mostly, it is too hard to imagine trying to explain to Xiao Mao and Zhang Jie all my layers of belief and disbelief. Although I am drawn to Buddhist teachings, I struggle with Tibetan Buddhism's more mystical or mythical elements. Despite my growing collection of dharma books and my attempts at meditation, I still do not call myself a Buddhist.

After eating our fill of hard stale dumplings, Zhang Jie asks Xiao Mao about something called *tian zang*. He nods. Yes. He has visited them before.

"Do you know what a *tian zang* is?" Zhang Jie turns to me.

I shake my head.

"You know, when Tibetans die and leave the bodies for the birds?"

"Oh. Yes." *Sky burials.*

"Can you take us to one?" Zhang Jie asks Xiao Mao.

He hesitates before nodding. "They have them every day. We can go later this afternoon if you'd like."

"Do you want to go?" Zhang Jie asks me.

I glance at Xiao Mao. "Are you sure it's okay?"

"It's fine," he says, staring at his hands. "They don't mind if people watch."

ا۳

We step out of the restaurant as a morning prayer session is just coming to an end. Monks and nuns spill out of a nearby temple's doorway, so Zhang Jie and I walk over to peek inside. All around an open courtyard, strands of pink, red, and yellow fake flowers wind around the railings of the wooden balcony. Chanting plays from a loudspeaker affixed somewhere above; a few older pilgrims, stand grasping prayer wheels, their leathery faces upturned, listening. The courtyard buzzes with small clusters of monks—no, wait; it is hard to tell with their shorn heads, but soon I realize they are women.

Zhang Jie and I drift apart taking photos, while the nuns chatter noisily and watch us approach. They nod and gather close together when I motion to my camera and ask permission in Chinese. *Zhao xiang?* Some smile shyly, others pose stiffly, and one stares brazenly, almost smirking, entertained. I can tell we are not the first tourists that have ever come through, and yet there probably haven't been many, for the nuns don't seem resentful yet toward our presence.

A young nun, maybe seven or eight years old, grabs my hand and tugs. With one hand, I take a photo of her face staring up at me, her hand holding my own, my arm outstretched, her dark brown eyes gazing directly into my camera. What do I represent to her? The vast unknown world outside this mountain valley? I glance at Zhang Jie, busy snapping away on the other side of the courtyard. Then, from my pocket, I take out a photo of the Dalai Lama and slip it to the little nun. Snatching it, she runs off to show the others. I can't be sure, but I sense she doesn't know who it is. No one mobs me afterward, begging for more. Could they have never seen the Dalai Lama's image? I know it is forbidden in the temples, although I thought most Tibetans would still have seen it before. But maybe not, especially in these Tibetan areas of western China that have long been assimilated, more removed from the politicization of Lhasa. I walk around slowly, taking more photos, exchanging more smiles, token connections. I pass out a few more Dalai Lama pictures to a similar muted appreciation, and then it is time to go.

ا

Xiao Mao leads us away from the monastery to a path that travels around a hillside to another valley. Approaching the sky burial site from afar, I see a small gathering of Tibetans, a horse grazing to their side. Smoke drifts from somewhere near a small white *choten* draped with prayer flags. Drawing closer, I am hit by a thick, pungent, slightly sweet smell—bodies and decay. Also juniper burning. A few heads turn our way, but no one pays us much attention. I try to take slow, careful steps, not wanting my presence to be more obtrusive than it is.

Then I see the vultures.

They are so huge I mistake them at first for goats. They wait on the hillside above. Zhang Jie, Xiao Mao, and I sit near the base of the hill, keeping our distance from the family members and sky burial site, yet still close enough that I can see clearly the two corpses laying in a crumpled heap on the ground. Their tufts of matted black hair, their ribs exposed: a young man and an old woman, their sex and age still roughly discernable. Tattered remnants of old clothes lay scattered nearby, colors faded.

A Tibetan monk walks back and forth casually between the bodies, carrying a leg here, an arm there, placing them on a flat rock and then hacking them into smaller pieces. The man moves slowly, nonchalantly, as if he is going about the actions of an ordinary day. Which he is. This is his job.

I stare. With the exception of seeing my uncle in a funeral casket when I was nine, made up and pasty in full-suit attire, this is the first time I've seen a dead body. Zhang Jie and Xiao Mao move in closer to stand near a small group of people up front, but I stay back on the hillside, near the others, family members I assume, who sit clustered in two small groups. I don't sense in them the same solemn nature that one would expect from a funeral service, but instead they recline as if hanging out at a picnic. Sitting with my knees pulled up in front of me, I notice how the grass is dotted with delicate yellow and white flowers. Looking closer, I see it is also scattered with feathers and small shards of bone.

Covering my mouth and nose with my sleeve, I watch as the burial man shuffles back and forth. My eyes insistently return to the corpses, as if trying to convince myself that I am really staring at what just days or weeks ago were two live human beings. I don't know much about sky burials, only that they are as common as cremation is to us in the West. Do the Tibetans see this ritual as an offering, I wonder, a continuation of the food chain, a relationship between the cycles of life and death? Do they believe the birds will carry the spirits of the dead to the heavens? Or have the spirits already departed in the days before? But Buddhism doesn't believe in a fixed, unchanging spirit or self or soul. The Buddha taught that what we refer to as our "selves" is a combination of physical and mental aggregates, something like energies that are constantly changing from one moment to the next. If there is never one fixed, unchanging self or soul to begin with, then there can be no fixed person or self to be reborn. Instead, life and death is a continuous unbroken series of change.

Buddhism, of course, has changed since it spread to Tibet from India around the end of the 8th century, morphing with the gods and rituals of Tibet's native Bon religion. I know nothing about what form of Buddhism the Tibetans at Seda believe in or what they trust will happen to their loved ones when they die. I also won't learn until later that sky burials are a ritual that grew out of practical necessity, for there is a high death rate in Tibet, little firewood for cremation, and scarce land suitable for burial in the ground. Sky burials are thus a logical solution, believed to have emerged sometime after Buddhism was introduced to Tibet.

At some point, the vultures stir. I didn't notice the burial man give a signal, but somehow, the birds know he is ready. Before I realize what is happening, they begin to rush down the hillside—half flying, half running and hopping—leaping with an ancient, prehistoric gait.

"My God!" I cry as I jump to my feet, hurrying out of their way. Squawking and vying for position, they swoop in to pick and tear at scraps of flesh. Zhang Jie begins taking pictures, and I take out my camera as well. Some birds wait at the edge of the flock. Others dive right into the center, the greediest or hungriest of them all.

The burial man turns toward us and waves angrily. "No pictures," Xiao Mao says quietly. Of course. I should've known better and guiltily put my camera away.

After about five minutes of watching the birds' frenzied feeding from the side, the burial man wanders back into their midst. They scatter, allowing him to retrieve some pieces of bone and smash them even more. Was the last thing he produced the head? He cracks something with his mallet that sounds like a skull, then throws it toward the birds, who dive in with increased fervor. Zhang Jie takes out her camera to sneak in a few more photos. I motion to her, annoyed. *Who cares*, she shrugs. *He's not looking.*

The whole ritual lasts about thirty minutes. Afterward, the birds begin to fly into the sky, circling in wide arcs above the valley. Hundreds of them, or so it seems. As the vultures fly off, family members rise and gradually disperse. A young couple approaches us, leading a horse behind them. They nod and give us each a piece of hard candy. Another part of the ritual? Candy for the attendees? I take off the wrapper and suck on the sweetness, the smell of death lingering all around.

As the three of us leave, Zhang Jie lags behind Xiao Mao and me, taking more pictures of the sky burial site and the valley. I feel a weight in my chest for my own photos, and Zhang Jie's flippant shrug rubs in my shame all the more. What does she see in this ritual? Some savage act of uncivilized beasts? Something she can show her friends back home so they will be impressed by her bravery? But am I really that different? I resent her influence on me, and yet in many ways we are the same—swooping in to ingest this world with our hungry questions and eyes, wanting to take a piece of it home so we can try to remember what we saw and felt. A moment of reckoning: *this is what will happen to us*—whether we choose to face it or not.

I let myself drift away from Zhang Jie, not wanting to wait for her as she continues to take photos. Xiao Mao walks silently ahead. I wonder if he regrets taking us here, with our need to document and preserve.

"Look!" Zhang Jie calls out as she runs to catch up with us, pointing up into the sky. I look. The clouds have parted to shape the perfect arc of a bird with its wings outstretched. I can't resist. One last shot.

But I should have known better. For when I develop the pictures months later, the sky and the clouds hover overhead, but the bird is nowhere to be found.

3

Mirror Face

Every woman who lives in a house has a mirror face. A way she examines her reflection, tilts her head, casts her eyes, gauges her own appearance. After putting on makeup or combing her hair, she makes a final assessment of how she appears—or rather, what she thinks she looks like to others—before she walks out the door into public.

My mirror face took hold in middle school, a time when I became obsessed by how I was seen. Every morning I rushed to the bathroom mirror to see whether my eyes would match or not. The left lid always had a crease in the middle, like a Westerner's eye, but the right eyelid would sometimes grow puffy and fail to fold on days when I hadn't gotten enough rest. At the time, I did not think of my creaseless eye as looking more "Chinese," but I did know it made me look sleepier—or uglier. Before long I figured out that if I held my finger to my lid for several minutes, I could train my eye to fold again as it should. My mom also assured me that a simple surgery could correct this when I got older. I don't remember if this made me feel better, but it did affirm that my fold-less "Chinese eye" was indeed a problem.

心

No one in my family wanted me to go to China the first time—not my mother, not my grandmother, nor the rest of my Chinese relatives.

They said the mainland was dangerous, dirty, and backwards. I was twenty-one and bought my ticket anyway, with an open-ended return, thinking I might stay and teach English in Taiwan, where one of my uncles still lived, but first I would travel in China with no real plan except to head west.

It felt amazing to speak Chinese again. So much started flooding back to me, so much vocabulary, but most of all the *feeling* of living and breathing inside this language, this language I spoke as a child but less and less as an adult. I proudly took the lead at times with other travelers, ordering up big feasts in restaurants with no menus, buying bus tickets, or negotiating rides. I loved to impress the locals with my good pronunciation. *Ni shi nali ren?* Where are you from? people would ask, confused by my Western features yet Chinese resemblance and the fluent tones coming out of my mouth. I'm American, I'd explain (knowing they equate "American" with white), but my mother is Chinese. *Ah, guaibude!* They'd say, eyes lighting in comprehension. *Hunxue!* Mixed blood. I'd go on to explain how my mom was born in Chongqing, but grew up in Taiwan, and their eyes would shift slightly—*ah, one of those.* Yet still I felt welcomed into their fold. And on the morning when I woke and realized that I'd actually been *dreaming* in Chinese, I knew I'd finally re-inhabited a part of myself that I hadn't even realized I'd lost.

This first trip was only the beginning. I knew I had to come back.

From fourth through twelfth grade I was bussed from the mostly white neighborhood where I lived to the mostly black neighborhood where I attended school. Steeped in Martin Luther King Day assemblies, not to mention post-Rodney King school-wide discussions, I was proud to go to a high school that was more integrated than most in segregated Seattle. But it wasn't until many years down the road that I'd learn to look more critically at the racial divisions in my school, with most of the students in the honors classes being white, and most of the students in the "regular" classes being black—and where I fit into that picture.

In high school, conversations around race were mostly framed around black and white, and when I looked at my friends, my neighborhood, my privilege, my speech, my musical tastes, it was clear that I belonged to the white side of this discussion. As a bussed-in from the north end, upper-middle class, half-Chinese and half-white girl, my claim to being a cultural minority seemed vaguely interesting in a "we eat these foods" sort of way, but to identify with those who had been oppressed seemed laughable. Sure, there was that Ching Chong Chinaman joke made once in gym class by a black classmate, and another "fresh off the boat" comment made years later by a white guy, but they were comments overheard, not lobbed directly at me, and I don't remember feeling that hurt or implicated since I clearly was not "that" kind of Asian. This, too, is probably why I didn't think twice about mimicking the character Long Duk Dong from *Sixteen Candles* along with my friends, evoking a stereotypical "Asian accent." Whiteness, assimilation, and the model minority myth had taught me to distance myself from my Chinese roots, well before I even knew any of those terms.

If you'd asked me then, I probably would have said I was proud of being half Chinese, for on a conscious level, I was; after all, I'd been schooled by my fierce and educated mother since I was little and grew up playing with many Chinese families. And yet, once I reached puberty, I wasn't so keen on being picked up from the movie theatre with a packed car full of Chinese relatives. And I rarely spoke Chinese in public. As a young child my sister and I had been spoken to primarily in Chinese, yet every year that I spent in school served to imprint English as my dominant language. Over time I grew more and more reluctant to speak Chinese, ashamed of how poorly I spoke with my grandmother. At home my mother still spoke to me in her native tongue, but mostly I answered her in English.

Then came college, when I chose to go to a largely white, private liberal arts school in Minnesota. Now, despite my college's purported focus on multiculturalism, I was aware of my presence as one of the few non-white people in the classroom, and the implicit expectation that I should now represent from this place of identity. I began to examine the ways in which I'd distanced myself from my childhood Chinese friends and from speaking Chinese as I grew older. I thought about how Chinese was my first language, since I was primarily raised by my grandmother who lived with us when I was young, yet now I could barely speak it. I knew next to nothing about Asian-American history or China. And I hadn't, before now, thought about how Asian women were stereotyped and sexualized as either exotic "dragon ladies" or shy, meek, and demure. And most of all, we were simply absent: absent from the books and media I consumed; absent from the public eye, much less from positions of power. I'd never had anyone point this out to me before. And nor had anyone ever talked to me about what it was like to grow up *multiracial*—neither white nor fully Chinese, nor yet invited into a wider inclusivity as a person of color. Instead, everywhere I went, even at family reunions, I was simply reminded of my difference.

心

Race and ethnicity, of course, were only part of my evolving identity. Practiced at the art of obsessively combing my hair and checking myself out in the mirror since I was young, by college I was all too aware of how men watched me while walking down the streets or halls, and by the way my face and body seemed to be my greatest assets. Self-consciousness and a desire to please others had shadowed me for years—who liked me, how I sounded, how I was seen. I barely spoke in class and had to force myself to participate even a tiny bit. How much of this had to do with gender, and how much had to do with race? That wasn't a question I knew how to ask back then. All I knew was, once I was away from home, apart from my tight circle of high school girlfriends, I became painfully aware of how afraid I was of speaking out in a group, whether sitting in class or around a crowded cafeteria table.

Something shifted for me, however, the summer after my freshman year when my old friend Beth and I went to Alaska to work in a cannery in Bristol Bay. Here, we wandered the beach during the slow periods or worked 18-hour shifts during peak. Mostly we worked the night shift in the frozen section, tossing, sorting, bagging, and weighing huge, rock-solid salmon for hours at a time. But most significant to me was that, for the first time in eight years, I didn't wear eyeliner, a ritual I'd adopted since I was eleven, never going out without it. I'd learned it from my sister who was a year and a half older—a dark thin line painted near the lashes with a little brush dipped first in water and then in the black cake of makeup, all of which was stored in a rectangular silver box. The only problem, however, was when my right eye would fail to fold properly, I could no longer apply makeup on that eye in the same way. Instead, I needed to draw the line in the middle of my lid so the line could be seen, like my mother did with her eyeliner. "You messed up your makeup," a boy I liked said to me one day in class. I can't remember my reply, just my shame, unable to tell him that I'd drawn it that way on purpose.

In Alaska, however, I knew how ridiculous it would be to primp before slinging dead fish, and it didn't take long for me to feel liberated from this practice, comfortable in my uniform of hiking boots and yellow waders.

Later that fall, when I returned to college, I chose a single dorm room and began spending more time alone. I grew disillusioned with my routine of intensive studying on weekdays and drunken weekend nights, but I felt claustrophobic staying in my tiny jail cell of a room on the weekends. Inspired by the Buddhist and Taoist texts I was reading for class, I tried to meditate for the first time, sitting on my bed on a Friday night, listening to the sounds of doors slamming up and down the halls—but my mind could not stop thinking for even five seconds. Minnesota was cold, I didn't have a car, I felt trapped on campus. I missed the Northwest, the trees, the air, the salt water, and I envied the hippy wandering lifestyle that some of my old friends were adopting. I was tired of being the good girl, trapped in a shell of shyness and perfectionism, so groomed to strive for others' acceptance that she was afraid to speak spontaneously.

What would it be like if I could truly live from the present moment? Eating psychedelic mushrooms a couple times with friends gave me a taste of this feeling, a taste of an experience where my strong sense of ego—in other words my fear of what others thought of me and my self-esteem's dependency on their approval—began to dissolve; where instead all of my senses felt heightened and alive, where my whole body felt intrinsically connected to—inseperable from—the rest of humanity, nature, the cosmos. But, of course, I could not sustain this kind of awareness. I suspected that meditation and Buddhism could be a path toward learning to live within the present moment that did not involve drugs. And although I was a novice when it came to owning a desire to embrace a spiritual path, I also intuited that I would not find what I needed if I stayed at this small, mostly white, private college.

It was around this time that I knew I needed to go to China. After initially studying Russian, I'd switched to beginning Chinese, realizing it was much more important that I become fluent in my mother tongue. In class, however, I was far more advanced than my peers with the spoken language, but I had to start at the beginning like everyone else since I couldn't write more than a few characters. I knew I could learn Chinese much faster through immersion. I also knew I could learn more from traveling than from staying in this enclave of privileged youth. So I decided to go on leave for a year, to save money and then travel through China. Inside, however, I already knew I wouldn't be back.

心

On my first trip to China, I really began to understand for the first time how it could be an advantage to belong to more than one culture and language. The longer and further west I traveled, the more I could go days without speaking to another foreigner, sometimes avoiding them altogether, even when staying in their midst. Alone, I found that locals opened up more easily, inviting me into their homes for a meal or as an overnight guest. Over many months, I moved in between solitude and companionship—proud of my ability to offer up advice to other English-speaking travelers, drinking and telling stories into the late hours, as well as my ability to turn down invitations and embrace solitude when I pleased. The less boxed in I felt to the old version of "me"—the approval-seeking schoolgirl plagued by a self-consciousness whose source she couldn't yet name—the more I felt confident and free. And the more I experienced a fluid identity, drifting between languages and different people each day, the easier it was to share myself anew.

In 1996, e-mail was not available in China (even in the US it was still a novelty) and international calls were hard to make, so instead I wrote long letters and went weeks without speaking to my family. With no one to report to, no business to check up on, and no agenda except to make my few thousand dollars last as long as possible, I felt released of obligations to others and free to truly live in the moment, in a way that maybe only a monastic or a really young person can. At times I felt incredibly lonely, but I also could choose to stay or move on whenever I wanted. My sense of self was not hinged upon who I was with, or whether or not I remained with a companion or crowd.

Of course, much of this would fade in time, after I went back to America. Of course, it would take more than six months of backpacking for me to shift my fundamental relationship to myself. But for now, I knew that I was adaptable. Resilient. And patient—unfazed by hours of waiting on the side of a one-lane mountain road due to some rockslide or engine failure, undisturbed by unexpected detours or a change of plans. I knew now that I could arrive by myself in an unknown town and walk through the dark with a pack on my back in search of lodging, then climb under filthy covers in all of my clothes because the room was too cold for anything less, and reach for my journal to keep me company.

I had no idea what my life would become after I returned to the States, but I knew I was not done with China and Tibet. I longed more than ever to give with my life, to give something back to all the people who had welcomed me. And I longed to let others see more of the real me, behind the ways I still withheld myself, behind the words I chose to say.

Near the end of my six months of backpacking, when I looked in the mirror one day, it dawned on me that I had not seen my reflection for weeks. My skin had grown darker, my face thinner, my light blue t-shirt faded and worn. My hair hung in a long, greasy braid down my back, and I hadn't showered for days, but I didn't care. For now, when I looked at myself, I saw a woman, bright-eyed and clear. A woman who was not well groomed, but raw and transparent. She was interesting to me. And no matter who I might still morph into when in another's presence, no matter how many years it might take for me to speak my truth with greater ease, I knew now that I could always find myself when I paused to meet my own gaze.

You again. You who have been hiding for so long.

4

Small Offerings

On the immigration form, they only let you check one box: tourism, visiting family, business, or work. None of these feel accurate. There is no category for what I want to do here. On one hand, I want a plan, an easy blueprint for how I can create a life for myself in China—and teaching English seems like the best way. On the other hand, I don't want to commit. I still want to travel to Lhasa and beyond, to connect with more people, to stay open to circumstance, a sense of fate whispering in my ear: *This is what you are here for. . .*

It is 1999, late July, and I've been in China for nearly a month now. After I return to Chengdu from the monastery in Seda, I am finally offered the teaching job at the university. Relieved that I can now move on and go to Tibet for the rest of the summer, I sign a contract to work for six months, starting in September, with an option to renew. I even agree to pay my way back to Hong Kong to change my visa from tourism to work, saving the school the hassle and cost. I don't care; I am mobile again. Soon, I will be back in Tibetan land. Soon I will be in Lhasa!

In 1999, there are only two ways for foreigners to officially travel to Tibet from China. You can either take a two-hour flight from Chengdu to Lhasa, or you can travel overland by bus via Golmud—a long, rough trip that supposedly helps to ease the altitude sickness.

All foreign travelers are required to join a tour group and are only given a two-week visa. Once you are in Tibet, however, the group is free to disband and you can extend your visa for another two weeks. I plan to fly, stay for a month, then return to Chengdu with a few weeks left to settle in before the school year begins.

But my first week in Lhasa my head aches, my nose is runny, my breath shallow, and I have a sore throat. Probably altitude sickness. I also just feel drained after weeks of uncertainty in Chengdu, all while fighting off a cold and staying with strangers in a dank, mosquito-infested hotel room. Now, I am finally here in this mythical capital, yet all I can do is nap and read in my hostel dorm bed for hours before dragging myself to sit in one of the many cafés that cater to foreigners, eating comfort food like fried potatoes and cheesecake.

Eventually, I pull myself out to explore the old Tibetan quarter and the cobblestone alleyways that surround Barkhor Square. Here, Chinese and Tibetan vendors line the narrow corridors displaying bags of bright yellow turmeric and cumin, measuring out huge sides of meat, chunks of rancid yak butter, and thick blocks of dried tea leaves on ancient scales. Merchants spread tarps on the ground with their wares—olive green canvas tennis shoes, cassette tapes, cowboy hats, bolts of cloth, buckets, brushes, socks, mugs—a multitude of everyday made-in-China goods.

In Barkhor Square itself, Chinese and Western tourists wander amidst vendors who sell more of everything from rows of numbered blue booths, especially fake antiques, turquoise and coral, hand-held prayer wheels, incense, and prayer flags. Tibetan pilgrims circle through continuously, since the square is a part of a larger pilgrimage path. Old women and young children in tattered clothes also pass through, begging, yet not aggressively. I willingly hand out small bills; their obvious poverty, not to mention the gratitude with which they receive, makes it easy for me to give.

As much as I don't want to lump the Tibetans and Chinese into big, overarching categories as backpackers often do (Tibetans: kind and peaceful; Chinese: rude and materialistic), I can't help but acknowledge the differences I feel. I notice that the Tibetans themselves often give to beggars, and the ease with which they meet my smile with a smile in return, sometimes pointing at my round cheeks and giving me a thumbs up. Such a welcome relief after Chengdu, where I felt a coldness on the streets. Sometimes on a good day in Chengdu, if I was feeling outgoing and energetic, I might smile at people or even say hello, and this breach of etiquette might be enough to shock someone into an embarrassed grin or slack-jaw of amazement. But more and more, I found myself just training my eyes to stare straight ahead, ignoring the blatant gawking.

In Lhasa, however, even the vendors have a kinder edge. I am finally in Tibet, so-called real Tibet; not just the Tibetan regions of China, not just sort of or used-to-be Tibet, but the Tibet that is recognized by most of the world as its own entity, if not country. I walk up to the Jokhang, considered the holiest temple, and ingest its white-washed stone walls and golden archways on the rooftop. Red and white fabric hangs around the entryway, some printed with images of Buddhas. At the top of the entrance sits a golden Wheel of Dharma statue with a deer perched on either side. I watch as Tibetan pilgrims prostrate in the forecourt, raising their palms to touch their foreheads, throats, and hearts, then getting down on their knees to stretch their entire bodies on the ground. Some wear kneepads or tie wooden blocks around their hands for protection; perhaps they've prostrated like this for weeks already just to get here, a once in a lifetime pilgrimage.

I take a breath and step inside, making my way down darkened corridors that lead from altar to altar where hundreds of butter lamps flicker and glow. A murmur of mantras and prayers echo through the hallways. Some pilgrims carry small bags from which they spoon out dollops of yak butter to add to butter lamps as offerings. Others leave small bills before various Buddhas and bodhisattvas on altars already overflowing with candles, money, and fruit. The devotional presence infusing this space is palpable. A wave of emotion rises in my chest. Even if my relationship to this place is so different from that of the Tibetan pilgrims, I also feel myself a pilgrim here. Or at least more a pilgrim than a tourist.

ॐ

Ani means nun in Tibetan. About halfway through my first trip to China, after spending a couple of months in the Tibetan areas in the Western provinces, I started going by Ani. In part, it was because the flat "eh" sound of Anne was hard for Chinese and Tibetans to pronounce. And my Chinese name, Ke Yi'an, felt too familial and childlike, only ever uttered by relatives. So Ani felt like the perfect hybrid. And while I wasn't claiming to be a nun, I liked the way the eyes of the Tibetans would light up when I told them my adopted name.

Could I become a nun someday? I asked myself this during the period that followed my first return to the US, when I became obsessed with reading about Chinese and Tibetan history, about Buddhism, and the Dalai Lama. I transferred colleges to a school in Olympia, WA, back in the Pacific Northwest, closer to the forests and saltwater I'd come to miss in Minnesota, and here I helped to start a Students for Free Tibet chapter on campus. I attended talks with visiting Tibetan Buddhists and tried meditating with a few local Buddhist sanghas. All of this led me to join the peace march for Tibet, walking from my Olympia to Vancouver, B.C. and staying in churches or in people's homes along the way. During this march, I became close to Ani-la, who had joined us from Dharamsala, India, where the Dalai Lama's government-in-exile has been based since he left Tibet in 1959. Ani-la now lived there as a nun, after fleeing Tibet in 1982 at age eighteen.

The others who marched the whole way—mostly white Americans, as well as one Tibetan man, and a father and son from Inner Mongolia—let me and Ani-la stay in a room together by ourselves. Ani-la had been given her own room since the march's starting point in Portland, but once I joined, for some reason I began staying with her as well. I was not a nun, but we were both quiet. I was not Tibetan, but we were both Asian. And somehow it was accepted that we both could use the extra privacy. So at the end of each day of walking and giving presentations and helping with dishes, Ani-la and I retreated. She lay on her mat and recited Buddhist chants, and I lay on my own, reading, writing, or just breathing. We formed a quiet friendship, communicating with gestures or with the few words of Chinese or English that she knew. Her calm, clear presence was a balm to me, and to many in our group as well. The Americans on the march often felt so noisy and dogmatic with their chants and slogans. Ani-la, on the other hand, exuded a feeling of kindness and compassion I'd come to associate with Tibetan culture. When we walked, I tried to not always be by her side, to give others a chance to be with her too.

Now, from inside the darkened interior of the Jokhang, I make my way up the stairs to the rooftop, then look out across Barkhor Square and beyond to the sprawl of the new Chinese development to the west, and to the brown mountains and majestic Potala Palace to the north. I eavesdrop as a monk explains some of the Jokhang's history to a group of Western tourists. They snap away with fancy cameras, capturing the classic imagery of a monk's burgundy robes, the glint of golden roof-top arches, white stone, and blue sky in the background.

Of course, there is so much that this monk can never say in his official tour, so much I barely grasp myself. Like how in 1959, several hundred Tibetans were killed inside this temple, while hundreds more were stormed out and forcibly marched to a prison. Or how in 1966, during the Cultural Revolution, the Jokhang was invaded by Red Guards who defaced, burned, or otherwise destroyed hundreds of ancient frescoes, images, and scriptures, as they did across all of China and Tibet. Or how after a period of leniency in the 1980s, which included China allowing visitors to Tibet again starting in 1984, thirty monks staged a protest in 1987 right below where I now stand, crying out "Independence for Tibet!" and "Long live the Dalai Lama!", leading to days of more protest, arrests, public beatings by the police, between six and twenty deaths, and a crowd of two to three thousand who swelled in support of the monks. Then, a couple years later in 1989, more demonstrations led to the death of up to 400 Tibetans, with over 700 injured and 1000 imprisoned. China declared martial law and expelled all foreigners again. Late that year, the Dalai Lama was awarded the Nobel Peace Prize—and the world began paying attention to his calls for compassion, non-violence, and Tibet's struggle for human rights.

Now, ten years later, I know some form of underground resistance in Tibet still exists, groups who communicate covertly with the Tibetan independence movement based in Dharamsala. Yet in recent years there have been no large protests—or at least none that the world has heard about. I look around the edges of the buildings, searching for hidden cameras positioned around the square, but they are invisible to my untrained eyes. Despite all the reading I've done, I realize I know very little about the true state of affairs here. How does the average citizen in Lhasa feel about Tibetan independence? Have most given up hope by now, or are fervent dreams still tended in private? How much political unrest exists beneath the surface that a traveler like me cannot see?

ॐ

It is already my fourth day in Lhasa. Although still weak and fatigued, I force myself to walk to the western part of town and join a procession of tourists climbing the stairs to enter the Potala Palace: a quarter-mile-long fortress of white and red walls with steep steps and golden rooftops set against a backdrop of barren mountains and open sky. One of the few important buildings in Tibet spared during the Cultural Revolution, the Potala contains close to a thousand rooms, but most are closed to visitors. It once served as the winter quarters for the Dalai Lama and also once housed chapels, government offices, living quarters for hundreds of monks, kitchens, dungeons, store-rooms, and the tombs of several former Dalai Lamas. Now, the Potala is more or less a museum, storing the remaining relics that haven't been carted off to Beijing. Tourists and pilgrims alike are herded through just a few sections.

The entrance fee for foreigners is forty yuan, about five dollars, but if you want to take pictures, you must pay another fifty. It angers me that the Chinese government is capitalizing on the absence of Tibet's rightful leader, so I don't pay. Instead, I walk quickly from room to room with the rest of the crowd and sneak a couple photos—one of a Chinese slogan and image of Chairman Mao painted on a wall; another from the rooftop, looking south across the four-lane road to the cement Communist-built Potala Square, where kids drive toy cars. The squat grey Worker's Cultural Palace, an exhibition hall built by the Chinese, sits behind the square, and beyond that, the suburbs sprawl and the mountains rise.

"What do you think of Tibet?" a young monk asks me in English as I stand looking out at the view. I pause, considering what answer to give. I've read that the government often plants spies disguised as monks to try and elicit the true feelings of foreigners. "Many things," I say. "Hard to say." I hate that I feel so paranoid. He stares at me curiously before I walk away.

What do I think of Tibet? Not the Tibet I've read about, but the one before me? It is hard to separate what I truly know from all I've ingested through our collective imagination. Most of us tourists,

Western and Chinese alike, have arrived with some preconceived vision, whether a snow-peaked Shangri-la filled with friendly, spiritually evolved people, or a country that has been violently oppressed and barely survived a genocide. But I am not interested in having these conversations now. Each day I shy away from opinions tossed back and forth about the future of Tibet over a few beers at a cafe. My confusion over what I am doing here (*Just seeing the sights? On a spiritual pilgrimage? On a covert fact-finding mission?*) makes me retreat into my own bubble of self-judgment. Am I truly an activist? Am I even a Buddhist?

After my first trip to China, I promised I'd return to this region and learn to speak both Tibetan and Chinese. After the peace march, I also attended three days of teachings with the Dalai Lama in Madison, Wisconsin, at the same time that I visited my grandmother whom I'd recently learned was dying. Ani-la went as well and slept on my grandma's couch. My dad's mother was an open-minded Catholic woman who encouraged my own spiritual searching. At the teachings, because of my friendship with Ani-la, I was allowed to sit up front with the monks and nuns. One day I joined Ani-la in greeting the Dalai Lama personally, each of us placing a ceremonial silk scarf, a *khata,* around his neck as a sign of our gratitude and respect. He in turn placed the *khatas* back around our own necks, a blessing.

So many things kept happening during this period that felt like gifts from the Universe: Ani-la's friendship, the timing of the Dalai Lama's teachings and my need to visit my grandmother, the way in which people fed us and welcomed us into their homes—both on the march and throughout my first trip to China. Increasingly, I felt called to be of service with my life, and my work felt tied to this part of the world. Yet when I sat with my feelings of heartache about Tibet and China's shared history, alongside my resistance to simplistic renderings of good and evil, as well as the idea that I was joining a recent trend (the Tibetan cause had been taken up by the likes of Harrison

Ford, Oliver Stone, and the Beastie Boys), I didn't know how to express myself. I knew I wanted to contribute to others with my life. But the grand question of whether Tibet could be saved, or what my role in this was, or if I was a Buddhist—all of this became too much for me. After the march, I stopped being involved with the activist groups and stopped attending Buddhist meditations. I wanted nothing to do with public posturing or identities. Instead, I retreated into my own solitary world of writing, art, and Butoh dance. But, deep down, I never abandoned the questions.

What was my connection to this land and culture? Could it be karmic; could I have been a Tibetan in a past life? I never said that aloud to anyone, for I still was not sure I completely believed in reincarnation, even though the idea that everything goes on in some form, and nothing ever truly dies feels right me. I envied the way Ani-la did not seem to question her path in life; did not question if being a nun was a worthy pursuit, acting in the service of all beings, as her culture espoused—or whether it was a selfish one that was too passive to be of help to the world, as many in my culture believed. Could I ever give away all my possessions and live as a nun? Or could I become a translator or some kind of diplomat for peace? Beneath these lofty ideas and my willingness to take risks with solo travel, I was still my parents' daughter. Their voices of caution reminded me that I should still think in terms of a career path—that I needed a plan, not just faith and intuition. On the surface I resisted their pressure, but beneath my "go with the flow" style of travel, my questions around my spiritual path came from a similar place of wanting to know or to somehow control the trajectory of my life.

"What do you think of Tibet?" the monk had asked. Now that I am finally here, I feel afraid to expose my conflicted beliefs. I shy from conversation with other opinionated foreigners, yet secretly believe myself more enlightened. On a level I am loathe to admit, I know I too want to be changed by this trip, to receive some sort of sign that I am *meant* to be here, that I am somehow more special in my feelings of connection to this culture than all of the others who are drawn to Tibet too. But knowing I am planning to teach in Chengdu, to settle into one place and one community in China, it is confusing to be temporarily swept back into the momentum of traveling and Tibet. I know that one month will not be enough to transcend my role as visitor here, yet somehow I still hope it will. While tour groups are whisked around by guides, I insist on traveling by myself, but ultimately we end up in the same few places.

Everything is so restricted. Besides Lhasa, there are a few other "open" towns in Tibet, which I plan to bus to later, but otherwise I will need to band with others and rent an expensive jeep and driver if I want to go to the other officially sanctioned destinations—a handful of monasteries and pristine lakes. I feel like I should do this; after all, why would I come all this way and just stay in Lhasa? But more and more, all I want to do is sit in cafes, journal, people-watch, check e-mail, do laundry, and simply be; to take a break from the endless quest to photograph more temples, barter for more trinkets, or otherwise play the role of a productive traveler.

ॐ

One morning over breakfast, I join a group of two young German men, a Turkish woman, and Dietmar, a white-haired Austrian Catholic priest whom I befriended a few days ago while visiting Sera temple, and together we spent the afternoon chatting and meditating. They are planning to rent a jeep to go to a festival at Ganden monastery, an hour's ride southeast of the city, and they invite me to come along.

Ganden, which means "Joyful Paradise," is one of Lhasa's three great monastic universities—along with Sera and Drepung. Today, the monks will unfurl a giant *thangka* (a religious cloth painting) in an annual ceremony. I've heard that auspicious signs often appear when *thangkas* are unveiled—a break in the clouds with light pouring through, a double rainbow, sudden winds. Tibet's history is full of so many fantastical tales of oracles, visions, reincarnated lamas, and flying monks that I temper such lore with a dose of skepticism, although I also believe in the unexplainable mystery of such signs.

When we arrive at Ganden, I wander ahead of our group, wanting to be on my own; sharing a ride is one thing, but I don't enjoy touring sites in packs. Briefly, I pause to squat and pee in a covered shed with holes in the ground, before continuing along the dusty path toward the monastery. During the Cultural Revolution, Ganden was completely destroyed—not a single building left standing. Today, the monastery's stone buildings have been rebuilt into the hillside, although undoubtedly much smaller in scope, the main hall painted white and the temples a warm terracotta. Tibetans—monks, pilgrims, and families, some in Western dress, some in traditional, and most wearing a mixture of the two—mingle excitedly on the grounds. Many perch on the steps of the temple trying to get a better view of a ritual song and dance performance in one of the courtyards. Western and Chinese tourists are also present, identifiable by their sporty caps, daypacks, and hiking boots. The sun beats down. As I draw closer to the heart of the crowd, a young monk begins to wave at me.

"You, you!" he calls out in Chinese.

I turn. Does he mean me?

"Did you lose your passport?"

I shake my head.

"Yes, yes. It's you." The monk nods, pointing to the small blue book that a Tibetan man holds at his side.

No way. I've only been here long enough to use the toilet, and that was back near the road. Even if I dropped it then, how could it have made its way all the way over here? I doubt it is mine, but I have to look. Sure enough, there is my face staring out from inside the small blue book I put beneath my pillow each night and otherwise keep strapped to my waist.

"Where—how—where did you find it?"

"He found it," the monk says, pointing to the Tibetan man in his forties wearing a cowboy hat who is watching me. "In Lhasa. On the street."

What? My head spins. In Lhasa? How could it be? When was the last time I had used it? Yesterday. I had gone to the travel agent to extend my visa so I could stay a full month. I must have thought I'd slipped it back into my money belt, but really it fell to the ground. How could I have been so careless? Or could it have been stolen? How exactly I can't imagine since I guard it vigilantly.

"Thank you," I say. Confused and relieved, I reach out for my passport.

The Tibetan man shakes his head, holding it tightly.

"He wants money," the monk translates.

What? No. "Please give it back."

The Tibetan man shakes his head again, his face tensing.

"He wants one hundred kwai," the monk says.

A hundred kwai. The PRC has recently issued brand new red and white one-hundred kwai bills with a fresh image of Mao and a special watermark to prevent counterfeiting. I have several of them in my money belt, but I don't want to reveal where I keep my secret stash to the good-sized crowd that now surrounds us. Plus, this pisses me off. It is my passport. For all I know, he took it from me.

"I'll give him fifty," I say, knowing I have a fifty in my wallet in my pocket.

The Tibetan man shakes his head and looks off into the distance. Fifty isn't enough. But I've said my price and now I can't back down. Neither can he. This is the game. Yet I am worried that he'll get scared and take off with it. And then I'll be the stupid one!

"Wait here," the monk says. "I'll go get a policeman."

Police? Evil Communist police? No—I shake my head. No need to get the police involved.

The monk insists. "He'll make him give you the passport back. I'll be right back."

I stand next to the Tibetan man who holds my passport tightly, waiting. Nervous. Someone in the crowd tells me not to worry, I'll get it back. I am not so sure. In a few minutes, the monk returns with a young man in a green army uniform.

"What's the problem?" the policeman barks. I explain in Chinese.

"She said she'd give you fifty kwai?" the policeman asks the Tibetan. He nods meekly.

"Then take it."

I pull the yellow bill from my wallet and hand it over. The Tibetan man hands me my passport. Relieved, I stuff it inside my money belt as discreetly as I can.

The policeman walks off and leaves the monk, the Tibetan man, and myself standing there, now engulfed in a much larger group since we happen to be standing right in front of the temple wall where they will unfurl the *thangka*. I don't have a clue now where my fellow travelers are, so I sit down where I am. Right next to me sits the Tibetan man who held my passport moments before, perhaps even fingered its pages for an entire night, dreaming of the money he could make on the black market. We look at each other and exchange sheepish grins, then wait for the ceremony to begin.

Minutes later, a group of monks walk out along the roof of the temple in mustard and burgundy robes and tall curved feathery hats, blowing on conch shells and banging cymbals. They are followed by a row of monks who carry the giant *thangka*, rolled up and heavy on their shoulders. I clap and cry out in gratitude with the crowd as the giant image of the Buddha is unfurled, as it is every year on this day in July. Later, I find the group I came with and explain what happened.

Dietmar shakes his head. "You know what that was? That was a miracle."

I nod, humbled again into belief.

ᡐ

With the exception of the Tibetan district, the Potala, and the mountains looming in the background, Lhasa looks and feels like many other provincial cities in China. Everywhere you see square cement buildings covered with small rectangular white tiles, the windows made of cheap blue glass. Pop music blares from CD shops or karaoke bars; young women in tight shirts sporting fake designer logos or random misspelled English words make their way along uneven muddy pathways in platform heels; young men swagger in cheap oversized suits with the brand-name tag often left on the sleeves. Taxis honk impatiently, shiny black Land Cruisers with tinted windows zoom by arrogantly, and mini-buses from the eighties chortle along spewing black smoke.

Today, my plan is to visit the Norbulingka, the Dalai Lama's former summer palace, now known to the Chinese as "People's Park," a park that the Communists had initially, after the Dalai Lama fled to exile in India, turned into a prison. Upon arrival, however, I discover that the buildings are closed for another hour until three, so I wander over to buy water from a Tibetan vendor. His name is Nima and he appears to be in his late thirties. He speaks decent Chinese, so I sit down to talk to him and his wife, who smiles shyly but doesn't meet my eyes. Soon, an old woman who runs a stand next door offers me peanuts and salty yak butter tea. From my backpack, I take out, for the first time while in Tibet, a small album of photos I've brought to share. Hidden behind the images of my family are pictures of my Tibetan friends in the States, many of whom I met while on the peace march. "What do they do?" Nima asks, as all three peer intently.

"Work, go to school . . ." I watch as they stare and grapple with the idea of people like them living in America. Then, I finger for the few Dalai Lama photos I've tucked away in the very back, looking around to see if anyone is watching. I take out two—one for Nima and his wife, and one for the old woman.

Nima and his wife thank me and quickly hide their photo in their bag, but the old woman leaves hers out. She keeps covering it with her hand, taking a quick peek, then covering it again. Tears stream down her face. I give her a photocopy of one my drawings (which I've brought as gifts) to fold around the photo, which she then wraps in toilet paper, ties a pink string around the bundle, and slips it inside the folds of her *chuba*. Worship of the Dalai Lama, along with all public religious devotion, was banned during the Cultural Revolution and not allowed again until the 1980s, when religious restrictions in Tibet were relaxed. But by the early nineties, the liberal wing of the Communist party had disappeared, and now, since 1994, the Dalai Lama's photo has once again been officially banned. As the old woman continues to peek at her photo, I feel grateful I didn't give in to my paranoia and leave them at home. In fact, I wish I'd brought more.

Before long, the grounds to Norbulingka open and I say goodbye to my new friends. First, I follow along and listen from the periphery as a Dutch tour group examines the artifacts left behind by the Dalai Lamas. But soon I realize I've had enough of official tours, so I trail off to wander the grounds on my own. It is hard to imagine this place in its glory, with wooded meadows and splendid gardens, birds, flowers, and wildlife. Now, the trees are withered, the grass dry, and the only animals are the panda bear garbage cans and a deranged screeching coming from the adjacent zoo. I decide to go over and have a look, even though my *Lonely Planet* guidebook advises to "avoid it at all costs." Soon, I discover why.

A drugged-looking brown bear sits in a cage the size of a

bathroom. A chained eagle stares from a cage the size of a stove. Monkeys, the source of the screeching, live in the bottom of a giant cement pit, scrambling over a mound of rocks in the middle. Tibetan and Chinese couples and families lean on the railing surrounding the pit, laughing and throwing pop cans, food scraps, and empty water bottles at the monkeys. The monkeys scamper over to grab the cans and sip the last drops before throwing them down and shrieking. The people laugh, take aim, and throw more, adults and children alike.

Lhasa has succeeded in depressing me, but it is a kind of depression that feels all too familiar: this place reminds me of urban China. The same China where I witnessed a crowd in Chengdu pointing and laughing at the scene of a traffic accident, or where I watched a policeman kick over an illegal vendor's cart full of apples and encourage bystanders to help themselves from the ground. The same China that is bent on getting rich and forgetting the past, watching out for one's self at the expense of all others. The same China that I read so much about back at home, but that I still barely understand in person.

ॐ

On my first trip, it was easier to befriend Tibetans, to get off the beaten path and visit people's homes. But here in the "official Tibet" there are so many more restrictions, and after each new excursion I take—to the cities of Shigatse and Gyantse, to Namtso Lake, and to a nunnery and hot springs—I just want to return to Lhasa. At least in Lhasa my face is recognized by a few I can actually call friends— like Dietmar, the Austrian priest, or like a group of three artists, one Chinese and two Tibetans, whom I spent several days hanging out with in their studio. Their stories of friendships between Tibetans and Chinese here challenge my pre-conceived notions of Tibet, and I am grateful for these conversations. I envy the other foreigners I've met who have figured out how to stay here longer and to give back—whether by turning an old castle outside of Lhasa into a school of traditional Tibetan arts and crafts for nomadic children; building a solar-powered monastery in central Tibet; or opening a school for blind children. Is there a way I could change course and stay longer too? No. That would be too hard. This is not where I'm meant to stay. I've signed a contract in Chengdu. My main destination is still China.

On my last night in Lhasa, I visit the Jokhang temple one last time. I sit on the ground in the waning evening light, lean my back against a stone wall, and watch a steady hum of people pass by—walking, turning prayer wheels, chanting mantras. A teenaged Tibetan girl in Fila sneakers pushes a mountain bike, pausing before the temple to raise her hands in prayer before continuing on. An old black dog with a bad leg growls at a man rolling a cart, then nuzzles up to an old Tibetan woman who gives him an absent-minded stroke on the head.

Next to me sits a young affluent Chinese couple. They tell me they are from Shenzhen, and with faces aglow, they recount how they rode horses for ten yuan an hour today, then drank *chang* with Tibetans. *The Tibetans are so kind*, they gush, and I agree. Then, a small huddle of foreigners approach, and one of them lets off a giant flash from his camera, momentarily illuminating a group of prostrating Tibetans who glance up in surprise. All around, vendors close up shop, pack wares into boxes, strap chairs to their backs. Near me stands a man from Portugal whom I met the other day, but we don't greet each other. The sky is pale blue and dark grey with hints of pink, growing darker. Another day in Lhasa is coming to an end. Tufts of coal smoke rise throughout the city, dinner prepared in the privacy of homes.

In my bag, I carry a white silk *khata* and a pouch of Tibetan medicine. My friend, Sonam, a Tibetan I met on the peace march, gave these to me to bring to Tibet. "They will value this more than money," he said of the tiny black pellets in the plastic bag. I've held on to these gifts for the last four weeks, waiting to find the right person to give them to. Now, I realize, anyone will do. I rise to tie the *khata* around a mass of other *khatas* and prayer flags already tied to the stone wall against which I've been leaning. Then I walk to the first old woman I see and hold out the medicine in my hand. She mumbles and nods as she accepts my offering, then turns and walks away.

Slowly, I make my way back to my guesthouse where I will pack and spend my last night in Tibet. Whatever my tie is or isn't to this place, I know I have given what I can for today, and for today, this has to be enough.

5

Foreign Expert

When I return to Chengdu from Lhasa, I am relieved to have an apartment waiting. A place to unpack my things, to wake slowly and make a cup of tea, to light incense and write in my journal. A place to finally be alone again, to finally make my own.

It's early August and school won't start for another few weeks. The first thing I do is rearrange the furniture—move the extra twin bed into the living room to use as a couch; the wooden dining table in front of the balcony to serve as a desk; and the small wooden coffee table into my bedroom to become my altar. Back in the States, I experimented with creating my first altar during college. It started with just a few candles and objects from nature, as well as a postcard of the Dalai Lama's smiling image. But before long it expanded into a whole table, before which I'd bow or sit cross-legged trying to meditate. I was self-conscious about what these acts meant to me; after all I didn't worship the Dalai Lama as a God-King in the way that Tibetans did; his image was more symbolic. Nevertheless I wanted to create a space that announced my intentions to live a more spiritual life. And now, in Chengdu, I can tell I'm going to need this: this physical reminder to stay connected to my deeper self.

My apartment is nice by Chinese standards, complete with a Western sit-down toilet, but it feels institutional with its harsh fluorescent lighting and grey worn carpet. To counter this, I "borrow" a few potted plants from the courtyard below, drape a woven Tibetan cloth over the television, and scatter the trinkets and artwork that I collected in Tibet all around. On the walls I tape my photographs of the grasslands, *chotens*, prayer flags and mani stones over spots where the pale green paint has peeled away to reveal grey cement. On my altar, I place a small Buddha statue, my prayer beads, a candle, and a photo of the Dalai Lama. All of this helps, but it does not yet feel like home.

My apartment is on the third floor of the foreign teachers' building, located within a small gated compound, which also includes the foreign students' dorm and the office of the *waiban*, the staff who deal with us *laowai*. My first week here, I don't go out except to buy food or take short walks around campus, not wanting to leave my small bubble of retreat. After my writing and tea each morning, I've been experimenting with watercolors, playing with a small set I picked up in the city. I love this feeling of being unseen and alone. I am the first foreign teacher to have arrived, so when I do go out, I feel even more on display here than I did in the city proper. As more and more students arrive, calling out to each other excitedly and mingling near the dorms, I become less anonymous each day. I am only a few years older than some of them, yet my lighter hair, my wider eyes, my larger breasts and thicker thighs—all of this marks me as a *laowai*. Some stare, obviously curious, but I don't feel like speaking to them yet, nor inhabiting my official role as "foreign expert."

Sichuan Normal University is a teacher's college in the suburbs, about a thirty-minute cab ride from downtown Chengdu. The school has a provincial air to it, surrounded by farmland and only a few streets with businesses that cater to the students. I enjoy picking out vegetables, tofu, eggs, and fresh flowers from the farmers who sometimes sell their goods from an alleyway near my apartment. I buy a wok, dishes, and condiments to start making my own meals. But the air is still polluted, the ground littered with plastic and garbage, the sky a muted shade of blue. This is still urban, crowded China, only now I am completely removed from the occasional glimpses of other foreign faces. In many ways, this place feels more remote than Lhasa.

When I got the lead for this job it felt fortuitious, for not only was Chengdu relatively close to Tibet, but it also seemed like a lively and cultured city that was not already teeming with expats, like Beijing or Shanghai. I'd set out wanting to have more of an immersion experience in China, but now I am no longer so sure. However, I've signed a contract. I will teach English composition—two senior level classes, three sophomore, and one graduate level—and for this I will be paid an average Chinese teacher's salary: 1,500 remenbi a month, roughly $200. Despite not having arrived with any teaching materials or clothes, much less a laptop, I still feel up for the challenge. In college, I worked as a writing tutor and taught ESL to small groups as a volunteer. And I am eager to share my love of writing. I tell myself I'll be okay.

二

Before long, I meet the other foreign teachers. Altogether, there are five of us, all Americans, and all in our twenties to early thirties. Robin, from Michigan, is Korean American and returning for her third year. The others are white: Josh, from the San Francisco Bay Area, returning for his second term; Chris, from a small town in New Jersey, his first time out of America; and Vicki, from Pennsylvania, placed here through the same Christian organization that placed Robin.

Actually, one other apartment in the foreign teacher's building is occupied—not by a single person, but by a family: a couple with two young kids. We call them the Monkees since that is what it sounds like when Mr. Yang, the man in charge of us foreigners, pronounces their name. They are from Alabama and have been here for a year. Four pairs of cowboy boots line up in the hallway near the door of their first floor, one-bedroom apartment. It is a mystery to me what exactly they are doing here. Someone said that the husband works for a foreign firm, and they are here studying Chinese. But I only ever interact with the kids when they play in the grass in front of the building, speaking to me in a Southern drawl. One day, I tell the younger boy that I am half Chinese. "My mom is Chinese and my dad is American," I say. He looks at me strangely. "My parents say God doesn't like that." The older sister hushes him, "We're not supposed to talk about God." That's when I come to suspect that they are missionaries. I guess we all have our secrets.

Robin, who has been here the longest, warns me that my teaching load is a lot. She has a similar schedule, but she's been teaching here for two years already and has her lesson plans mapped out. I didn't bring any books with me because I didn't want to lug them around over the summer, especially if I didn't even end up teaching for some reason. But now I am starting to realize how unprepared I am, so I eagerly borrow books from Robin's shelves before diving into planning my first lessons.

I am happy that the school isn't assigning textbooks so I can teach however I want. I plan to introduce my students to freewriting—writing without editing from prompts, whatever comes up about themselves and their lives. I want to be the kind of teacher who will shake up their ideas of how a teacher is supposed to act, like in *Dead Poet's Society* when Robin Williams jumps up on the desks, reciting poetry. Maybe not quite that dramatic, but I *do* want to help them discover the beauty of self-expression, of finding the poetry and meaning in their own stories.

First I'll have them keep journals, and then we'll progress to personal essays, while reading examples by American writers. I look for essays that might spark interesting conversations about cultural differences between America and China, about ethics and values, about young people today. I want to get them talking and expressing their opinions. I figure I'll follow the same format for all my classes, adjusting the difficulty as we go along. Beyond this, it is hard for me to plan more until I get a better sense of their comprehension level.

In the meantime, I've been initiated into the Chengdu nightlife, going into the city with the other teachers. The most happening spot is the High Fly, a bar/café popular with expats, travelers, and young Chinese alike. Every Saturday night, a Chinese man with long hair deejays, nodding his head as he looks out at the crowd from beneath a huge pair of earphones. I am amazed to hear this music in China: reggae, hip-hop, Arabic-French pop, Alpha Blondy, Manu Chao, Nirvana . . . I hear that the deejay used to live in France, which explains why he sticks out as so different.

Another hot spot is The Little Bar. Robin and Josh introduce me one night to this oasis, where a punk band wails from a tiny stage in the corner and the room is packed with young, trendy Chinese, standing room only. Votives glow atop small wooden tables, crowded with men and woman smoking cigarettes and sipping drinks. Waitresses pushing Bacardi circle the room in tight silver skirts. The walls are covered with modern Chinese paintings. Built-in shelves hold art catalogues and books. In the center of the room is a square bar, commanded by a round-faced woman in her forties with a short bob and a cigarette clutched between her fingers. She nods her head to the music, smiling and confident, occasionally greeting someone or pouring a drink. A white woman also bartends, dressed in a tight black shirt and taking orders in Chinese. I ask for a Tsingtao, the only Chinese beer I know by name, and try not to stare too hard at it all. *What is this world I am in?*

At the end of the night, I learn from the other teachers how to climb over the iron gates that surround the foreigners' compound, for they are locked each night at eleven for our "safety and protection."

Thankfully, they are easy enough to scale, and the school turns a blind eye to our comings and goings. Once you are over the gates, you have to then knock on the glass door to the foreign teachers' apartment building to wake up the grumpy bald old man (nicknamed Mao) who sleeps on a cot in the foyer. He stirs from his sleep, then shuffles over to unlock the door. *Xie xie*, I thank him, wondering if he can smell the smoke and alcohol on my breath, feeling like a deviant Western woman.

心

After two weeks here, I am relieved to learn that the foreign teachers' classes will be starting a week later than planned. Now I have one more week to pore over Robin's resources, to go shopping in the city for more clothes to wear in the classroom, to explore Chengdu's nightlife, and to paint. Painting has become my new favorite mode of expression. I've finally finished my first creation: a circle in which rich shades of brown and red, burnt like earth or blood, twist and swirl around each other like a mandala. I hang it over my altar in my bedroom, my altar which I've barely acknowledged with a cursory bow, but which gives me comfort all the same.

Meanwhile, I am enthralled by the city's nightlife. One Saturday at the High Fly, I notice Guang Hui, the deejay, watching me as I dance. He waves me over to his side and invites me to a party at his apartment. I can't understand his Mandarin very well, so he asks an Italian friend of his to help translate and give directions. I write my number and my name in Chinese on his card, and my cheeks grow hot when he laughs at my crude childlike strokes.

The next week, I invite Robin to come along to the party. Walking in, I feel like I've been transported to a hippie friend's place back home. Batiks hang on the walls, cushions are scattered across the floor, and a small group of foreign students I recognize from the bar mingle and chat. Robin and I head out to the deck which is covered with potted bamboo plants, while Guang Hui fetches us glasses of wine.

Before long, a group of Chinese show up, three men and one woman. I watch her curiously as she sits down across from me at our table. She is maybe in her 30s, her dark hair pulled back from her pale thin face and high cheekbones, except for a row of long thick bangs. She wears all black—a tight T-shirt, platform heeled sandals, and capris. Immediately she reaches for a pack of cigarettes from her purse—*Honghes*, the harsh brand usually smoked by men. I try to smile at her, but she avoids my gaze.

A few minutes later, leaning across the table, I extend my hand in an American style of greeting. "*Ni hao. Wo jiao Ani.*" Hi, my name is Ani, I say. She shakes my hand limply, shifting in her chair. "*Wo jiao Xie Ping.*" My name is Xie Ping. I tell her I am teaching English in Chengdu and ask what she does. "*Wo hua hua,*" she says. A painter! I've wanted to connect with local artists, and although I've met a couple, I haven't yet met a female artist. "*Wo ye xihuan hua hua.*" I tell her that I also like to paint, and she offers to show me her work. Exchanging numbers, we make plans to connect next weekend. I can't wait to glimpse the home of a Chengdu local—and not just any local, but a young woman artist to boot!

I don't talk to any of the other foreigners that night. They stay inside, clustered around Guang Hui, mostly talking in French, whereas I stay on the deck, sipping wine and practicing my Chinese. The men who are with Xie Ping are older, in their forties, and talk to me in a patronizing way, but who can blame them; I am only twenty-four, and my Chinese is pretty basic. People seem sympathetic when I tell them I am teaching at Chuan Si. *Why Chuan Si? That's so far away.* They suggest I look for a different job or get a moped so I can commute more easily to town. *Right,* I think, *there's no way I'll be learning to ride a motorcycle in crazy Chinese traffic or looking for a new job at this stage.* Classes are starting next week. I've committed and I'll make the best of it.

ٿ

On my first day of teaching, I wake early, tie my hair in a bun, and put on a long, flowing beige skirt and loose burgundy top. Sitting on my small balcony, I drink coffee and smoke while looking over my notes. Going to the bars has rekindled my old social habit, and recently I bought my own pack, tired of bumming from others. Now, I enjoy this little ritual more than anything: stepping outside and sitting and smoking where no one can see me, whether in the morning or late at night.

Of course, I brush my teeth and wash my hands to make sure I don't smell like smoke, then take one last look at myself in the bathroom mirror. I wonder if my glasses make me look more like a teacher. Even though I don't like the way they are so thick, I started wearing them again after I returned to the States following my first trip to China, in part because I was tired of the male gaze. Glasses and baggy clothes made me feel more invisible, and after years of dressing for others, this was a welcome reprieve. Now, back in China, I appreciate anew the sense of protection my glasses give me, less permeable and exposed to everyone's stares. I also prefer clothes that hide my curvy body, clothes that are more about comfort than fashion. And yet I'm also about to step onto a new stage as a teacher. I'll have to get a few nicer things, but for now what I have will do.

Outside, I make my way slowly to the English building. It isn't even ten o'clock, yet the air is already sticky. I walk slowly, passing a mix of building styles—from old rectangular brick structures to the common Chinese white-tiled buildings with blue, tinted-glass windows. I have one senior class this morning, and a sophomore class in the afternoon. Tomorrow I'll have two sophomore classes, and on

Wednesday another class of seniors and a small group of graduate students. It seems like a decent schedule, all in one block, with a long weekend to recover.

Entering the classroom through the back door, I am surprised at how full it already is. Students chat excitedly. Heads turn as I walk up the aisle. Whispers. *Is she our teacher? She's so young...* I imagine they say. I take my place on the raised platform before the podium and set down my folder, my water bottle, my notes.

Forty-five faces watch me expectantly. "Good morning!" I smile and write my name on the blackboard.

Everyone settles at once. "Good morning!" they chime in response.

I take a breath. "My name is Anne," I say in English, "and I'm your new foreign teacher. I'm from America, from Seattle. Do you know where Seattle is?" Yes, nods. I draw a quick map of the US and a star in the upper NW corner. More nods and *ohhs*.

"My mother is Chinese . . ." The room gasps with familiar surprise and approval, ". . . and my father is American." The room echoes with oohs, aaahs, and "*guaibude,*" no wonder!

"*Suoyi, wo keyi jiang yi dian Zhongwen.*" So I can speak a little Chinese.

The students erupt into more gasps and applause. I knew they would like that; I've been through this routine each time I introduce myself to a Chinese person. "My mother went to America to study, met my father, they fell in love, and here I am." Everyone laughs. So far, so good.

I tell them how I have been to China once before, and I've wanted to come back ever since. And how I studied writing at my university. I wonder if my language is too difficult, or is it too basic? I must speak loudly to reach the ones in back, mostly boys. Otherwise, the class is almost all female.

"Okay, let's talk about writing. In this class, we're going to do a lot of writing. In America, I love to write. I've liked to write ever since I was little, and I still write in my journal every day. Do any of you keep a journal or a diary?" Some nods. "Great! In this class, I'm going to have all of you keep journals. We're also going to do a lot of freewriting." I write this word on the board. "Do you know what freewriting is?"

They shake their heads, some blank stares.

"It's when—when you write anything you want to, when one thought leads to another, in a 'stream of consciousness' way." I write this down, too. "Do you know 'stream of consciousness'?" *Why am I introducing this concept right now?* A few students nod. "You know, like a stream, or river, that goes in any direction? Well, your mind can also flow like this . . ." The students in the front row nod. "Okay, so when you freewrite, you don't worry about grammar, spelling, or mistakes. You just keep your hand moving and get your ideas down. Freewriting is a very important step in writing. Before you start to write an essay, you first need to explore your ideas. And brainstorm. Have you ever heard of brainstorming?"

Confused looks. *Brain + storm*, I write on the board. "This is when you make a list of ideas, you put anything and everything down that you can think of, like a big storm . . . of ideas . . . in your brain." I make wild gestures around my head. The students laugh and scribble in their notebooks. I glance again at my pages of notes. I ramble. They stare. I imagine them thinking, *She's so young. Has she taught before? Not like a real teacher.* These are seniors. They've had a foreign teacher before; maybe they are comparing me to her. Was she better than me? I'm sure she was older. Did she have a clue in hell what she was doing?

"Okay, now it's your turn," I say. "Tell me your name and something about yourself." They groan. "It can be anything. Not just where you're from. It can be what you had for breakfast or something you did when you were a child. Anything. Okay?"

I point to a girl in the front row to begin. She stands up, turning red.

"Hello, teacher Anne. My name is Susan. I come from Zigong. It is a lovely town in Sichuan. I am very happy to meet you, our foreign teacher. I hope you come visit my town. Welcome to stay in China."

I smile and nod, then turn to the next student.

"Hello, Miss Teacher Anne. My name is Lucy. I come from Leshan, it's the city with the giant Buddha. I hope you can come visit my hometown with me someday. I think you will like it. I hope I can study good English with you this year. When I graduate I hope to become English teacher for children in my town. I very much enjoy learning and reading. Thank you."

After the first row of ten has spoken, each completing their own welcome-to-China speech, I realize how long this is going to take. They've been in the university together for three years now, moving from subject to subject as their own class unit—they must have heard their classmates' mini-speeches a thousand times before.

By eleven a.m., the room has grown stifling and hot, the windows letting in little breeze. Some fidget in their seats or stare into space. By the time we've gotten through all forty-five students, I can barely feign enthusiasm myself. Relieved, I pass out 5x7 note cards and introduce their first exercise, "I remember". I ask them to write down their names and a few memories. "Any memories, anything you think of. It doesn't matter what they are. It can be a memory from this morning: *I remember I ate* baozi *for breakfast*, or a memory from when you were three years old. Just begin each line with 'I remember' and every time you come to the end of a thought, begin again with 'I remember.'"

The students stir, having been given a task. As they write, I walk around and take pictures of each one. Most seem shy and embarrassed, but as they pose, I glimpse their personalities lurking beneath the formal polite greetings. Some can barely look at the camera, laughing and turning their heads down at the last minute while covering their mouths. Others face the camera directly or smile demurely as if for a fashion magazine. A few of the boys clown or smirk before finally posing with upright seriousness. I introduce myself personally and shake hands with each of them, forgetting their names the moment I move on to the next. It doesn't matter; that's what the photos are for. Later, I can match each note card with a face, and slowly get to know them as individuals.

As the week goes on, each class gets easier. My confidence grows. I learn that I need to give my students a break midway and limit their self-introductions. I find myself repeating the same jokes that entertained the last group. I can play this role, I even like it: part kind, encouraging supporter and part wacky, enthusiastic performer. They like me, I can tell. One girl even says she likes my smile.

Most of my students already have English names that they chose or were given by their previous foreign teacher. Most are common, like Lily or Jane, but others crack me up, like Cinderella, Seaman, Young Fish, and Greengirl. Fruits and vegetables are popular— Pumpkin, Plum, Lemon, Peachman. Those who don't have names ask me to choose for them, and I promise next week I'll return with a list. Only a few students opt to be called by their Chinese names, which I respect, yet admittedly these are harder for me to remember.

For now, I am doing pretty much the same thing in all my classes—introductions and freewriting. But I enjoy my sophomore classes the most; they are smaller and more intimate—35 students instead of 50, and for many I am their first foreign teacher. Most of my sophomores are from smaller, provincial towns in Sichuan, which means they are probably poorer—and thus possibly brighter. (I've heard that wealthier students can sometimes buy a slot at the university, so if you are poor, you've earned your place here.) Despite my own youth, my students seem so young to me, more like American high school students than college aged—at least socially, the way they giggle, whisper, and cluster in groups. They seem so innocent; I feel like I would shock them if I revealed my recent social life filled with drinking and smoking, or my old life in the States dancing Butoh, going on peace marches, and making art.

My graduate students, however, are a different story. There are nine, four men and five women, and most are older than me. We meet in a small room in one of the newer, white-tiled buildings on campus, and sit in plump brown leather rolling chairs around an oval wooden table. After introductions, I ask them to write a short paragraph about how they hope I can help them this term. I want to get a sense of their writing abilities—which vary quite a bit. They are getting degrees in linguistics, translation, and English or American literature. Many want help with their critical theses: how to choose a good topic and organize it, how to find resources.

What do I know about the theory of linguistics or the work of Edith Wharton? What do I know about how to find resources while in China? One woman is studying Amy Tan; at least I've read her. What I *do* know is how to edit and structure a paper. What I *do* know is how to listen to their requests, nod, and tell them I will help.

心

By my last class of my first week, I am anxious to step out of the teacher role. I've arranged for Ms. Gao, an English professor on campus, to come tutor me in Chinese once a week, so my Thursdays are now devoted to studying characters. I love talking to her in Chinese, especially since she speaks English and can thus coach me when I am reaching for an unfamiliar new word. After she leaves my apartment, I write down a long list of words I want to learn how to say in Chinese, imagining using them someday with Guang Hui, the deejay—or with someone intriguing like him. For hours I sit and copy characters over and over, relaxing into the simplicity of repetition.

The next day, Friday, I declare as all mine—no lesson planning, no visits, no studying. No awareness of a public identity, just sitting at the desk, painting and writing, sinking back into a quiet space. I am on to my second painting—shades of pale green, blue, and purple swirled together, washes of color muted by white, then accented by thin strokes of black. A tangle of roots or branches surrounding a bright heart of fuchsia in the middle. A rose, or maybe a lotus, inside a labyrinth of water and weeds.

Painting has become my new favorite meditation, but still I crave something more. Later that night, I retreat to my bedroom, finally lighting candles on my altar and stretching my back and shoulders out on the carpeted floor. It's been too long since I've sunk into my breath and body. After a while, I stand and begin swinging my arms, going through qi gong movements that I used to practice on the shores of an inlet of the Puget Sound, near my home during my last year of college. Ever since I've arrived in China, however, I haven't practiced qi gong or tai chi. There isn't enough space in my apartment to do the full form without running into something, and I don't feel comfortable practicing in public. People in China are too curious about everything a foreigner does—*Look, the foreigner is eating hot pot! Look, the foreigner is taking a picture of the billboard! Look the foreigner is doing tai chi!* I can't imagine losing myself in the flow of the form while trying to shut out this awareness of people watching. It is hard enough just to walk down the street. I don't want to make myself more of a spectacle.

Now, my fingertips begin to vibrate, the air I pull them through thickening with resistance. Swinging my body freely for the first time since I left Olympia, I find myself merging from qi going into Butoh, a dance form I studied in college, strange and other-worldly. My lids lower, my limbs soften, my breath grows more audible, my center rooted. Legs bowing, feet turning inward, movement drawing out of my body as if pulled by an infinite number of strings. *Now: mouth open and gaping, eyes half closed, hands rising to chest. Now: pulling out my heart, cupping it in my palms, holding out an offering.*

Now: body hunching forward, huddling in close. Now: limbs gangly, extending like wings.

Heavy, awkward bird. Earthbound and restricted.

6

Butoh Vision

If my students saw me dancing Butoh, I have no idea what they'd think. That I was on drugs? Mentally ill? Wildly unknowable like other foreign ghosts? Out on the crowded streets or standing in front of class, I must be smiling, friendly, keeping an open diplomatic face. But in the privacy of my apartment, I seek to hold onto my rawness, the intensity of how I feel things, the parts of me that feel most real, the parts that are least exposed.

Born out of post-World War II Japan, Butoh feels weighted and hunched over, dark and emotive, the antithesis of ballet. Imagine your body is made up of infinite points, and each point has a string attached to it. In Butoh, every movement is pulled from these strings. Your dance comes from within, but *you* don't control your dance. Instead, you allow your body to become a vessel, open and ready to be led by emotion, memory, images from nature, dreamscape, intuition and the unconscious.

I started dancing Butoh in my last year of college, following the period I went on the Tibet march. After the march, after visiting the Dalai Lama, after saying goodbye to Ani-la and my grandmother, I wanted nothing to do with grand questions of what I would do with my life. I only wanted to journal, to draw, and to be in my body. I spent most days silent and alone, walking in the woods or biking to school to attend classes. Wearing thick glasses and baggy clothes, I moved around quietly, not wanting to be noticed. At night, I came home to my rented room in a house in the woods I shared with roommates. This tiny room was my sanctuary. I filled its white walls with my drawings and danced or sat on the hardwood floor before my altar. Most of all, I loved the skylight above my bed. I lay there most mornings and looked out at a giant maple, one hand on my belly and one on my heart, breathing into my body.

Back then, I was so often alone that it felt like a huge departure just to go to class a few times a week. Every Thursday evening ten of us would meet in a studio on campus and begin with an "honoring ceremony." Here, we silently paired with another and "pulled strings" from parts of the other's bodies—the crown of the head, the third eye, the mouth, neck, chest, belly, legs, and feet. The choice of what strings to pull exactly was our own, but we always moved downwards, from head to feet. The person being honored just stood there, still, as the other gently awakened and honored their being. Then the partners switched places. I always found it harder to be honored than to do the honoring. Harder to stand there, open and exposed to the full gaze and touch of a near stranger. Harder to let myself be seen.

Aside from the voice of our teacher and, at times, music, the class was conducted in silence. Often we just walked very slowly, toes pointed inward, each footstep set down carefully, mouths open, breath heavy and deep. Sometimes we cradled dead birds in our hands. Other times we pulled out our hearts and held them as offerings. Usually, Butoh was slow, but it could also be fast, jagged, electric, like the time we were hungry ghosts, hurling across the room with manic fury. For *Hanging Woman*, we imagined a hook in the back of our necks, slowly drawing us upward, shoulders slouching forward, head dropping. For *Baby in the Light,* we balanced low to the ground on our bottoms, before raising our arms and legs up to an imagined light, as if seeing it for the first time, then slowly sinking back down again, up and down: an embryonic form.

In Butoh vision, you keep your eyes half-lidded, so while you can still see everything around you, you also sink deeper into your own body and breath. When I danced I didn't wear my glasses. While going without them in any other public context would feel far too vulnerable, having blurry vision while I danced helped me more fully enter my body. Others around me could transform into energy, darkness, and light. I didn't have to try so hard to shut out their influences—or rather my mind's constant thoughts and judgments that were triggered when I was with others. Instead I could just focus on opening.

7

Red Bird

Xie Ping lives in Yulin, a central neighborhood populated with cafes, bars, expats, and Chinese artsy types. I take a cab to her apartment on Saturday afternoon, after spending most of Friday and Saturday morning painting, unable to pull myself away from my new creation. She answers the door wearing a short black sundress and leads me to her studio, a small bare room, the lighting harsh and fluorescent. On the floor in the corner sits a narrow mattress; canvases are stacked against the wall. At first glance, they look almost exactly the same—all the same shade of sage green, and all with a bird, a thin elongated ghost of a bird, like a heron or crane, standing enclosed in a room.

My vocabulary to describe art is limited, but even in English I wouldn't know how to respond. Xie Ping pulls out some of her older paintings, hidden behind the birds. They are mostly in shades of black and grey. In these, wispy, stick-figured people perch on top or within everyday objects; a man and a woman balance on two spoons or stand inside vessels like a flowerpot or wine bottle, or are enclosed within boxes. Lots of angles and shadows, walls and mirrors.

I also notice a small muddled mass of strokes that hover above the birds or other objects, attached to them by a thin wispy line, almost like some sort of plant form with a stem. When I ask Xie Ping what it is, she shakes her head and says she can't say exactly, it's just something that always appears in her paintings, something that has to be there. Her eyes ask me if she'll be forced to elaborate. I nod, thinking of how certain images unconsciously reappear in my own drawings, assuming this is what she means.

Back in the living room, Xie Ping offers me tea. As she boils water in the kitchen, I sit on her rickety wicker couch and look around. Her living room, like her studio, is mostly unadorned, the walls bare, the floor concrete. A table and two chairs are pushed up against the wall to the right; a narrow, antique wooden table sits at my feet before the couch; and a stereo and big-screen TV loom large against the white wall across from me.

Xie Ping sits beside me, setting a pot of tea and two cups on the table. "Here." She holds out a catalogue of her paintings. "You can have it. It's from a show I had in Singapore a few years ago." The title reads *Loneliness in Grey*. The introduction describes how Xie Ping is not formally trained and how her unique "smudging technique tainted the melancholy tone with a feel of expressionism." I gather she must be about ten years older than me. I flip through the pictures which are more or less the same as the ones I've seen in her studio and scan the titles: *Man in the Flower Pot, Man on the Plate, The Grey House*. Most are called *Bird in the House*. I want to get to know this woman.

٢

That Sunday, I try to get ahead with lesson plans and figure out a course of action. I decide we'll focus on descriptive writing during the second week—writing from the senses, writing about people and places. But first I have my students lay their heads on their desk. They giggle and oblige. As I walk up and down the aisles, I ask them to visualize a favorite place, what it feels like, looks like, sounds and smells like. Then I have them write about it. Finally, we read a poem together and talk about metaphors. It seems to go pretty well.

With my graduate students, however, I am stumped. I find an essay by James Baldwin about language and dialect, hoping it might spark a conversation relevant to their studies in linguistics and get them reading and thinking more in English. The conversation goes okay, but I can tell they are wondering what this has to do with their papers.

By the next weekend, I've collected a huge stack of my students' journals and spend hours at my desk reading their first entries, some of which are interesting, but most are short and poorly written. Whereas one student writes about her fondness for Jane Eyre, others can hardly form a correct sentence. How can I teach to the middle, when the low and high ends are so extreme? The star students have been especially friendly to me, inviting me to eat lunch with them, but mostly I've declined their invitations, needing every non-required moment to be alone. To sit and write, paint, or listen to music. Or to plan lessons for the weeks to come.

I go into my third week of teaching feeling heavy and defeated, almost wishing the school had assigned me a textbook. Although I still have faith in the intention behind my methods, I am starting to realize that I need to give my students more structure. I borrow Robin's laptop and finally type up a syllabus—the bulk of which describes their first essay assignment and gives tips on revision and peer critique groups. My grading scale reads: *Journals, Attendance, and Participation: 25%; Personal Essay: 25%; Other Projects and Assignments to be Announced: 50%.* It will have to do for now.

The next day, I give my students their first major assignment: write a personal essay about a person or experience that changed them. As I walk through the formula for an essay—introduction, thesis, body, conclusion—my students obediently take notes. But when I try to get classroom discussions started, all eyes go down, with the exception of the few who sit up front. Finally I resort to calling on people, but I can only remember a handful of names. When I call on some of those who never speak, I begin to realize they probably haven't understood half of what I've said this whole time.

I want to be accessible to my students, to accept more of their invitations out to lunch, or invite them over to my place for tea, but this job is draining me, and I am protective of my time. I also want to have *real* conversations with them about China and America, history and oppression, Tibet and Taiwan, relationships, youth, rebellion, rock and roll, but I feel censored in my role as their teacher. My contract states I am not to talk about politics or religion in the classroom, and it is dawning on me that there are so few topics of substance that *aren't* related to those subjects—from China's one-child policy to the country's recent tenuous relationship with America, to my student's personal philosophies about life, love, spirituality, or death. On top of this, I know there is an assigned "classroom monitor" whose job has something to do with reporting to the administration what goes on, and knowing this makes me all the more cautious.

One day I spontaneously tell my students that I went to Tibet over the summer, and their eyes light up with envy and surprise. I learn that many of them dream of going there too, yet I still don't feel I can share my true feelings since I know most Chinese believe what they've been taught: that Tibet has always been a part of the motherland. That day after class, one of my bolder sophomore students, Jack, approaches me.

"What do you think of Tibet? Have you seen the movie, *Seven Years in Tibet*?"

I nod. Here it is, the question I've been hoping for and dreading. "Do you believe it, what the Chinese did?"

My mind flashes to images of Brad Pitt, who played the German mountaineer Heinrich Harrer, a friend of the young Dalai Lama, and to the scene where Chinese soldiers murdered monks in front of the

Potala and blew up the homes of villagers. I've read the book as well, and was annoyed by the liberties Hollywood took to add a romantic interest between Brad Pitt and a Tibetan. But of course, this was not what he was asking. Here is my opportunity to engage, but instead I hem and haw, unsure how honest I can be. Is he a typical nationalistic Chinese ready to set the foreign imperialist straight, or does he really want to know? If I reveal my sympathy for Tibetans will it somehow get back to the school authorities? In the end, I say something vague and Chinese, like "I think some things are probably true, but it is not so simple."

The next week, I collect their personal essays. One boy copies straight out of a text: *And then, my teacher Annie put the water under my hand and spelled into my palm, W-A-T-E-R . . ..* I laugh, then write in the margins: *I know you are not blind, and I know your name is not Helen Keller.* But not everyone's papers are bad; in fact many are decent, if not good. Several write of failing an exam or strict authoritarian fathers. Others write about their first time teaching English in a middle school as a part of their practicum, or their first job selling things door-to-door. One writes of getting lost in a train station as a child, and another of the death of a classmate. As I read, I flip through my stacks of photos to remind myself who they were. *Keep it a secret, Anne?* a student named Julie writes at the end of her paper about how her mother just died. All I remember of Julie was that she looked sullen and I thought maybe she didn't like me. Now, I realize her expression had nothing to do with me.

I can tell I am connecting with some of them who listen with rapt attention when I reveal bits of information about myself—like Normany, Tolby, and Gordon, the only boys who ever sit in front. They are endearing and often invite me to eat lunch with them, but I am afraid to tell them too much—afraid they'll find out how little experience I have, afraid to reveal my real intentions behind being in

China, which have nothing to do with teaching English and everything to do with my own longing.

ن

The next weekend, I go back to Xie Ping's for dinner. "This is He Mei," she motions to a young woman who greets me shyly before disappearing into the kitchen. I didn't know Xie Ping had a roommate. As if to answer my confusion, she explains, "He Mei used to work for me and my ex-husband. But when we got divorced, we had to let her go. A year later, she called me looking for work. I don't really need a maid," Xie Ping's eyes search for my approval, "but she'd didn't have anywhere else to go." She holds out her cigarettes, lights one for me, then sucks deeply on her own. Exhaling, she sighs.

"I used to be a good cook, you know. I cooked every night for my husband. I taught He Mei all kinds of dishes. Now, she makes them better than I do."

As she finishes her sentence, He Mei comes out of the kitchen and sets down a pot of tea and two cups. Her face is round, her shoulder-length hair pulled back in a messy ponytail. She glances at me with a shy smile, then quickly looks away. "*Xie xie*," I thank her, and she shakes her head quickly, barely meeting my eyes.

That night I learn that Xie Ping's ex-husband was also a painter, successful and internationally recognized. Xie Ping's energy grows heavy as she talks about him. In the silence that follows, I suggest we study English; Xie Ping mentioned last week that she wanted to learn. "Okay," she agrees, "but my English is terrible."

"Don't worry," I say. *Mei guanxi.* "We can just study a little." With a black marker, I write down basic words and phrases on a piece of paper. *Hello, how are you, my name is*—she knows these. *I'm from Chengdu, I am a painter, I like to dance*—these are familiar, but need review. Like most Chinese, Xie Ping learned a little English in high school, but that was a long time ago, and she hasn't had any schooling since. It is clear she doesn't even have a basic grasp of letter sounds. I decide we'll just focus on memorizing a few phrases for now.

As we study at the dining room table, He Mei begins to bring out steaming hot bowls of vegetables and diced meats. She keeps her eyes lowered and doesn't speak, but I can tell she is interested in what is going on.

"*Chi*," Xie Ping says when all the dishes and chopsticks are in place. Eat.

"Thank you." I smile at both of them, and pick up my bowl and chopsticks. I am self-conscious about the way I use chopsticks; even though I grew up using them as a child, I still don't hold them the "proper way." Well-meaning Chinese often make comments about my skills, lumping me together with other inexperienced foreigners, which annoys me. But Xie Ping doesn't say anything. The three of us eat silently, helping ourselves from the dishes at the center of the table.

After dinner, I sip on lukewarm tea as Xie Ping talks on her cell phone, making plans with a few of her girlfriends who we are to meet later at the High Fly. I listen as she talks in *Chengdu hua*, the local dialect, her voice more animated and coy as she teases her friends. With me, she seems more reserved, speaking in slow and simple standard Mandarin. Later she tells me that she doesn't feel natural in Mandarin—it feels too formal, almost like a second language.

That night I meet more of Xie Ping's friends. They are stylish, made-up women who are constantly answering their cell phones, then tucking them away in their purses. One is a photographer who took part in a show in LA, another is a fashion designer who studied in Holland, and another hosts a local television talk show. I feel young around them, dowdy in my thick glasses, loose khaki pants and Birkenstocks, the remnants of my traveling wardrobe. They banter back and forth and crack jokes with dramatic flair, always speaking in *Chengdu hua*. I get the gist of what they are saying, but most details fly past me. Every so often they turn and ask me a question in nice proper Mandarin, smiling and nodding in a saccharin sweet kind of way, before turning back to each other with more gossip, forgetting I am here. But I don't really care. I am content just to go out with them, sip on some beer and eye the dance floor, wait for a song to lure me out of my seat. It is better than going to the bar alone, which I've forced myself to do before. I need to dance, to have this weekend release away from campus, to be in a place where I feel more free.

Most of Xie Ping's friends don't dance, but after the crowd grows, she joins me on the dance floor when a Middle Eastern/electronic fusion song comes on that she likes. Together we twirl our wrists above our heads and wind our hips from side to side, flashing each other eyes of seduction. Usually I like to close my eyes when I dance in public, so I can more easily lose my awareness of people watching and merge with the music, but dancing with Xie Ping I keep them open so I can connect with her and encourage her to loosen up all the more. The dance floor is the one place in China where I feel bold, where I don't want to simply blend in.

ؖ

For the National Day holiday on October 1st, the students have a full week off. This is a special year, the 50th anniversary of the founding of the People's Republic of China, otherwise known as *jiefang*, liberation. Hurrah. I am relieved at the chance to rest and then do some hardcore lesson planning—get beyond this week-by-week scramble. I also need a cleanse—no more smoking, less drinking, time to center and breathe.

I already know what my next painting will be. I want to paint the feeling I had when I started dancing Butoh that night in my bedroom. The feeling of a bird with long, gangly red wings, expanding, not enclosed. I want to paint the colors of a sunset: glowing orange, deep blue, purple. *Red Bird*, I think as I wash a stroke of translucent color over the thick paper. In the middle of the painting, a white face with a gaping mouth, an anguished face, a Butoh face, emerges. As I paint, I feel like something is trying to get out of me, something fierce and red, the dark underbelly of my own sweet and smiling face. I start adding black for contrast. Twisted, elongated lines, like the grain of wood. I sit at the table for hours, forgetting to eat, painting until my fingers grow cramped, my eyes hard to focus.

I hide this painting when the repairman comes to fix my toilet later that afternoon. I don't want anyone to see it, much less some random Chinese person like him, or like the older Chinese woman who comes twice a month to collect my sheets—bedding that smells of mildew, complimentary from the school. Maybe they will shake their heads and think, *I can't understand art*, like my sophomore girls said when they came over for tea—the one time I managed to have anyone over. Maybe they'll think, *strange foreign woman*. Or maybe they won't even notice it, too absorbed in their tasks. But to have a creation in progress exposed, incomplete, still in mystification of what has come out of me, feels too vulnerable. It'd be different if I were painting flowers or scenic landscapes that people hang in their living rooms. But this is some raw part of me—wet, frayed, lingering strands still connected to my soul.

That Friday, I make the hour-long bus commute with two of my sophomores, Candy and Jean, to Tianfu Square. Candy is bubbly and sweet, with a high voice, short hair, round face, and glasses. Jean is quieter, with more depth. Both feel extremely innocent. We arrive downtown with the throngs of others before the giant Mao statue framed by flashing lights and giant billboards advertising cell phones and pagers. A wide busy street separates Mao from the square itself, a huge block of green grass with a smaller concrete area to stand on. Candy and Jean, both from provincial cities in Sichuan, gawk and exclaim at how *beautiful* the square is, especially the grass, which is guarded by stout middle-aged women in red vests who will yell and fine you if you dare step on its surface. (Grass was once declared bourgeois by Mao and torn out from every place in sight, but now it is okay.) We squeeze through the masses of bodies and pose for photos before freshly potted chrysanthemums and draping red banners with yellow characters proclaiming the glory of the motherland.

The crowds are ten times thicker than usual for the streets of Chengdu—and the usual is already the equivalent of being at a crowded summer music festival back home. Besides my Saturday night excursions, I've barely come into the city once since school started because it exhausts me to be around so many people, never mind the commute. The Chinese, however, seem to thrive on big crowds, gawking at each other, talking excitedly, taking photos. I stay close to Candy and Jean, not wanting to lose them in the sea of people carrying little red plastic flags proclaiming "50 Years." My students buy one for me and I carry it the rest of the afternoon like a decoy. I notice a Tibetan monk in the midst of the commotion and catch his eyes for a moment, wondering what he makes of the scene. But I do not greet him, "*Tashi Delek.*" I feel so removed from Tibet and all my idealistic longing to become some kind of peacemaker, much less fluent in Tibetan and Chinese; learning Chinese is hard enough. Nowadays, I don't even try to meet the eyes of people I pass on the street, never mind reaching out to greet a stranger with words.

In the evening there will be fireworks and on TV you can watch the parade, floats, and military marches broadcast from Tiananmen Square in Beijing. I want no part of it. This giant display of nationalism only saddens me. It makes me sick that some of my students don't even know about the Tiananmen Square massacre of June 4, 1989. My sophomores would have been around nine years old, easily sheltered from the media—whatever media might have reached them in their small towns in Sichuan or through the filter of wary parents.

Too many years of suspicion and betrayal, of being constantly monitored and asked to prove ones' loyalty to the party, too many political campaigns where even family members were pressured to turn against their own has created a nation of silent back-turning. *Better to not get involved, better to quietly go about one's business.*

No one has an official number of how many were killed. The Chinese government claims several hundred, but many years later inside sources will reveal it was closer to *ten thousand*. Tanks rolled into the city to clear the square, but tens of thousands of Beijing citizens stood in their way. They set up barricades with their bodies and bikes. They told the young, frightened soldiers, many brought in from the countryside, what was really going on; they read to them from newspapers, they offered them bowls of soup; they pleaded and initially succeeded in stopping the tanks from entering the city.

The moderates in the government argued and begged with the students to leave the square. They knew what was going to happen, although they weren't allowed to say. They knew the old guard could not lose face, could not concede one inch lest their whole faulty foundation start to crack and erode. They saw the students' idealistic naivety. The students hadn't thought things through; they didn't really know what they wanted beyond the abstract: human rights, freedom of press, speech, assembly, and travel. They had been in the square for weeks now and were sleep deprived, running on adrenaline, and still, every day, more busloads of students from outlying provinces arrived. But they should go home now, the moderates pleaded, take heart from what they'd already accomplished: the attention of the world, the attention of their countrymen. They should go back to school, finish their education, before it was too late.

On June 4, 1989, the tanks rolled in at night. People threw their bicycles together in piles to try and stop the inevitable. Crushed. Shots were fired. Fires blazed. Chaos. Blood. Hysteria. Those are real bullets. Running away, bystanders caught in crossfire, can't run away.

Even the next day, in broad daylight. One lone man stood still with briefcase in hand, his image immortalized by the press: a man facing a tank. Rigid, erect. No one knows what happened to him.

Now, as Candy, Jean, and I push our way through the narrow pathways in Tianfu Square, I wonder if any in the crowd also look upon this day with sadness, or if everyone is too steeped in nationalistic pride. From what I've read, ever since the Tiananmen clampdown in 1989, the idealism and opening up of the eighties has all but disappeared, activists and outspoken critics have gone into hiding, and everyone has became more focused on accumulating their own wealth. Cynicism and capitalism reign; who wants to be a martyr?

After posing for more photos in front of Mao and the potted yellow and orange chrysanthemums, I suggest to Candy and Jean that we walk to Renmin Gongyuan, People's Park, up the street. They have never been there before, so we wander through the park's teahouse and around the small, polluted pond, taking pictures. They want to make sure I get the tall ugly building in the background in the frame, the one I would have tried to crop out.

All I want now is to go home, back to the privacy of my own apartment. I can't handle the thought of another long, crowded bus ride, so I offer to pay for a cab back to campus—about $5. I can tell Candy and Jean think this is extravagant, but they quietly agree. Neither of them know what the taxi meter is, and they can barely figure out how to open the car door. I feel ashamed that I come from such a different world than they do.

Back in my apartment, I put on Indian sitar music and open a bottle of Red Dynasty wine. Gulping mouthfuls of the vinegar-like drink, I work on *Red Bird*, adding depth and layers of color. In the distance I hear fireworks and I laugh, toasting to the debauchery of the foreign teacher getting drunk by herself. When I am tired of painting, I go out on the balcony to search for a cigarette butt, but there are none worth smoking. I hate this trapped feeling of not being able to just walk out my door, but it is past eleven so I can't leave without disturbing the old man who keeps watch in the foyer, and I don't feel like climbing the gates.

I go into my bedroom and sit on the floor before my altar, this altar the purpose of which I no longer know. If anything, my desk is more my altar right now, a place I come to with mindfulness each day, whereas this bedroom altar feels like a mere symbol, an early yet futile attempt to announce what I wanted my life here to become.

When I arrived in Chengdu, I imagined my whole self spilling into this room, this school, this job, slowly sharing my ideas and stories with people, inviting them into my heart and home. But now, this apartment feels like a hideout, a refuge that isn't even fully mine. My altar, my paintings, Butoh, my writing, my love for the people of Tibet, my mourning over the history of this country, and my longing for all people to wake up and see more clearly the nature of their own suffering—the deepest, most authentic parts of myself all feel like secrets. There is so much I can't explain, so much I fear sharing with others, so much I can't even understand myself.

I light a candle, watching its flame flicker wildly from the air that comes in my open window. I sit on the floor, pull my knees against my chest, rock myself, and begin to cry. My breath heaves, in and out, quickening. Outside, a warm rain begins to fall. A gust of wind sends the long white translucent drapes sweeping forward, knocking my wine glass to the floor. Red wine on institution carpet. I leap up to get a towel, but my body sways and I no longer care if it stains. This room is only borrowed. Shaped by my efforts to try and hide the fact that it is surrounded by eyes on all sides, a locked gate, an imposed identity: foreigner. Teacher. Woman. Slightly odd. Not like us. *I'll be what you want me to be.*

I go into the bathroom and stare at my reflection in the mirror. You again. *You. What do you want?* I lean against the cold smooth counter. Sobbing now. If someone could hear me, I would have no words to explain. But I know no one can hear me, for all the other teachers are away. It is safe. I sprawl across the bed and bite on my pillow, heaving, gasping. No surface can absorb my weight. Putting my hand to my chest, I feel a concentration of pain. *Heart strings.* Strings being yanked—purging, wrenching. A pain that is not separate from my love for the world, only when I feel I must hide it, it becomes heavy and compressing, knows only the weight of sinking and nothing of gratitude or flight.

So dependent on my body for release. Only breath to channel. Slow, steady, finding my center of gravity. Body rising. Mouth dropping, breath transforming, heavy, long, deep. Lids lowering, focus softening. Limbs loosening, arms rising. Hunched old woman, angular wings, distorted cries, croaking gasps. Wind, dirt, decaying leaves. Shifting current, turning head, beating heart, listening. Burning chest, gagging throat, gnarled anguished birth. Red Bird...

She knows more than I do. About the pain of love, grief, and birth.

The locals say the weather turns every year around National Day. As I sleep that night the rain comes down hard, and in my dreams a massive flood surrounds me, water pouring in on all sides. *Hold your breath*, a woman says as we both go under.

The rain continues to pour the next morning. I wonder if the heavens are in mourning, crying for all the unnamed blood spilled, for stories still waiting to be unearthed and spoken.

Later that week, I catch a cab into the city and dance hard and furious at the High Fly, even to the music I don't care for. Xie Ping arrives and I sit with her and her friends between numbers, smoking way too many cigarettes as I half-listen to their conversations. Xie Ping is still the closest thing I have to a friend in Chengdu, but she still doesn't really know me. Surrounded day and night by the bodies and sounds of millions, I have never felt more alone.

Late that night back on campus, I weave drunkenly along the empty path back to my apartment. What would my students think if they saw me now? I climb over the gate to the foreigners' compound, knock loudly, and the old man eventually stirs, lets out a muted groan from somewhere in the depths of his dreams, shuffles to the glass door to let me in. After replacing the lock, he returns to his cot. The odor of mosquito repellent is thick in the air. I creep up the three stories to my apartment.

Is this what my life in China is meant to be? This repetitive cycle of cramming to get by and then trying to lose myself in one bingeing swoop? It is as if I want to go to some edge so that I can finally say, *enough*, and come back to my old slower rhythms. I miss my friends, my family, my small community of artists and spiritual seekers back in the States. If you'd asked me before if I had much community, I would have said no. But now I'm starting to realize how much I did have. Even if my closest friends no longer lived in the same town as I did, at least I could pick up the phone and call them. At least I could go home to watch bad TV, eat my mom's leftovers, and do laundry at my parents. At least I could walk outside and wander through mossy damp forests or along quiet sheltered shorelines, glimpsing magestic herons fly by, embraced by the beauty of nature.

I know now that I am definitely not going to renew my contract come February. I don't want to spend my whole time in China teaching English; I want to be learning and speaking Chinese. Maybe I can get a part-time job in the city, something that will leave more time for exploring this country and myself on other levels. But now it is only October, and four months from now feels so far away.

I grow sick that week while on break, my nose stuffed, my head dizzy, body worn. Mostly, I just lay in bed reading *Red Sorghum*, a novel I borrowed from Robin about the brutal Japanese invasion of

Manchuria. I pull myself out of the apartment once in four days to get a bowl of noodles, too tired to cook. I have plans to meet with two of my students who aren't going home for the break, Plum and Jane, but when their calls come, I don't answer the phone. When I receive a note saying that one of the Chinese artists I'd met in Lhasa stopped by, I also don't return his call.

By the end of the week I feel a little better, but still drained. I force myself to face the stack of student journals and essays waiting to be graded, heading with them to a teahouse in town. Then on Saturday, I make plans to have dinner with Xie Ping at her apartment. I promise to give her an English lesson, and then we'll go dancing at the Flamingo, a bar near her apartment where Guang Hui now deejays.

Over the last couple months, my crush on him has festered and grown. Mostly, it is his music that moves me, but also his style and aloof mystery—his long dark hair and funky wardrobe of hippy Nepali shirts, black leather pants, and sporty zip-up sweatshirts—all of which stick out uniquely amidst the sea of typical boring male Chinese dress. He flirted with me at one point, telling me as I left his party that we should go out for tea. I began to fantasize about entering a relationship with him, writing down lists of all the words I'd need to learn in order to reveal myself—words like spirit, inspiration, and meditation. Or simple phrases like, "Do you want to hang out sometime?" that I still don't know how to pull off smoothly in Chinese. But when Guang Hui did finally call, he invited Xie Ping to join us for our date, which was fine, but then in person he barely met my eyes or spoke to me directly. Since his Mandarin was hard to understand, we spent most of the afternoon talking through Xie Ping, looking up occasional words in the dictionary.

Now, it has become clear that Guang Hui is not interested in me, and that in fact he can be extremely arrogant, an entourage of foreigner girls always hanging at his side. I've stopped approaching him at the bar, and instead try to ignore him completely as I dance, yet secretly I still hope he is watching.

More than anything, I crave intimacy, to look into someone's eyes and feel seen. These artists and bar-frequenters seem like my closest kin here. Yet even though I can relate to many of them more than I can to my students, their emphasis on fashion, status, and cynical gossip often makes me feel like I am back in high school. Something is missing here, some spark of vitality or optimism, a desire to share transparently, to tell your story and connect from a deeper place.

I smoke thirteen cigarettes that night at the Flamingo, and the next morning my throat feels like hell. Twice now, I've triumphantly thrown away a pack, only to go digging for it the next day in the garbage. I am also now re-addicted to coffee (instant, sugary Nescafé), whereas I arrived here drinking only tea. I planned to buy a bike so I could get some exercise, but never got around to it. Now, I've sunken into a cycle of unhealthiness. I miss my friends and family; I haven't gotten a letter or good e-mail in weeks, and it is too expensive to call.

All I want is to crawl into bed and read or sleep. But I have too much to do. So I shower, make coffee, and eat cookies for breakfast since there is nothing else in my kitchen. I light a stick of incense and reach for the stack of my sophomores' journals. I will get through this. Only fifty-six more to go.

ای

Monday marks the beginning of my fifth week of teaching, and I am not refreshed nor better organized after the break. I barely managed to get through everyone's journals and personal essays the night before, and then I couldn't sleep, knowing I had to get up early today. Before class, I need to go to the copy center and wait for the staff to print the week's handouts with ancient ditto machines on soft recycled paper that reminds me of grade school. Now, I am beginning to understand the degenerative cycle of bad teaching. *Overwhelmed and unprepared? Give them worksheets!* Something to keep them busy.

When I arrive in my first senior class, my students are abuzz with fresh energy. They watch me without quieting down, until I assume my role at the podium.

"Good morning," I say, and smile.

"Good morning!" they call back in unison. I write down the word *insomnia*. "Do you know what this means?" Some nod. Great, I can't even teach them a new word. "Well, I had insomnia last night. I couldn't sleep." They stare. I feel like they can see right through me.

Toward the end of the class I hand back their essays, watching as they hungrily read my comments. Later, as they leave, Julie comes up to me with a huge smile. She tells me this is the most any teacher has ever responded to anything she's written. Others give me smiles as well. But some students are surprised that I am asking them to revise, even though it is stated in the syllabus. I've intended to draw out the stages of writing and this was only meant to be a rough draft, but they seem to think they are already finished.

In my sophomore classes, I hand back their journals and then tell them they will be writing their autobiographies. Their eyes grow wide. I say that maybe we can even find pen-pals for them in America to send them to. They gasp. I don't know where to find the pen-pals, but I hope the idea will get them excited.

Thankfully, the weekend finally rolls around again. And Saturday night, I am excited, for I have plans to get together with my friend, Tamara. She is from San Francisco, in her late twenties, and here studying traditional Chinese medicine. I met her back in June when we were both staying at the guesthouse near the medicine college while I was looking for a job. She'd gone to Beijing for a couple of months, but now she is back in Chengdu.

I meet Tamara at her hotel that night and she gives me a hug. Her big brown eyes and gentle voice feel so welcoming. Over dinner, she

listens as I tell her about my months living and teaching at *Chuan Si*.
It is a huge relief to finally vent to someone from outside school about
my class load, my isolation, my overall unhappiness. I didn't know
how bad it was until I recounted it out loud. As much as I appreciate
chatting with the other teachers like Robin or Chris over an occasional meal, I haven't been able to fully confide in them how much I
have been struggling. After all, they have similar loads. I feel weak for
not being able to handle mine.

After dinner we go to the Little Bar, where Tamara introduces me
to a Chinese painter with long hair and an endearing grin, someone
she met briefly the week before. I love the feeling of being out on
the town, interacting with locals and other young people, but not
so young as my students. Urban Chengdu feels a world apart from
the suburbs where I teach. Later, we go dancing at the Flamingo, but
Tamara grows tired and leaves early. I stay on, dancing by myself
amidst the other expats and students. By now, their faces are all
familiar, but I've only ever spoken to a few. A drunken French businessman tries to pull me into a salsa number, but I don't like to partner dance. Dancing is spiritual for me, the closest thing I have to
church.

By three a.m., I am one of the last ones still here and the bartender
offers us free shots. These days it feels like I could keep drinking and
drinking and still not feel drunk. At least not happy drunk. Later the
bartender offers me a ride home.

Back on campus, only a few lights are on. I walk slowly up the
main tree-lined street, during the day crowded with students, but
now refreshingly empty. I walk past the building in which I teach,
swaying as I turn left onto the familiar path to the foreigners' compound. *Here we go again.* I climb the gate. It creaks and rattles as I
make my way over and drop lightly to the other side. *Piece of cake.*
Wake up the old man. *Xie, xie.* Climb the three stories. *My apartment, just as I left it.*

Still buzzing from an evening of drinking and conversation, I do not feel like going to sleep. I do not want to wake up to the stack of papers waiting to be graded and the new week of teaching that lays ahead. I open the doors to my balcony and pick through the ashtray for a salvageable butt. Lighting and inhaling—and then the taste of the filter already, the pleasure gone. In the distance I hear a train, melancholy, the sound of coming and going, strangers sleeping in compartments passing through this dark spot of earth. I look through the ashtray one last time, sigh, then go inside and shut the door.

In my room, I lay on my bed, but I can't sleep, head still buzzing. I turn on the lamp and start to write in my journal. *I wish I could just leave. I could, you know, I could just leave right now...* Double take on what I've just written. *I could pack my things, leave a note, "Sorry, didn't work out," and just leave.* My pen starts to get excited. *What the hell are you talking about, Anne? You've got 200-something students, you've got papers to grade, you've got a responsibility.*

Yeah, but you know, I could, if I really wanted to, just leave. After all, Chris told me about his friend who had just done the same thing. Couldn't stand it. Had to go be with his girlfriend in Guatemala. Just picked up and left his job.

This is ridiculous, irrational, you're drunk.

Still, the thought remains. *I could just leave . . .*

I go into the bathroom and stare in the mirror. *Do you know what you're talking about? Are you serious?* I go back to my journal and write, *You have to really know yourself in this moment, Anne. If you do this, there's no turning back. You have to know this is what you really want.*

I test the theory. Opening my closet door, I stare at my clothes. I could pack them first, just see how it feels; they'll be easy to put back if I realize halfway through that this is crazy. I get out a cardboard box and start pulling clothes off their hangers. Faster now. It feels good. *Don't worry about packing neatly.* Clothes packed, I am not yet dissuaded. Next, the books. Those will be easy to put back on the shelf too. One sweep, swift and neat, and they are in the box as well. *What next?* My trinkets from Tibet, special things. The things on my altar. More frantic now. Writing tools, paints, toiletries, thrown in bags and boxes. A few kitchen things, the expensive Tupperware and Ziploc bags. The rest can stay, too bulky. I turn on music for inspiration. It is happening.

I save the things on the walls for last. Carefully arranged and taped photos, drawings, posters, I peel away. With the walls now bare, it feels sealed—this is going to happen. All the effort I've taken to make this place feel like a home, destroyed. In the middle of the living room my few boxes and bags sit in a small pile. I go into the kitchen and wash the dishes. Don't want the staff to come in and think that I am irresponsible, now do I? Dishes done, I stack and order my students' journals and papers in neat piles, so they can be returned to them after I leave. My other notes I pile together—won't be needing these anymore. Now it is done. There is no way I am holding class on Monday. Otherwise tomorrow will be a headache of backtracking preparation. I am behind enough as it is.

At five-thirty a.m., more sober but spacey from lack of sleep, I realize I need support. I need to tell someone what I've done, what I am doing. Make it seem less crazy, more real. Otherwise, there is always the possibility of pretending it never happened. I decide to wait until six to call Tamara. I make a cup of Nescafé to sip while I wait, which only makes me jittery. Finally, six o'clock comes.

"Tamara?" Of course I wake her. "You'll never believe what I've just done."

Tamara tries to talk sense in me. "Now, Anne," she says in a kind, motherly voice, "maybe you should go to sleep for a few hours, get some rest, and decide when you're feeling a little more, uh, normal."

No, no, that's not what I want to hear.

"Maybe you should think this over a little, maybe you should give them two weeks' notice or something."

No, no, no, two weeks' notice was ridiculous. I need to leave NOW. I can barely wait until sunrise. I can not wait two *weeks*. They would try and talk me out of leaving. They would lighten my class load. They would say, "We can work this out together." I would not be able to say no. I would not be able to explain my real reasons for leaving—how trapped I feel on campus, climbing over locked gates, everything monitored and watched; how false I feel when I can not share all of me, openly, who I really am—a writer, an artist, a seeker, a tentative Buddhist and activist, a woman still in her infancy of discovering her voice and place in this world, an authentic way of being.

I can not handle the pressure of so many classes to plan, journals to read, papers to grade, stories to ingest, people to please or let down with my performance. I came to China trusting that I could keep my core of awareness and compassion intact, yet now I am learning how hard it is to live here, and how easy I've had it back home. How quickly my equilibrium can crumble when no longer supported by the beauty of the earth at my doorstep, by ample time to pursue my creative outlets, or by the company of friends who share the same language as I do, as well as a similar spiritual worldview. I've lost my core of nourishment, and without this, I have nothing sustainable to give. I can't be a teacher right now, at least not here, in this way. There is too much I still have to learn. And I am too young to compromise.

"Tamara, please listen to me. I've already decided. I just need your support. Just tell me you'll come help me move my stuff. Tell me you'll help me out. I'll go to sleep for a couple hours and call you at eight."

"Okay," she says.

As I suspected, with the morning light come my own suspicions and doubts. I feel strung out. My apartment is a mess. I almost consider backing out, but then I think of what it'd take to put it all back together, and I know I can't. I sit down at the table and write two notes. One to Mr. Yang, the man who hired me, telling him how sorry I am but that I have to leave due to a "crisis of the heart." I do not want to lie, but I also do not know how else to explain. The other letter I write to the other teachers, also saying how sorry I am. How I know I am leaving them with an unfortunate situation, because someone will get stuck with my classes. With them I am a little more honest, but still vague. We have never grown close.

I call Chris upstairs, the teacher I sense will be the most supportive, and wake him, telling him what I am doing and asking him to show my note to the other teachers. He is surprised, but not *that* surprised. "You know what you're doing," he says. "You're following your heart." I love him for saying that. He walks me down to the main gates, where we wait for Tamara's taxi to arrive. I direct the driver to my compound and tell him to wait as Chris and Tamara help me carry my few boxes and bags down the stairs and stuff them into the back seat. I run to tape the other note on Mr. Yang's door. It is Sunday, eight-thirty a.m. I know he will not be there, but I am terrified of running into anyone. This has to be done quickly, with no second thoughts, or else it could still be undone. I still am not sure what I am doing. All I know is, once my bags were packed, I had to go.

In the apartment, I leave a few discarded tapes, some clothes, a lamp, wok, rice cooker, dishes, stolen plants, and on the wall I leave a poster I bought in Lhasa, a painted mythical rendering of the Potala Palace. Some things I leave because I can not carry them or do not care about them, but the poster, that is meant to be a sort of gift—an object of beauty, a reminder of a spiritual place that is far away, yet also still within reach.

"I'll send you an e-mail," I tell Chris, and then we are off, Tamara crammed in the back seat amidst my stuff, me in the front. The doors slam shut. In the taxi, I feel almost safe, though I can't fully breathe till we get off the campus grounds, afraid someone will see me. My heart pounding, my mind dazed. I eye the taxi driver's pack of 555's and ask him if I can have one, discarding my usual reluctance at bumming smokes from random locals. In broken Chinese I tell him triumphantly that I quit my job as a teacher! He looks at me strangely and holds out the pack. I light it, victorious. It is harsh and burns in my throat, but I don't care.

8

Seeking Intimacy

When I was in high school, my mother used to smell me when I came home late at night. My bedroom was across from my parents' and I was supposed to knock and say, "I'm home." She'd come out into the hallway in her pajamas to give me a hug, which was her way of getting close to me, hunting for the scent of cigarettes or alcohol.

The Chinese like to say to their kids (or their pets), "*Guai guai*," an endearing coo of approval that means you're good and well-behaved. My sister and I had been groomed to be *guai* since we were little—to behave politely toward adults, to never contradict our elders, to do our chores when asked. On the surface, I was always a good girl who got good grades and was on her way to a good college. But inside, I was drawn to the rule-breakers and I loved the feeling of being wild, out at night with my peers. Whereas my sister frequently got in yelling matches with my parents or otherwise openly defied their rule, my rebellions took place largely in silence, away from home, or within the confines of my journal. I did get grounded a few times for drinking or sneaking out at night, but for the most part I partied hard throughout my teenaged years without my parents having a clue. My sister would later claim I got off easy because she'd paved the way, which may have been true to some extent, but mostly I think it was because I was better at hiding.

To avoid my mother's smell test, I often spent the night with my friends who had later curfews and less suspicious parents. My friends and I went to keg parties held in woodsy parks, ran from the police who'd inevitably break up these "kegs," then roamed the streets of Montlake, high on the rush of running around on our own. We asked adults to bootleg us beer or wine coolers at small markets in Seattle's Central District, drove drunk from party to party, and skipped class and drank pots of coffee at IHOP until our hands shook. Sometimes after school we'd get stoned in the private worlds of our bedrooms while listening to Tracy Chapman, Alpha Blondy, Nirvana, and Neil Young, revealing secrets about heartbreak, or how my friend's dad was gay, or how we couldn't wait to graduate and live on our own.

My experimentations started before high school, however. My friend Beth and I both had sisters two grades ahead and had heard enough of their tales of partying that we were game to follow in their footsteps. At age twelve we started stealing a few cigarettes from her dad, which we'd share and then spin around in circles, our buzz immediate and dizzying; or we'd do "whip-its," inhaling the nitrous oxide from cans of whipping cream for a quick little high. Soon we began preparing for our frequent sleepovers at her place by slowly pilfering alcohol from our parents, mixing together whatever we found, be it brandy, gin, or wine, in a small jar. After forcing down these nasty concoctions we'd go out on an adventure, maybe t.p.'ing someone's house or meeting up with our guy friends at a nearby park, sometimes walking for miles. On one such outing, I took a long-neglected bottle of Crème de Menthe from my parents' stash and drank enough to make me sick. My shit the next morning was green. The following week, I gave a speech to my school, as I was running for eighth grade vice president. My guy friends who had been with us that night heckled me from the bleachers, laughing, "A.A!" (*Alcoholic Anne!*). I blushed, hoping others had no idea what they were talking about. But I was also a tiny bit proud to be a part of their rebellious crowd.

Despite my frequent partying, I only ever got in trouble a few times. The first time came in eighth grade when my mom read my journal, inside of which I talked about sneaking out and drinking with Beth. She yelled at me when I came home from school that day, her dark eyes flashing from behind her big owl glasses as she pointed to the offending page. "Kid! What is this? You are in big trouble!" I felt violated and powerless. She would never understand me. I was grounded for a month—no phone, no going out. We didn't otherwise discuss it.

Another time, I was out with friends one day as a freshman. We were drinking 40s of Old E at someone's house. When the time came to go home, I knew I was too drunk. Did I call my parents to tell them so? I must have, for no one had cell phones then so they couldn't have called me. I can't remember what I said exactly now, only that the conversation ended for the first time with me screaming, "I hate you!" at my dad.

What did I hate? Was it my parents' cluelessness, the distance I felt from them now that I was no longer their little girl? Or was it witnessing their own irrepressible bursts of anger—indications of their own deeper fears and emotions, feelings that usually were usually unexpressed or buried? It would take me decades to begin to see all the layers of experience that went into my need to feel more unconditionally loved, and to slowly learn how to give more witnessing words of acceptance and appreciation to myself. But as a teen, I just felt my need to break free from their controlling influence and from my need to seek their approval. To stop trying to be so *guai*. All I knew that night was that I was not going home. I was spending the night with my friend, I told them. And they must have said okay. Because all I remember is, they didn't yell back this time. Maybe they were afraid. They actually seemed to listen.

٢

I come from a family of planners. Of fret about your future, worry about your health, beware of taking risks, kind of people. Of try to closely monitor and account for all things that could possibly go wrong kind of people. Every time I left the house or came home they never failed to remind me to double-lock the door. Fear and a desire to control things ruled. Following one's gut without a plan was not to be trusted. Although my dad was raised Catholic, he didn't adopt any faith as an adult. And my mom, too, was raised without religion, unless you count the Confucian ideals of working hard, and honoring education and family. As such, I did not know how to share with my parents my growing relationship with my own spirituality, nor my growing trust in my own intuitive choices, rational thinking be damned.

When I was born, my dad was working as a campus planner for the University of Washington and my mom was getting her PhD in urban planning. She'd immigrated to the US for grad school, where she met my dad at the University of Wisconsin-Madison. They moved out west, and before long, my grandmother, Popo, moved from Taiwan to help take care of newborn me and my one-and-a-half-year-old sister. My grandfather had insisted she come help my mother, even though she didn't want to move by herself. Eventually, my mom began working as a policy analyst for the city council, and my parents also helped my mom's siblings come to the States, including my uncle's family who lived with us for a couple years. After school, Popo would warm up steamed *mantou*, soft white rolls that we'd slather with margarine and eat in front of the TV. At night we'd watch Popo as she did her exercises in front of her TV in the basement. Weekends we were often left on our own to roam the neighborhood and play with the neighbors.

I have few memories of being with my parents as a young child. I know my dad used to play with us, pretending he was a bear lumbering down the stairwell as we screamed in waiting, or holding us upside down so we could "walk" on the ceiling. And I can recall my mom helping me to get dressed or combing my hair in the mornings, then cooking me a fried egg with soy sauce, the morning news droning in the background. My dad came to every one of my basketball games from third through twelfth grade, and my mom sat us down to practice piano every week or Chinese characters every Sunday morning. Yet most of my early memories relate to hours of imaginary play—whether alone, pretending I was a teacher in front of a blackboard in the basement; with my best friend next door playing private detectives or with our Barbies and stuffed animals; or with my sister up in the treehouse my dad built, pretending we were a family like Swiss Family Robinson, mixing concoctions of grass and berries for our meals.

I know my parents were loving. But they were also stressed, working full-time, and supporting both of their families financially. My mom was doing research and writing reports in her second language. And then my grandfather grew ill with hepatitis in Taiwan when I was five. A couple years later after, he moved to Seattle and my parents helped him and my grandma move into a house up the street. But he died about two years later of liver cirrhosis, just before I turned nine.

I remember the wailing cry of my grandmother and the flurry of movement that followed as the adults rushed out of the house and a close neighbor came over to watch us children. Although I'd learned of death a year prior when a distant uncle from my dad's side had died, this was the first time I witnessed the sudden eruption of my family's grief and emotion, what was usually stuffed inside. My mom was the only one to speak at her dad's funeral. "My father would be very happy that you are all here," she said, her voice cracking—the only time I ever remember seeing her cry. To this day, I don't recall seeing my dad shed a tear.

Certainly, a tension must have permeated the household during this time, but no one talked about it. My parents did not know how to talk about feelings—whether theirs or ours. And as such, although I know I was loved as a child, as an adult I mostly think about what was missing and why. At family reunions I'd hear accounts of my dad and his ten siblings growing up poor, working at their family store and eating sandwiches made of sugar and lard. But I heard little about the traumatic events, like how it affected him after his dad died from lung cancer when he was twenty-six, or how his almost-three-year-old brother died when he was in high school, falling out of their family's moving car. I'd long known about that moment, but it would take over four decades of being alive until I learned that after little Doug fell out, he was then hit by an oncoming car. No counseling was given to the children. No one talked to them about the death, puberty, or sorrow, I suspect. Just like no one talked to me.

My mother has shared even fewer recollections from her youth, except the occasional anecdote, like how she doesn't enjoy candle-light because she used to have to study by it—and how it will ruin our eyes not to read with proper light. I know that after fleeing the mainland during the civil war when she was seven, her family with five young children lived in Hong Kong, and a couple years later they moved to Taiwan, outside of Taipei. They lived in the countryside in a house made of mud, though they were neither rich nor poor when compared to those around them. I never used to think of my mom as a refugee. But when she speaks of her childhood now and relays how they would have been "slaughtered" had they stayed on the mainland, I can only imagine what that awareness felt like as a young child. Whether anyone ever told her directly what was going on, or if she overhead adult conversations, or simply ingested their fear and followed along with their directives—all of the chaos was nevertheless felt acutely, but never addressed directly.

My parents were present throughout my childhood, yet they were also absent. Did I seek more of their time and attention? I must have. Especially from my mom who did not play with us like my dad did. My most tender memories of her are from when I was sick and she would bring me toast and 7 Up or rub Vicks on my chest in bed. I also loved to go to the bookstore at the mall with my parents to pick out a hard-backed Nancy Drew, my reward for my good report cards each quarter. On weekend mornings, I'd put on my favorite *Swan Lake/ Sleeping Beauty* Tchaikovsky album from their collection of classical records, then prance around in front of them as they read the paper and looked up every so often, smiling and nodding. In these times I knew I could make them happy. In these times I knew I was *guai*.

I also learned how to shut the door to my room and escape into books—fantasies, mysteries, stories of young girls solving crimes or going on journeys, little people hiding in the walls, children wandering through forests or museums at night, resilient and fending for themselves. I'd find cozy hiding spots in my closet or snuggle with our dog in the basement. I'd write in my diary and learn to stay quiet, to let the others do the worrying or arguing. To disappear and get out of everyone's way.

My sister and I were only one and a half years apart, and I looked up to her—copying her every move in fashion or music—as much as I also resented her. So close in age and both hungry for affection, maybe it was inevitable that we would grow up comparing ourselves to one another, for we'd hear the praise given to the other or the ways our accomplishments were listed off to our parents' friends. And while my parents did their best to try to make sure that everything was distributed equally between us, counting down to the last dollar how much they spent on us for Christmas, I wonder now if this meticulous accounting only caused us to compare ourselves even more. After elementary school, once I started in an honors' program, I attended different schools than my sister—and for this I was relieved. I didn't like always being known as her little sister or being mistaken for twins. I hated the way she talked down to me or stood over me while I was laying on the floor watching TV, pretending she was going to spit. We fought often—whether with words, cold water tossed on the other while showering, or by grabbing hair and clawing with nails. We fought the worst after school as tweens when no one was home to mediate. But even when my parents were home, they'd just yell at us to knock it off, rarely intervening unless it got ugly.

When I started middle school a year early with a special class of fifth graders in a gifted program, our class was mostly boys and as such I was eager to find girlfriends among the "big" sixth graders. As a lowly fifth grader, I desperately wanted to be chosen and cool despite the fact that I still wore dorky thick plastic glasses and had a gap between my front teeth. One day I took home a circulating "slam book" (where people anonymously write their opinions about you), reading it on my hour-long bus ride home to North Seattle. I was crushed by one of the comments under my name where someone wrote, "tries too hard." My sister must have at some point read my journal too, for she taunted me, "No friends!" Maybe she said this only once, maybe more, but the echo rang in my head for years.

Yet as sisters it was easy to go from all-out battle to acting normal again the next day. Although we sometimes hated each other, we also knew each other intimately. At night we'd knock on the wall in our own secret code of communication—*Are you awake? Yes. Goodnight.* Our voices sounded the same, our expressions, our laughs. We read the same books, wore the same clothes, listened to the same music, shared the same jokes, and stayed loyal when it came to not disclosing one another's transgressions. In this we were united against my parents' fury when we disobeyed.

My mother's temper was the worst, yelling without reserve when she was set off. And although my dad was ordinarily the more patient one, his anger could feel equally explosive when it suddenly arrived. Afterwards, once punishments were doled out, no one would talk about any of it—or if my parents ever tried to get us to open up, they failed. We saw their lack of emotional control, their tipping points. We didn't know what lay beneath, but maybe we intuitively knew it was something they didn't even fully understand. And although we'd accept our punishments, we never respected them; they only made us more determined not to get caught. Breaking rules gave us a small amount of agency during a time when we otherwise had none.

My mom now tells me that she worries she was too lenient with us, more lenient than most of her Chinese friends. At the time, I thought the opposite, for I had the earliest curfew of my mostly white friends. Now, however, I can appreciate her dilemma, how raising American teenagers was radically different than any experience she'd known. As kids, however, we were already indoctrinated into a white, affluent culture that glorified youth partying and rebellion. We grew up watching movies like *Sixteen Candles*, *Ferris Bueller's Day Off*, and *The Breakfast Club*. My parents tried their best to raise us right, but ultimately they had no idea how to talk to us about feelings, insecurities, bodies, or desires. And as such, we were lost to them.

I never told my parents about my difficulties adjusting to middle school, and they never knew how to ask. Meanwhile, sexual innuendo was inserted into the school terrain seemingly overnight, yet everything I knew about sex was gleaned from TV, my sister, my peers, *Sweet Valley High* or Danielle Steele books, and from the men who now honked their horns at me on the street. Boys snapped my bra, commented on my bubble butt, or wrote things in my yearbook about "hot beef injections." I learned from watching my sister how to apply my dark eyeliner, how to obsessively brush my hair, and how to shave my legs, even though they barely had any hair. At age eleven, I also watched my first porno in my parents' basement when some guys my sister knew paid us a midnight visit. Only once, years later in high school, did my mom attempt to give me a "sex talk" by saying, "You know about AIDS and all that, right?" That was a little too late.

I loved my parents, yet I no longer turned to them for affection nor understanding. Instead, I gravitated towards rawness, towards conversations that exposed vulnerability, places where exteriors could be cracked and emotions expressed—places I now found with my peers. I longed for the rest of my life spreading out before me: flickers of authenticity surfacing, glimmers of how much I didn't know.

9

Sex, in Chinese

The farther the taxi gets from the college, the more anonymous and free I begin to feel. I smoke the harsh cigarette the driver gave me till its very end, flicking the butt out the window. When we pull up at Tamara's hotel in the east-central part of Chengdu, we pull my plastic bags, boxes, and backpacks out on the curb, then lug all my stuff into the lobby. The people at the front desk look at us strangely, but don't ask questions. I figure I'll stay with Tamara for a week or so, until I figure out a new plan.

Without a job, I've lost my anchor, not to mention my visa status. But I also feel blissfully released. Released from the responsibility of teaching 200-some students, released from being on stage. Back to just searching for my purpose. Waiting for the right signs to appear. By day, as Tamara attends class at the traditional medicine college, I once again take to wandering the streets of Chengdu, writing e-mails from crowded Internet cafes, running errands, and trying to figure out what the hell I am going to do. It's mid-October, the air is cooler, and the season has definitely shifted.

On my second day of my new freedom, I drift into Carol's, a café/bar by the river and sit near the window, staring out at the bleak grey of the city, doodling in my journal and sipping a cup of weak coffee. A few minutes later, a Chinese man walks in who looks familiar. Yes, he is the guy I met at the Little Bar just a little over a week ago, the painter. Yizhong. I even remember his name. Tamara had introduced us that night, although she had only met him once before. He knew a little English, so we stuck to English. I remember thinking he looked more South American, Peruvian perhaps, than Chinese. Maybe it was his hair, long and flowing, or his wide nose, or the brown glow of his skin. Or maybe it was his friendliness, so much less less guarded than many of the hip, young Chinese I've met so far.

I probably would have never thought of him again though if he didn't walk into Carol's just now, along with Roman, an older French guy I also know from the bars. I nod when they see me, and Yizhong invites me to join them at their table.

"*Ni hao,*" I say as I sit down across from him.

"Hello," Yizhong answers me in English.

"*Women keyi jiang Zhongwen,*" I say. We can speak in Chinese.

He looks surprised and smiles brightly. "*Hao.*" Okay.

They order drinks and we start talking in Chinese. I explain how I quit my job, and they nod sympathetically but don't act that shocked.

"There are lots of opportunities for teaching English here," Roman says. "You will be able to find something else."

I nod, but don't say that I am not sure if I even want to.

They order spaghetti and coffee and I watch them eat as we continue to chat. I keep thinking that Yizhong has something in his teeth, but then I realize that his front tooth is actually broken. Every so often he meets my eyes, but then looks away shyly at his food. After Roman signals to the waitress for the bill, Yizhong asks if I want to tag along with them, looking for picture frames for paintings that Roman bought from Yizhong and his parents (a family of painters). I agree, eager to have the company and distraction. Later, after we shop, Yizhong invites me to have dinner at a friend's place.

"Everyone's going to cook a dish. My friend plays the guitar. People will probably just be sitting around, hanging out."

"Sure," I agree, intrigued by the opportunity to meet more Chinese artists.

We walk to the street market that sells live fish and freshwater shrimp, a labyrinth of narrow lanes, entrepreneurs, and farmers. I follow Yizhong as he picks out fresh ginger, green onions, garlic, hot peppers, and spices, impressed by his navigation among the vendors and stalls, thrilled to be here with a real Chinese "intellectual," buying ingredients for dinner.

None of Yizhong's friends say much to me when we arrive; I think they are surprised by my presence. Instead, they sit mutely in the living room watching Chinese MTV while Yizhong takes his turn in the kitchen to prepare his famous spicy fish. I sit beside them on the couch, awkwardly trying to make conversation, before finally wandering over to stand in the doorway and watch Yizhong cook. He whips up egg yolks, coats the slices of fish, dusts them with a light layer of flour, and then heats up the oil in the wok to fry the ginger and spices for a few seconds before throwing in the fish.

"Sorry it's not more exciting," he apologizes.

I shake my head. *"Mei you, mei guanxi."* No, no, it's fine.

But I feel relieved when we finally leave to go home, back out into the cool night air. We ride the bus and make plans to meet the next day at two in front of Tamara's hotel, for he happens to live right nearby. Tomorrow he will show me his paintings, and I will get to see his home.

The next day at ten after two Yizhong runs up, out of breath, hair flying loose, wearing a pink button-up shirt, brown pants, and tan New Balance tennis shoes, apologizing for being late.

"Ni chi le ma?" Have you eaten? he asks, a typical Chinese greeting. *"Chi le,"* I assure him.

As we walk back to his apartment, he motions with his hand to a vendor at the side of the road selling golden apples from a bicycle cart. "Do you like apples?"

"Xihuan." I nod. He picks through the selection, choosing each carefully for the farmer to place in a plastic bag and weigh, before pulling out a few kwai to pay. We walk on, past the buzz and crowds of vendors, shoppers, and idlers on the sides of the street, then turn the corner to face his apartment complex. A dingy grey six-story cement building, it is surrounded by others that look exactly the same. A scattering of people gather in the courtyard below; laundry hangs from windows to dry. We climb five flights of stairs, he opens two locks on his metal door, and we step inside.

"Should I take off my shoes?"

He nods. *"You tuoxie."* He motions to a pair of slippers near the door.

His apartment is small, but larger than I expected. To the right of the entryway is a tiny kitchen, to the left is the living room, and in front of us, two other small rooms. I peek at the bathroom, the size of a tiny closet.

"Do you want to drink some tea?" he asks.

"Sure."

"Go ahead and have a seat." He motions to the living room. "I'll heat some water."

As he disappears, I look around. On the walls hang several colorful batiks next to a few framed works of calligraphy and two long carved wooden totems. Against the far wall sit stacks of tapes and two speakers, empty wine bottles serving as candle holder perched on top. A vase of fresh red flowers rests on a square coffee table; a spider plant hangs near the window. I sit on the dark green leather couch and look at a collage of pictures arranged underneath the glass covering the table—a black and white postcard of what looks like old Shanghai; a photo of an old doorway; some tall blonde foreigners in a green field with a cow and Yizhong dressed in a blazer, smiling at their side.

Soon Yizhong returns with two cups of tea and a plate of washed apples, then sits on the chair diagonal from me. With a paring knife, he begins to shave off an apple's skin in one long curling strip, then holds it out, an offering.

"For me? Aren't you having any?"

"No problem, I'll peel another." He smiles, then cocks his head to the side. "Do you want to hear some music?"

"*Hao.*" I nod.

Squatting beside his stacks of tapes and CDs against the wall, he asks, "What do you want to listen to?"

"I don't know. You choose."

"*Hmm,*" he runs his finger along the spine of the plastic cases and pulls out a tape. "Do you want to hear some Chinese rock 'n' roll?"

"Okay."

"Have you ever heard Cui Jian?"

I shake my head.

He pops it into the boom box, presses rewind, and explains, "He was China's first real rock star. In college, he was all we'd listen to."

The tape cued, Yizhong comes back over to sit on the floor near my side.

"I'll sit on the floor too," I say, pushing the table forward a bit and pulling a cushion off the couch. "I like to sit on the floor."

"Me, too."

The music sounds like it is from the early eighties, a poppy, synthesizer-heavy piece with more of a reggae rhythm than hard rock. The singer's voice is deep and gruff. I can't understand the lyrics.

Yizhong reaches for his cigarettes, a gold box of Hilton Lights, and offers me one. Pulling out a lighter, he lights mine and then his own.

"Who are they?" I motion to the foreigners in the photos under the glass on the table.

"Oh, my German friends. They were studying here at Chuan Da last year. I went to Munich for my friend Mike's wedding last spring. He married a girl from Chengdu."

I nod, scanning the rest of the photos and notice one in black and white of a white girl looking out a window, but I don't ask who she is.

Yizhong takes the cover off his porcelain cup, then picks it up by the saucer and blows. I do the same.

"How long did you stay in Germany?"

"Two months. That's all my visa was for. But I'm going back next month."

"Really? What for?"

"To study painting, I hope. First I need to learn some German. But then the university is free."

"Free? Even for foreigners?"

"*Dui.*" He nods. "I've been waiting eight months for my visa." He smiles, then stubs out his half-smoked cigarette. "I'll go get my paintings," he says while leaping up, suddenly remembering the premise of my visit. Soon he returns with a small album.

"They're not very good." He hands them over.

I open the book and turn the plastic pages filled with original ink drawings and watercolors, most of them a combination of the two mediums—abstract portraits of people, highlighted with delicate washes of orange, green, blue, and violet. They are interesting and playful with a definite influence of traditional Chinese brushwork, yet far from the classic paintings of flowers and bamboo, or mountains and water.

"These are from several years ago." Yizhong reaches for another cigarette. "I have some newer ones I'll show you later."

I nod and turn the page.

I feel like I've stepped into another world, so far from the country

vendors and chaos of the streets below, and so far from the class-
rooms full of shy students where I taught a mere couple weeks ago.
Yizhong also has a shy, innocent quality to him, but he seems a different species than my students—in touch with the world, in touch with
himself. And I don't feel with him the same awkward hesitation that
I often do in this language—in fact I feel like I could talk for hours,
really introducing myself for the first time in Chinese.

He tells me about what Chengdu was like when he was a child,
how they'd swim in the river that is now so polluted, and about the
courtyard his family used to live in filled with insects and birds.
"Now, the city is so different. The traffic is terrible. That's how I got
this," he says, then laughs, pointing to his tooth.

"What?" I'm not sure what he means.

"I got hit by a car a year ago. Broke my tooth on the car."

I make a face and shake my head.

"I was okay though."

"That's good," I say. Our eyes meet for a moment, before he looks
away.

Later that night we go out to dinner at the High Fly, ordering spaghetti—often the safest Western fare at Chinese restaurants— and
Chinese beer. We talk about his upcoming departure for Germany, and
my uncertainties; how I fled my job and don't know now whether I'll
stay or go home. We talk about the masks people wear, the disguises, so
much fakeness, especially here in China. I've never had these kinds of
conversations before in Chinese, yet with Yizhong they seem to come
easily. After dinner, we walk down the wide boulevard of Renmin Lu
to a tiny bar near the university where he says a lot of writers hang out.
Our shoulders bump against each other in the darkness.

At the bar, Yizhong greets a few people and we drink a few toasts
with them. I can tell they are curious about who I am, but beyond
my name, they don't ask me any questions. I stand at Yizhong's side,
trying to look friendly and engaged, even though I can't follow much

of their conversation. I'm relieved when Yizhong finally excuses us to our own table. Here, we both seem to relax and even though my vocabulary is small, somehow we manage to keep talking. Mostly I enjoy the sense of warmth and intimacy between us, as if we've both found someone we've been waiting to meet. In the taxi on the way home I take his hand, feeling bold after a few beers. We sit silently behind the driver and his metal cage, watching the other red taxis and streaks of light stream by in the night, everything concentrated in our fingertips.

When we get close to the neighborhood where he lives, I suggest that I could go back to his place. He agrees, with shy conspiracy. Everything about Yizhong feels so safe. In his apartment, sitting on the couch, I kiss him. He kisses me back, timidly, without offering me his tongue. I am not sure if he feels I am being too forward, or if he is just tired, so I don't pursue it further. It is late.

"*Shui jiao, ma?*" Sleep? He suggests.

I nod.

We brush our teeth over the kitchen sink, then lay on his lumpy twin bed pushed up into one corner of his bedroom/studio. He keeps his white long underwear on, and I wear my smoky clothes from the bar. We lay close to each other, arms reaching out to hold tighter in the night.

One day I am an English teacher, a "foreign expert" with over 200 students and a contract that states I can not talk about politics or religion in the classroom. The next day I am a wanderer again, an American girl dating a Chinese painter, free to do anything I please. *What are you doing here?* People keep asking me, and I keep changing my story: *Traveling, teaching, learning how to say things in Chinese . . .*

I really don't know what I am doing anymore. Should I try to find another job in Chengdu, or maybe enroll in a Chinese school? Or should I go home? It feels too early to give up on China, too early to admit defeat, but I've been here for six months and already I feel drained. I decide it would be good for me to get out of Chengdu in order to gain perspective.

I plan to go to Dali, a small laid-back town nestled in the mountains of Yunnan province, a place I visited three years ago on my first trip to China. Dali is filled with cafes where backpackers sip coffee by day, drink sweet tall bottles of Dali beer by night, and smoke ganja that grows up in the hills for the picking—there is no other place in China quite like it. When I tell my friend Xie Ping that I am thinking of going, she says she's always wanted to go as well and decides to come along.

Dali has changed a lot since I was last here. Now, there are even more bars and cafes, and young transplants from cities like Beijing or Guangdong who've come seeking a slower pace of life. After Xie Ping and I check into a local guesthouse, we immediately smell the sweet waft of marijuana coming from next door. Xie Ping says she's smoked a few times before, and I haven't since I left the States. We look at each other with conspiratorial smiles.

We knock on the door of our neighbor, and he happily treats us to a round with his tall bamboo bong. He's from Beijing, and his tiny room is filled with pot, plastic bags, and a sealing device—all of which he plans to transport back to Beijing on the train. We thank him, then excuse ourselves to our room. The pot is mellow, nothing like the stuff of my native Northwest, but still Xie Ping and I lay on our beds laughing at the words coming out of our mouths. Sunlight pours through our window, dust particles swirl in slow motion.

Wandering out into the cobblestone streets, our senses heightened, it feels like Xie Ping and I have been friends a long time. We are also on more equal turf here, since the backpacker culture is familiar to me, the mingling of accents in the background; just a few words and I can guess where people are from. *Australia. England. Israel.* But now, hanging out and speaking Chinese with Xie Ping, no one guesses I am American, and I like this. I am pleased to be taken as an insider, to be Chinese by association. We plan to stay in Dali for a week. In the mornings, we sit underneath the small gazebo in the courtyard sipping green tea (Xie Ping) and coffee (me). I keep my little red dictionary by my side and eagerly listen for new words to jot in my notebook. She tells me more about her painting and I try to tell her more about what I write. I tell her about Yizhong, whom I was hanging out with almost every day before we left Chengdu. Xie Ping knows who he is, but has never spoken to him before. She wastes no time digging out the dirt.

"*Ani,*" she smiles mischievously, a glint in her eye. "*Ni youhuo le, ma?*" Have you . . . *something* . . . yet?

"*Shenme?*" What? I am not sure what she said, but I have an idea. And so begins our vocabulary lesson, the two of us giggling as I studiously write down words.

Penis: *xiao di di* "little brother," or *xiao pengyou* "little friend," or *nan de shengzhiqi* "male genitals," or *jiba*, something like "cock."

Vagina: *nu de shengziqi*, "female genitals", or *bi*, something like "cunt." (It seems there are no choices in between.)

Xiongzhao: bra. *Rufang:* breasts. *Rutou:* nipples. *Xingjiao:* intercourse. *Bi yun tao:* "avoid pregnancy cover," otherwise known as a condom.

I am not sure how many of these words I will actually get to use with Yizhong, but I relish learning them all the same. Likewise, I make sure Xie Ping knows the difference between "penis" and "peanuts." *Now repeat after me, stress on the second syllable so you don't confuse the two*: Penis. Peanuts. Penis. Peanuts. We practice diligently, trying to keep our voices low, even if it is doubtful that any of the Chinese at our sides have a clue what we are saying. "*Penis, peanuts, penis, peanuts* . . ." Xie Ping whispers, trying out these foreign sounds. I

tease her, trying to get her to say them louder. When penis gets old
we move on to other words, each eliciting a new round of laughter, as
if we are schoolgirls trying out dirty words aloud for the first time.

When Xie Ping laughs, she covers her mouth with her hand like
I've noticed most Chinese women do. From photos she's shown me, I
also noticed she never smiles with her mouth open, and her expression is always the same: eyes looking straight into the camera, confident yet subdued with a hint of melancholy, composed and aloof, a
face that does not reveal what she is thinking. Now she explains by
pointing to her teeth—they are yellow, some blackened. "*Wo de yachi
bu hao,*" she says, looking ashamed. My teeth are bad.

In the morning, I cringe as I listen to her cough up phlegm, then
reach over to light a smoke before she's even gotten out of bed. In
Chengdu, the way Xie Ping snapped orders at cabbies or openly
smokes in a culture where women who smoke are looked down upon
had seemed almost admirable; she was the new young and liberated
Chinese woman, breaking out of a ten-thousand-year mold of the
chaste demure lady. But here in the fresh air and bright sun of Dali,
Xie Ping seems more vulnerable. She tells me about going to a board-
ing school as a child and being the only one who didn't go home
for the New Year holiday. Her parents were divorced, her mother a
comedic actress who traveled extensively performing, her father a
photographer, also mostly absent. It makes more sense to me now
that Xie Ping has become an artist, an uncommon path to follow in
China, especially for women. It also makes more sense that she is so
hard for me to penetrate, so hard to understand.

One morning, she teaches me the word *fengbi*. "It is the feeling I
try to convey in my paintings," she explains. I look it up in my dictionary. 封闭 *Fengbi*: 1.) to seal up, as in sealing a bottle up with wax;
2.) to close down, as in closing down a publishing house. *Fengbi*. I
think about Chengdu, the toxic air, tall buildings, endless construction and noise, people crowded into every corner of space, watching,

judging, forcing you deeper inside. *Fengbi*. I think of her paintings of thin stick figures or birds perched in boxes or on utensils or in empty rooms. *Fengbi*. I am becoming familiar with this feeling. An ordinary word, but it says so much. I write it down in my notebook.

心

Back in Chengdu, I return to stay with Tamara and I can't wait to see Yizhong. In Dali, I spontaneously started wearing my contacts again, and when Yizhong sees me without my glasses he smiles but doesn't make a big deal of it. He makes me an extra set of his keys so I can come and go as I please, but for the most part we start spending all of our time together. Maybe because he is leaving for Germany so soon it makes it easier to dive in and discard the usual caution and pacing that goes along with entering a new relationship.

Then, a few days after my return to Chengdu, my visa gets stolen, snatched out of my purse on a crowded city bus. Without a visa, I now can't register to stay at a hotel, and Tamara is leaving soon, so I can no longer crash with her either. If I go to the police they'll probably make me leave the country right away since I no longer teach but still carry a work visa. I know I have to sort this all out in the near future, but when Yizhong suggests I can stay with him for now, it seems like the obvious solution. I can relax and get to know him better, not have to decide what to do right away. As a foreigner, I am technically supposed to register with the police before staying with a local, but this isn't strictly enforced, Yizhong says. So I become the slutty, illegal, foreign woman pulling her suitcases down the street and up five flights of stairs to his apartment, neighbors gawking as we pass.

Most mornings, Yizhong and I laze around listening to music and drinking Nescafé. Afternoons, he brings me to tucked-away teahouses where locals chain-smoke and spit sunflower seed hulls on the floor, playing mahjong and cards all day long. And evenings, we visit more smoky bars where young artists and musicians converge.

One morning as I lie in bed with Yizhong he turns to me and says, *"Wo xihuan wen ni."* I like to *wen* you.

"Wen? What is *wen?"*

"This is *wen,"* he replies, giving me a deep kiss on the mouth. Kiss. But I thought kiss was *qin.* That was the word I always used as a child.

"It's not *qin?"*

"This is *qin."* He leans over to brush his lips lightly on my cheek.

Ah. I am beginning to understand. It makes sense that I never learned the other word for kiss, the passionate one, from my mother. *Wen.*

"Wo yao wen ni." I want to kiss you, I say, trying out my new word. I lean toward him and press my lips against his, hesitant to use my tongue. He wraps his arms around me tightly. It is strange and yet so natural to be in bed with a Chinese boy. Boy? Thirty-one-years old, hardly a boy, and yet something in the way he smiles and giggles, or maybe it is his smooth, lithe frame, something about him makes me call him a boy. It seems like all of this is new to him, just like it feels new to me. I don't even know the word yet for sex in Chinese, although when Yizhong tells me, I am not surprised: *zuo ai.* Make love. It's been so long since I've made love. In fact I wonder if I ever really have.

In recent years, I've tried not to fixate on finding a partner and instead wanted to trust that my time will eventually come. I haven't had a true boyfriend since high school, and besides that, only a few one-night-stands or short flings. Sometimes, when I listen to music and dance at the bars here in China, I close my eyes and replace the "you" (as in, *Baby, I love you*) with the "You" of a greater Beloved, trying to lose myself in a more rapturous dance, trying to funnel my longing for intimacy with another into my parallel longing for God. This helps, but it doesn't erase my loneliness. Now, with Yizhong, I am out of practice, but I am not afraid. His earnestness and kindness help me feel bolder. I don't have to worry about hasty advances or hidden intentions. If anything, I feel like I am the fast one, the one who has to make all the moves.

The first time we make love he is trembling so much that I wonder if it is his first time ever. I want him to wait, to touch me more before he enters me, but I don't want to interrupt and make such requests—not yet, too soon—these things are hard enough to say in English. He doesn't last long, and afterward he holds my body tightly against his own, shaking slightly, breathing heavily. I want to ask him if he is okay. I doubt this is really his first time, but I can tell he doesn't have a lot of experience. Does he feel the "pressure" of being with a foreign woman, rumored to be so forthright in bed? Is he worried I'm judging him? Or is he too overwhelmed to think about my nationality at all?

We lie next to each other, skin on skin, his body smooth, like a woman's. His limbs feel small and lean underneath my thighs and pushed up against my round belly. I want him to kiss me gently, on my face and the sides of my neck, nibble my earlobes, cup my breasts, work his way down my body, merge with me in a silent rhythm of give and take. But this all feels so delicate, so foreign and new. For now, it is enough just to lie here.

My hand resting on his stomach and touching his belly button, I ask, *"Zhege shi shenme?"* What's this?

He giggles.*"Duqi."*

"Duqi," I repeat.

"Yingwen, na?" And in English?

"Belly button. Beh-lee Buh-ton," I sound it out more slowly.

"Beh-lee Buh-ton," he repeats.

"Dui!" Good! *"Zhege na?"* And this? I ask, moving my hand up his body.

Chest: *xiong.*

We continue. Elbow: *wantou*. Shoulder: *jianbang*. Armpit: *yewo*.

"I'll tell you a secret," I say with the hint of a smile. *Gei ni jiang yi ge mimi.*

"*Shenme?*" His eyes light with curiosity.

"Xie Ping already taught me some words . . ." my voice trails off, teasing him.

He props himself up on his elbow, eyes wide, looking down at me. "What'd she teach you?"

"Oh, many, many . . ."

"Like what?" he cries impatiently.

I lay there, pondering which word I should choose. "Okay. *Xiao didi.*" Little brother.

"Xie Ping!" he groans, rolling his eyes, but then immediately asks, "What else did she teach you?"

"Ohh . . . *tai duo.*" Too many.

"Tell me!"

"*Hao, hao . . .*" Okay, okay . . . "*Jiba!*" I blurt, watching his eyes for reaction.

"Xie Ping!" He cries out again, scrunching his face in feigned exasperation. "*Na ge hui dan!*" That bad egg! "What else did she teach you?"

I think for a moment. "*Bi.*"

"*Ai ya . . .*" he groans, throwing himself back down on his back.

I have no idea how these words sound coming out of my mouth to his ears. Just like he sounds so funny saying penis, pee-*nis*, just two syllables to him, two sounds. For me *jiba* and *bi* are also just sounds, but to Yizhong they are words that people barely utter—except in crude jokes, perhaps, among those with "no culture"—*meiyou wenhua.*

"What else? What else did she teach you?"

He wants to know, so I list off what I remember, and with every new word he cries out *Xie Ping!!!* as if she were my corrupter, as if I weren't the one asking for the names. Secretly, I think he enjoys it, but he'd never admit it.

Lying in bed or with the help of the dictionary, I continue to collect words from Yizhong like "sperm," "ejaculation," and "orgasm"— *de dao gao chao*, "reaching the high wave"; I like that one. But beyond the purpose of these teasing vocabulary lessons, sex is hardly talked about and sexual organs are never named. I can think of many more examples in English for penis and vagina than he has shared with me in Chinese, but I am not used to saying the words either, and I am not about to begin with Yizhong. Surely there must also be a sexy way to use these words, a modern way, in this culture that's used peonies and moonlight to allude to sex and romance for hundreds of years. But if there is, it isn't a part of our vocabulary.

I do find out that Yizhong dated a German girl for a while and had a steady Chinese girlfriend throughout college. I tell him about my two-year relationship in high school, but I don't speak of the other people I've been with since then—the crushes, flings, and disappointments, the one-night stand I had with an American I met on the train on my way to Chengdu, nor how I fantasized about being Guang Hui's lover. I don't want Yizhong to think that what we are doing is casual for me, or any kind of ordinary.

心

"How do the two of you communicate?" Yizhong's friend Zhao Yang asks him one day as the three of us sit in the living room. I understand the question, but don't say anything, waiting to hear how Yizhong will reply.

"In Chinese," Yizhong says, as if it is obvious.

Zhao Yang nods, but seems unconvinced. He hasn't heard me say much since we've been together. My small talk is limited to a few subjects, and once those are exhausted, I grow silent. But with Yizhong, we have slow unhurried conversations, two dictionaries between us. One of us might say, "Describe yourself" or ask "What is important to you?" And together we look up words, one by one, sometimes spending an hour on just one question. We tell stories with simple adjectives and describe places we've lived or traveled. I lived in a house in a forest near my college; he lived in an apartment with friends in Beijing. I went on a march for Tibet in America; he demonstrated against the Tiananmen massacre in Chengdu. I studied writing; he studied painting. We both like music; we both like nature. Small things. Important things. Glances, smiles, and easy silences in between.

After staying with Yizhong for a few weeks, as his departure date for Germany approaches, I decide I will leave China as well. I am tired, winter is coming, and I can't imagine dealing with the hassle of finding a new job. I started out with such enthusiasm to forge my own life here, but after nestling into this soft private space with Yizhong, I feel more tender and aware of my needs. I need to go home, rest, be with my family. Yet I know I am not done with China. I will come back later and start anew. Or maybe I'll first visit Yizhong in Germany. His eyes light up when I speak this as a possibility. He is surprised, and I am too. I don't want to let go so soon.

There is so much I don't say to Yizhong, so much I can't explain. All I know is, he is the first boy, or man, that I've let myself trust in so long. It doesn't matter that our conversations are simple; it's almost a relief to be excused from the controlling grasp of language to define us. In this space, we can take our time in communicating one word, one thought, one emotion—like the first time he whispered to me, *baobei* . . . treasure, or baby, in Chinese. I turned to him, my body remembering being called by that name long ago. *Baobei*. A word reserved for children, or for lovers, or for some soft space in between.

10

What Goes Unsaid

Mama, I haven't talked to you in weeks. I e-mailed you and Daddy to let you know I quit my job, but beyond that you know nothing. I know nothing. I am floating, untethered, unmoored. I have no work, no residence, no official reason for staying in Chengdu. I thought that teaching English would be the easiest way to enter in here, but it was too much and I don't want to be the teacher. I want to be the student. I want to meet other writers and artists. I want to immerse myself in unsanctified versions of this place. I want to speak more Chinese.

Mama, do you remember that day when you visited my kindergarten class? You stood up there and told some story about Gong Gong chopping off the heads of chickens with a cleaver in a courtyard in Taiwan. *Whack!* I can see your hand cutting through the air in demonstration before our wide-eyed awe. With a smile on your face, you painted this funny picture of a far-away country. Then you sat at a table with big pieces of white paper, blank ink, and a bamboo brush. With smooth, sweeping strokes you found a character for each of my classmates—big majestic symbols they were told were their Chinese names. I stood silently to the side, watching you, my mother. Inside, I glowed. You were mine.

Mama, when did I stop speaking to you in Chinese? Was it in

elementary school, when it sunk in more how the world outside my home was so different? Or was it later, in 5th grade perhaps, around the same time I could no longer stand to hold your hand in public? Eventually I would only reply to you in English. But you still spoke to me in Chinese—or rather, Chinese and English intertwined. Enough so that I would never forget the sounds to which I first belonged.

English, of course, is now the dominant part of our daily life, your husband's language, my father's language, my own. But it was less prominent at first, a world I was a part of, yet did not belong to exclusively. A language that belonged more to the world outside than it did to our family and home.

Mama, I don't remember being conscious of gradually losing my Chinese, but I do remember that Sunday afternoon during my first year away at college when I walked through the dry, brittle Minnesota air to see *The Joy Luck Club* at the Grand Theater. There was one scene, a part of a flashback, where a mother fingers the earlobe of her daughter whom she has to leave and tells her she is lucky, she will be rich. I felt my own earlobes in the dark, thick and velvety smooth. Not long ago, you'd told me the same thing. I cried for you in the shadows of that theater, but not too loud. I wanted you, but not our English conversations. I wanted you deeper. The next quarter I started to study Chinese.

Mei Mei . . . you are the only one who still calls me Mei Mei, little sister. Not now, not over the phone, when we speak strictly in English; not in letters or e-mails where you are Mommy and I am Anne. But when we are in person and can feel each other's bodies close. A part of me turns to you and smiles, the child in me that loves to be held and stroked. Mama... I can still bask in your attention, feel an intimacy between us, our silent pleasure in reuniting. The last time I was home, I demanded a hug while we were watching TV on the couch, trying to fit again within your arms, but my body was too big.

Mama, I am almost the age that you were when you first came to the States for grad school. I remember those black and white photos from the airport runway in Taiwan, right before you were about to leave. You wore a tight, sixties polyester dress. Around your neck hung a flowered lei. You were soon to fly to Wisconsin. Your family stood around you in a series of posed shots—you with your four younger siblings, you with your parents, you alone. If you had fear, you did not show it. But the rest of them, their faces all say: they are saying goodbye to big sister, the one who holds things together, the one who is about to leave.

Of course, you did not leave them for long. One by one, you helped them come to the States. One by one, you became Americans, learning the hearty chuckles and smiling chit-chat of office, break room laughter. Your English is so good now that I forget you still carry the slightest hint of an accent that comes out most obviously when you get mad, and your English word orders or tenses lose their rational calm.

Mama, I miss you. It is not easy for me tell you this, and this letter I will never actually give you. But on some level I can't yet fully understand, I know I am here because of you. Not here to visit your literal birthplace or to find lost relatives, no. But the longer I am here the more I realize that I *am* here because I want to speak Chinese fluently, to transcend my childhood vocabulary, to merge the adult me with the earliest me.

To see where the part of me who once lived in this language has gone.

PART TWO

REFUGE

11

In Germany

Yizhong meets me at the airport outside Munich, his long hair flowing, his demeanor bashful and shy. He looks thinner and smaller than I remember, more feminine, especially next to the Germans. I feel distant, like we are different people now that we are in this vastly different place, and I worry I made a mistake, but it is too early to say. We get on one train, then transfer to another line. Clasping hands, we ride further and further into the countryside, quiet.

After our last days together in Chengdu, I decided to go home to the States for a reset, but I couldn't stop thinking about him. How could I finally connect with someone like this and then not see if it could go further? From Seattle, I wrote Yizhong a letter which my mom translated into Chinese. *I want to say so much to you, I want to tell you the story of my life. I want to ask you so many questions. Questions of the heart and of the spirit, things difficult to find words for even if we shared a fluent tongue . . .* He wrote back in Chinese. Again, my mother translated. She said she felt odd reading our letters, but I wouldn't have asked her to if I'd had another option. Soon, I decided to buy a ticket back to China that would allow for an indefinite stopover in Germany. Yizhong was thrilled.

Now, my plan is to stay in Munich for about a month—unless it goes really well and we fall madly in love. Of course I haven't said that last part aloud; I don't want to get his hopes up. Returning to China still feels more important to me than some guy, and yet, Yizhong also feels like more than "some guy."

On the bus, Yizhong tells me how he is renting a small room from a German couple who speak no English and have two children in college; staying way out of town is the only thing Yizhong can afford. His goal is to study painting at the university in Munich after he first learns enough German at a language school. Then he will search for a professor who can sponsor him to become a full-time student.

Two buses later, we finally arrive in Hohenlinden, the village near Yizhong's new home. Another half hour later, we get off at a rural stop in the midst of green farmland. Walking along a gravel path through open fields, Yizhong carries my heavy purple backpack while I drag my suitcase behind.

"Sorry there's not much room," Yizhong apologizes as we find a place for my bags once inside. Yizhong's rental has its own entrance, and a kitchen and bathroom he shares with another renter, a businessman from Croatia who is only there at night and goes home to his family on weekends. "Are you hungry? I can cook you something. How about fried rice?" He goes to the kitchen while I take in his new home.

In his bedroom, I unpack a few things, change, and then spy his drawings. He has started a new series since he arrived in Germany. Black and white sketches, abstract images of us together, a couple dozen. Two figures with long hair and moody expressions, inter-twined in various poses, with short thin angular lines for shading. Yizhong walks in and watches as I flip through the final few. "Do you like them?" he asks. I nod. "*Xihuan.*" I love being his muse, and I admire his skill. "This is the most I've created in a long time," he says.

When we were in Chengdu, Yizhong also painted a couple pictures of me. One was more generic, an Asian woman with long dark hair, her head turned demurely to the side, adorned by flowers. The other was obviously me: a woman with brown hair, glasses, and the burgundy shirt and mustard scarf I wear all the time. Her eyes are closed and palms raised, as if dancing. No one has ever drawn me before, especially in this way. I feel like Yizhong sees some essential part of me, some essential longing, or beauty. But I also feel like he barely knows me at all.

Over the next week, Yizhong senses my distance and tiptoes around me, catering to my needs, worried that I am unhappy, upset that this isolated apartment is all he can offer. While Yizhong goes to class by day, I mostly stay in his room—reading, writing, and studying Chinese characters. Sometimes I venture out to walk along the path that weaves through green pastures, the flatness punctuated by an occasional farmhouse or tree. Sometimes Felix, the German Shepherd that lives at the house, follows. I sing to myself as I walk, just toning, no words, a meditative song that I first experimented with while walking the empty shorelines of the Puget Sound.

When Yizhong comes home, we hang out at the table in the kitchen where I study more Chinese and he studies German. Occasionally, he helps me or I give him an English lesson, or we just talk, looking up words in the dictionary. Yizhong worries that, at thirty-two, he is too old to be a student. I worry that it will take him too long to learn enough German to attend school here, but I also admire the earnest, relaxed way in which he studies.

For dinner, Yizhong tries to replicate some of his favorite dishes from home—thinly sliced beef with green peppers, steamed egg custard with green onions, instant rice. They are tasty, even without all the proper seasonings, and I love to watch him methodically chop and cook. This is the only time when he doesn't defer to me, when he isn't hesitant or overly apologetic. Yizhong apologizes so much that I have taken to exaggeratedly slapping his butt to make a point every time he says *duibuqi*, which makes him chuckle and blush. His confidence in the kitchen, however, turns me on, and occasionally after we eat I lead him to the bedroom.

I am hot and cold with Yizhong, sometimes closing off, other times falling in love again with his sweetness. It's not fair, I know, but I indulge in his easy acceptance of my shifting moods. One night he says, "I'm afraid you're going to leave me," and I cannot bring myself to assure him that this is not true. I nod, then carefully craft my words. "I know I will eventually move on." When I am alone, connected to my source of deeper knowing, I know it is not going to work out with Yizhong. Some days I feel my affection growing for him, yet in my heart of hearts, it now is obvious. In Chengdu, I was needy and lonely. But after restoring my energy in Seattle, connecting with family and friends, the part of me who is confident in her solitude has reemerged. I am not meant to stay in Germany; I need to go back to China.

I mean to tell Yizhong that I will leave in a couple weeks, but then, unexpectedly, Yizhong is scheduled to have surgery. He has been suffering from a bad case of hemorrhoids, apparently genetic—his father had to have surgery in China a few years ago, too. Luckily, Yizhong has insurance, a requirement of the language school. So we borrow bikes from his landlady and ride for thirty minutes along country roads to the hospital so he can sign some forms. I am called upon to translate—from the doctor's rough English to my rough Chinese. I don't know the word for anesthesia, but I get the point across by saying "butt" and "numb," *pigu ma*. Yizhong laughs and nods, then signs. *Mingbai*. Understand.

"You have an American accent. Did you spend time there?" the doctor askes me. "I am American," I reply, watching his eyes grow wide with surprise. In Germany, I've grown used to people assuming I am Chinese, or rather, from some Asian country. A part of me likes this, becoming more Chinese at Yizhong's side, but I also feel an aversion to their easy assumptions. More than any place I've ever been, I am self-conscious here because I am Asian. In Seattle, my mixed-race appearance might gain me extra glances of curiosity, but more because I sense people are trying to figure me out or they find me attractive. Here, in Germany, the stares feel different. I feel lumped into some overarching category of "non-white, immigrant foreigner," in other words: ignorant, inferior, other. Perhaps some of this I project, interpreting the stares or cool dismissals from clerks as personal versus typical, aloof German etiquette. In any case, everywhere we go I now see things through a triple lens: my own direct perceptions; my perceptions of what Germany must be like through Yizhong's eyes; and my perceptions of what German people must think of me and him—all of this, mixed together.

Thankfully, the surgery goes fine, although Yizhong has to stay at the hospital for several days to recover. He shares his room with an old man behind a curtain on one side, and a ten-year-old boy on the other, whom Yizhong communicates with through simple words and gestures. The boy has grown fond of Yizhong (as have the nurses) and draws hilarious pictures of him with his long, dark hair, wearing a white gown and sitting on a toilet with anguished expressions. I suspect it is a novelty for everyone at the hospital to have a *real* Chinese person there, in the same way that it is a novelty for Yizhong to be served wienerschnitzel, mashed potatoes, iceberg lettuce, and jello on plastic trays. He is a little sore, but in good spirits. Each day I visit and we go outside to a picnic table and smoke Gauloises cigarettes, Yizhong's newly adopted brand, before I ride back to spend the night alone in his room.

After Yizhong returns from the hospital, I feel closer to him. I've helped him through something. I've seen how much people at the hospital enjoyed his presence, and how he took everything with such good spirits. And I've missed him. Each day, our connection grows deeper. One day as we walk together in the countryside, I begin to sing my wordless song. Its minor key reminds me of an old Chinese song, of a kind of intonation that I imagine I might have heard as a baby, being sung to by my grandmother. It also reminds me of the high wailing call of Tibetan songs that I came to love during my travels. Wherever my song comes from, this is the first time I've sung it in front of another.

"I heard a sadness in your voice," Yizhong says as we walk home. I try to tell him about where my sorrow comes from, about all the tears I've cried—for Tibet, for China, for all the stories of genocide and suffering I've read about in the world. For my longing to figure out how I can give something meaningful with my life, to find my path. He nods and I feel like I love him a little more. Yet later that night, when the subject of us and our future comes up, I warn him that I will still be moving on. And then, ironically, each time I confess my truth again, I feel closer to him all over.

Before long, I help Yizhong move into an apartment with a friend in central Munich, allowing us both more freedom to explore the city by foot and public transportation. One day I see a poster for two upcoming shows at a large venue in Munich: *The Dalai Lama* and *Iron Maiden*. I laugh at the juxtaposition, then decide to call to see if there are still tickets to hear the Dalai Lama in one month; maybe this is a sign, a reason I should stay a bit longer. After all, the last time I attended teachings with His Holiness it was so powerful, even though I didn't take formal refuge in Buddhism, didn't go through the ritual at the end and say the vows. Maybe it simply wasn't the right time. But alas, I learn that the event is sold out, and finally I acknowledge that it is time for me to move on. I can no longer put off the inevitable goodbye.

My plan is to fly to Hong Kong, get a new visa, and then I will head straight to Dali. Maybe in Dali I can settle into a community, write, and study Chinese. It no longer feels important to me to be closer to Tibet, nor to be in a big city. My experience in Chengdu humbled any grand ideas I arrived with about my purpose in China, and now it is clear to me that I am more suited to live in a smaller town, somewhere closer to nature, with fewer crowds and stares, but also with access to the Internet and the outside world. A place where I will not feel my presence so acutely as a foreigner.

Yizhong and I spend our last week together traveling through Austria. We go to Salzburg, as well as Bregenz, where we are hosted by Dietmar, my priest friend whom I met in Lhasa. Our time together is sweet, I care for Yizhong, can even say I love him. But he clings to me like I am the love of his life, whereas I am eager to take off again, to see what lies ahead. I try to explain this to him, but it is hard to find the perfect words in Chinese. Also, I don't want to close the door between us completely. After all, who knows where I'll be a year or two from now when Yizhong eventually returns to China. Maybe there is still a chance we will be together again, I say, but I try not to sound too promising.

12

Merging

Hong Kong. I have finally arrived after thirteen hours of air space. Coming from the Western world, I pass quickly through customs, claim my bags, follow the signs, and step outside into the night. The air warm and humid, the scent of rain, tropics, exhaust, sewage, *Asia*. Beautiful, bustling, combustible Asia. I've come back to your markets, your rows of fresh hanging meat, your steaming bowls of noodles, your underwear hanging out of windows to dry, your old-timers sitting at the side of the street, fanning themselves, watching the world pass by.

The sky is dark yet glows lavender, orange, pink from the city. I board the bus that goes to Tsim Sha Tsui, a neighborhood of shops, locals, immigrants, and cheap guesthouses. The bus is silent and almost empty, the air-conditioning turned on too high. I sit in a plush purple seat near the front and stare out the window; my reflection glows back. *You again.* We pass through darkness, suburbs, and wind between tall buildings that hide families asleep in their beds. Then we enter the bright lights of the city, head down Nathan Road into neighborhoods like Mongkok and Jordan, a blur of signs, shops, and Chinese characters. Even now at half past midnight people still stream up and down the street. Finally I see Kowloon Park and the white glow of the mosque's giant dome, the mosque that no longer surprises me but welcomes me, bright and familiar. I push the buzzer and heave on my pack, step out onto the concrete. *Here I am.*

A few of the diehard guesthouse touts are still out waiting for us night travelers, waiting to thrust out a card for their place of business and whisk us away before we can think. I've been here enough times now that I'm beginning to recognize their faces, but I'm sure they don't recognize me. I'm tired so I go with the first one that approaches me. He's in his late twenties, maybe Nepali. I let him carry my pack and lead me to an elevator inside Chungking Mansions—a seedy run-down hi-rise full of apartments, hostels, tourist shops, and food stalls selling fried rice or chapattis.

The guesthouses around here are more or less the same: ten bucks gets you a cubicle-sized room lit by a buzzing tube of fluorescent light. The bed fills most of the space; underneath you can find a complimentary pair of dirty flip-flops and on top an old ratty sheet and towel. There won't be any windows, except maybe one that opens out into some dark ventilation chute. But it doesn't matter; all I need is a place to sleep, shower, and store my bags while I hit the streets. I know I will crash hard tonight, dream of the women who are hidden inside corridors, cramped over sewing machines in rooms the size of closets or cooking pots of curried chicken for lunchtime specials, the fragrant drifts of Indian spices and hot stagnant air shooting out of a thousand vents and rising fourteen stories to meet the sky.

۳

I step outside, press play and adjust the volume on my Walkman, then merge into sidewalk traffic on Nathan Road. It's late morning and I'm listening to Massive Attack, walking past camera shops and bins of leather wallets, Chinese fans, silk boxers, postcards, and t-shirts. I walk past Watsons, Giordano, Gucci, Esprit, and the mosque on the corner. I pass heels and shiny loafers, fine cut suits, narrow straight skirts, little handbags, briefcases swinging, cell phones, lunch hour rush. I pass Snoopy, Hello Kitty, denim jackets, stretchy shirts, little stuffed animals hanging from chains off of backpacks.

I pass the African, Indian, and Pakistani men huddling on the steps near Chungking Mansions, eyes scanning the crisscross motion of tourists and locals, back and forth. *Custom-made suit, custom-made suit? Guesthouse? Guesthouse? Fake watch? You want fake watch? Just look, look, have a look.* Thrusting out a card, a man with a fast-talking accent latches on to the side of a white female as she walks and grasps her purse tighter. *What? No. I* have *watch. I have* real *watch,* she declares in a tight, defensive shrill.

I keep going, past newsstands, past bus stops, and past the old woman on the corner I've seen every time I've come through who sits hunched over in a wheelchair, dozing, her hand barely grasping a Styrofoam container for spare change, wheeled out by relatives to do her part for the family. I pass the open door of the Holiday Inn and a two-second air-con blast for a few step's stride—keep moving, in and out, turn my shoulders, eye the opening, squeeze around, get ahead. I join the crowd at the corner and wait for the familiar *ke-ke-ke-ke, ke-ke-ke-ke* rattle of the crosswalk to signal our bodies back in motion. Double-decked buses and long red cabs come to a halt as we pour forth into the streets.

Hong Kong. *Xianggang.* You are my layover, my resting ground of transition. Now, arriving from the West, you remind me again of Asia— humming, churning, chaotic. But when I am leaving China, you remind me of the West—modern, sanitized, and polite. You belong to Britain, you belong to China, you belong to neither, or both. I enter your blur of Chinese faces and smells, yet I am just another traveler, Eurasian love child, possibly a local, depends on your perspective. Here, the Chinese do not stare at me with wide gaping mouths. Here, they are used to seeing white, brown, and black faces. Here, they are too busy to care.

It's late afternoon and I lean against the railing by the water. I've made my necessary stops today; I've bought bananas, instant noodles, and bottled water at Welcome, browsed through books at Swindons, ordered a coffee at Friends, used their free Internet and scanned through listings of salsa, drum and bass, and jazz in the local weekly. Most importantly, I've applied for my six-month Chinese business visa at Happy Travel. With a tourist visa you can only stay for a few months. But so long as you've been to China before, any Westerner can get a much longer business visa through a travel agent, no questions asked—then come back here every six months to get it renewed.

Now, all that's left for me to do is wait. Wander and take things in. I stare out at old junks, speedboats, barges, and the small fleet of Star Ferries painted white with green trim. They crisscross through the channel, each at their own speed, and I feel like I'm on a movie set—the tall, angular buildings reflecting light in the background, the rocking surge of the waves, the ships, the salty sea. Maybe there are stowaways, gangsters, triads on board, secrecy and corruption in the pounding engine rooms, steaming beneath the surface.

A Western couple in their fifties take photos across the channel. A young Filipina woman pushes a white baby in a stroller along the smooth beige-tiled promenade. An older Chinese man sits near her on a bench. A plump Indian woman draped in a sari leans across the railing down my way. We all stare out at the bright, shiny high-rises of Central—land of banks and designer boutiques, little square shopping bags made of high-quality paper. The buildings crowd in on each other, competing for space. I hear the channel grows smaller each year—they call it "land reclamation"; got to push further, edge outward, build higher, add more angles and lights, outdo the ones that came before. The Indian woman comes close to my side. *Do you like this?* She asks, waving her arm towards the buildings and before I can answer she answers herself, *I don't like, I don't like.* She shakes her head back and forth, mouth pursed in disdain. I smile faintly and nod.

I don't think I could ever live here, but I love to pass through. This in-between place mirrors my in-between face, and soon I will be back in China, back on the other side.

13
Being Good

I never imagined I'd live with Yizhong again so soon, but he insists he wants to come back to Chengdu—regardless of whether or not I plan to be with him. He misses me. And I need him. Or I need somebody—someone who cares about me. After Hong Kong, I tried living in the small, artsy town of Dali in Yunnan province—and failed. In Dali, I'd settled into a community of Chinese artists and expats; spent an idyllic few months writing in cafes, drinking, making friends, getting stoned, wandering the picturesque hillsides—and falling for my good friends' husband. We kissed one night. He spoke of wanting to leave his wife. And I knew I had to leave. There was no life for us together. I was ashamed I'd betrayed my friend, and I knew Dali could never now be my home.

Although Yizhong had a vague idea of what happened (for I still called him once in a while from Dali), I told him that I didn't want him to come back to China just for me. He said this wasn't the case. He said he wasn't happy in Germany. And me? I couldn't just go home again to my parents' basement. I had to stick it out this time. I was not done in China. And so, grateful to have a place and person to turn to, I made plans to meet Yizhong in Chengdu.

Before I arrive, Yizhong paints the walls of his apartment in pale shades of grey, peach, and light blue. He also gets new carpeting and moves a bunch of stuff out to make more room. Our first few days together, he knows I am upset, so he gives me plenty of space and asks few questions. I stay up late, drinking and listening to moody music like Portishead and Mazzy Star. I lament in my journal about how badly I fucked up.

Eventually, though, I begin to let go of my time in Dali, and to tell Yizhong more about what happened. He listens without judgment and holds me when I cry. At first, I feel no desire to share a bed with him, but gradually I begin to melt into his enveloping safety. He is kind. Familiar. It is easy. The balance between us has shifted again, and all the things that bothered me while in Germany—his hesitancy, his timid nature—no longer stick out. We are back on Yizhong's turf again, back in his hometown where he takes the lead. Still, I don't think I will move back in with him for very long; maybe just a couple months until I figure out what's next. After all, I still know that Yizhong is not "the One" for me, and I tell him this, and he says he understands. But one night he says, "I don't want you to leave me." *Wo bu yao ni likai wo.* And I nod and stroke his head as he lays against my chest, unable to reassure him with any words. I cannot deny that the longer I stay here, the more I enjoy this feeling of settling into a relationship and a home. I am so tired of living out of my suitcase. I am so tired of starting over. Yizhong is welcoming me with open arms, and all I have to do is stay.

Our life falls into an easy rhythm. Mornings, Yizhong paints in his studio while I write in the living room. Afternoons, he makes us lunch before we hit the streets to go shopping, run errands, or seek a quiet spot in a teahouse. At night, we make dinner before settling in to watch a couple of DVDs, then go to bed late. Now that I am a part of a couple, Chengdu's night life is no longer so appealing. Occasionally we still meet up with Yizhong's friends or with Xie Ping for a hot pot meal and drinks, but for the most part we stay inside our own bubble.

"I think I'm going to stay a little longer," I say one night.

"So you can figure out if you want me?" he asks.

I don't answer. Deep down, I still suspect I will eventually move on, but the more I allow myself to be enveloped in our daily intimacies, the less I care to examine this seed of truth.

心

In traditional Chinese culture, a virtuous woman should follow the "Three Obediences." As a child, she is to obey her father; when she marries, she is to obey her husband; and when she is widowed, she is to obey her sons. Chinese culture is nowhere near that feudal anymore, and to Mao's credit, women have been integrated into the workforce and society in ways that were previously unthinkable. But still, in a civilization with thousands of years of history, fifty or a hundred years is nothing, and ultimately, Confucian standards of gender roles, filial piety, and social etiquette are still firmly in place. Couples are not supposed to live together before they get married, sons are supposed to listen to their fathers, and potential daughter-in-laws are supposed to be selfless and subservient to their future parents.

I first met Yizhong's parents after I quit my teaching job and was staying with Yizhong temporarily. We needed to use their shower, since his was broken. *This is Ani from America. Can she borrow a towel?* was not exactly the ideal way to be introduced, but Yizhong's parents didn't take issue with the fact that I was a foreigner, or that I moved in after knowing him less than a month. At least, they never said anything. Maybe they were just happy that their only son finally had a girlfriend again who might eventually give them a prized grandson to carry on the family name.

Now, every week we walk down the street to Yizhong's parents' apartment, loaded with bags full of laundry. I feel guilty, but things get dirty so quickly in Chengdu, and thick jeans are a pain to wash in a bucket. Plus, Yizhong's mom insists she doesn't mind. I always apologize about the number of bags we arrive with, and then apologize some more as we leave with the items from the week before. *Xiexie, xiexie.* "Thank you, thank you, it's really too much trouble," I repeat like a mantra. Don't worry, she beams back at me, it's no trouble at all. I have a machine and you don't.

The very least I can do is wash my own underwear. I enjoy this ritual: soaking, then scrubbing, rinsing, wringing, and hanging them up to dry over the sink. Occasionally, I'll wash Yizhong's too; it doesn't seem right that his mom should still be washing her thirty-two-year-old son's underwear. Sometimes he takes my hint and attempts to wash them himself, but rarely does he get past the soaking part, and all it takes is one day in stagnant water for clothes to develop a foul scent and emerge smelling worse than before. Better just to let his mom do it.

Yizhong tells me not to worry. "She likes to do things for us," he says, and I know this is true. She spends most of her days doing housework, her one foray into the outside world being a walk to the market to buy the evening's meat and vegetables. She's so excited when Yizhong and I finally call or stop by that it makes us feel that much worse; we know how easy it is to make her happy—just one compliment and her eyes light up with childlike delight. Our sense of guilt is magnified because they live so close. We walk by their apartment all the time, easily distinguishable from the street by the overgrowth of plants that reach through the bars on their windows, and by our freshly washed laundry hanging from the bars to dry.

Now, it is early fall, and the sweltering heat and humidity is finally giving way to more comfortable temperatures. Yizhong and I sit with wet hair on the couch in his parents' living room, across from his father. (Our shower has long since been fixed, but sometimes we still shower here when we come over for dinner, since their water pressure is much stronger.) Yizhong's mom is tucked away in the closet-sized kitchen preparing dinner. An uncomfortable silence fills the room until his father jumps up and announces he's going to get some red wine. His father normally never drinks red wine, so I know this gesture is for me. I feel both honored and a nuisance. Red wine is still an emerging market in China and few people know how to make it or drink it; most of the brands at the supermarket taste either like vinegar or syrup, and some Chinese even mix their wine with Coke. "It's okay, Ba, don't bother," Yizhong protests, but his father already has his coat on and is heading out the door.

Yizhong lights a cigarette and I reach my hand out for a drag. He insists it's okay for me to smoke in front of his parents, but whenever I've given in to this, I can't sit back and relax like I do at home. Instead, I make sure to blow my smoke up in the air or to the side when I exhale so it won't settle in the middle of the room in a thick haze. And inevitably, I stub out the end prematurely, wishing I just waited until we got home. I wouldn't smoke in front of my own parents or Chinese relatives, after all; it's something good Chinese girls just don't do.

I have become practiced at the art of cracking sunflower seeds, though, a skill that all Chinese women have mastered. Two deft clicks of the front teeth, suck out the small kernel of meat, discard the shell in the crystal ashtray, reach for another. Cracking seeds is the Chinese woman's substitute for smoking—a mindless, continuous, hand-to-mouth action.

When Yizhong's father comes back with the wine, sure enough, it is sickly sweet. I feel embarrassed, like the wine reflects badly on the taste of Westerners, and I want to tell him that good red wine is nothing like this. But instead, the three of us sit silently and sip sparingly, no one wanting to admit it tastes awful. I try to think of something to ask his father, but it's so hard for me to break the silence. Usually we exchange a few initial greetings when I first arrive and maybe a few questions about the classes he teaches at Sichuan University or the part-time conversational English classes I now teach at a private language school, but our conversations never go much further than this. It doesn't help that Yizhong grows quiet and defensive around him. The two of them grunt messages back and forth, in between lulls of silence.

I'm relieved when Yizhong's father finally turns on the TV, which dominates the small room with its huge screen. In our own apartment, Yizhong and I rarely watch TV, so these visits are my one weekly dose of Chinese mass media. Yizhong's father holds the remote and switches from channel to channel, searching for the news, about ninety percent of which reports on Communist party meetings and whatever new "Anti-crime," "Develop the West," or "Three Objectives" propaganda campaign Jiang Zemin is touting at the moment. Commercials are loud and annoying. An overwhelming number of them are for pharmaceuticals, a huge industry in a country with few regulations and a population wary of hospital bureaucracies. Also high in the commercial ranks are cell phones, shampoo, instant noodles, and young couples with one smiling child. They live in homes with sleek Western-style furniture and modern amenities, and worry about things like white teeth and leaking maxi pads.

I get up and poke my head into the kitchen to ask Yizhong's mother if she needs help. "*Tai duo le, tai duo le*," I say when I see how much she is preparing—too much, too much. But we both know this is only a token gesture, and in a minute I'll go and sit back down to wait with the men. The kitchen *is* too small for more than one person, but I still can't help but feel like a real Chinese girl would not give up so easily.

Dinner is always served in the living room, the only other two rooms being the bedroom and Yizhong's father's studio. Like his son, he is a painter, and his intricately detailed watercolors, mostly of people in traditional robes and gowns, dominate the small living room, crowded together in overbearing frames. Yizhong's mother is also a painter. Her watercolors are of mountains and streams with dark mottled patches suggesting shadows or trees. They are displayed on the living room walls too, but there are not as many as her husband's. Her workspace is a little converted balcony off to the side of their bedroom.

One by one, she starts to bring out the dishes—fried cucumber slices, fried green peppers with beef, chicken soup—before slipping back into the kitchen. Yizhong is in charge of the remote, and suddenly, amidst the blur of exuberant Chinese voices, I hear the familiar yet foreign-seeming sounds of English: a business show out of Beijing on CCTV. Yizhong stops here for me, and the specialized vocabulary of a financial analyst pierces into the dreamy haze of my Chinese life like an incision. I don't care about what the talking suit is saying; it is my English-speaking mind that is suddenly enthralled, the part of my brain that I process complex thought with, that I use to display my charm and wit. I am so used to being partially present, linguistically handicapped, reliant on smiles and nods to express myself that, while listening to this broadcast, I feel a vague sense of pride. *See, I'm not stupid. I have my own language and world back home. My vocabulary extends far beyond the simple messages I convey to you.* In the background, Yizhong starts talking to his father in Chinese, and I wonder when his father hears these garbled foreign sounds if he somehow sees me differently too. Is he suddenly reminded that I am of a different breed, or has he never forgotten? After a few minutes, however, I start to feel self-conscious about dominating the TV with a language they can't understand and insist on changing the channel.

Yizhong's father gets up to check on the status of dinner. "*Ni hai zai zuo cai? Gou le, gou le, ling wai cai yao leng le. Lai chi.*" You're still making more dishes? Enough, enough, the other dishes are growing cold. Come eat, he scolds his wife. "*Hao, hao.*" Okay, okay, it's almost ready, she hushes him back to his chair. Like a king waiting to be served, Yizhong's father never helps with dinner or the dishes. It bothers me the way he grunts impatiently or acts exasperated when Yizhong's mom makes a silly comment. I wish she wouldn't act so timid and apologetic. *"Dui, dui."* Right, right, she always says, smiling and agreeing with whatever her husband says.

This is the opposite of how my own mother usually behaves; if anything, she is the one scolding my dad for eating too much junk food or for making some unnecessary (to her) purchase, to which he'll either smile sheepishly, offer a quick retort, or otherwise ignore her criticism. If she's going overboard, sometimes I'll come to his defense, or meet his eyes and we'll both raise our eyebrows in a "What are you going to do?" kind of resigned shrug. We both know that my mother is the one who gets the last word.

In a few minutes, Yizhong's mother comes out with the last dish, a slow-braised pork, *hong sao zhu rou*, the dark red sauce glistening with oil, and sets it down on the table with pride. *"Chi,"* she motions—eat. *"Bu yao keqi."* Don't be polite. She takes off her apron and sits down. Yizhong's parents sit on the two chairs across from where we sit on the couch and the four of us crowd around a small square table with a floral cloth held in place by a glass top. His dad dives in, sucking noisily on chicken bones and slurping at the soup as if he hasn't eaten all day. I wait until his mom takes a few bites before reaching in with my own chopsticks and lifting food into my bowl. His mom picks sparingly at the dishes she has cooked, which are all too salty for her high blood pressure. "Ma," Yizhong complains, "you should cook a dish for yourself without salt." *"Dui, dui,"* she nods and agrees, but she never does. *"Chi, chi bao."* Eat, eat your fill, she smiles at me, and I smile back and give my compliments, "It's delicious." "Really?" she asks. *"Zhende,"* I insist. She is a wonderful cook, even though she uses a lot more oil than my mom—most mainlanders do. "If you like it, then I'm happy," she says. And I know she means it.

Meanwhile, a soap opera from Beijing now plays in the background, one of dozens of popular shows sweeping across China. Some are set in modern times with your typical hospital/crime scene/love affair dramas, and others like this one are set during the Tang dynasty with kung fu duels and men with long manes of hair swept up into round buns. They all have their beautiful woman, of course, with the Chinese prizes of fair skin and small delicate noses and lips. I can usually follow the general storyline, but their speech is still too fast and laced with too many unfamiliar words for me to fully understand. Yizhong's mom picks at her food at the same time that she continues to place food into our bowls with her chopsticks, a Chinese custom that shows endearment towards guests and loved ones. "*Chi, chi, chi bao,*" she smiles, and I nod, reaching for more as a sign of my gratitude.

After dinner I help clear the table, and Yizhong's mom brings out a plate of sliced Asian pears speared with toothpicks. Then, I offer to do the dishes, the one thing I *can* do to redeem myself. Yizhong's mom frets about, helping me tie on my apron and adjust the hot water valve, commenting on how *xinku*, tired, I must be. "Don't be silly, go sit down and rest," I insist, and she wrings her hands and tells me how helpful I am. But I never feel very helpful, nor do I feel like I am doing a stellar job at being their only son's girlfriend. I feel like I could wash their dishes for the rest of my life and it would never make up for the fact that I rarely cook, I smoke cigarettes, and I will never be as polite, servile, or feminine as a true Chinese girl.

In private, Yizhong complains to me about the sedentary nature of his parents' lives: the two of them pent up in their tiny fluorescent-lit apartment with its cold tile floors and big-screen TV. *They never read or think about things in depth. They never go out or have any friends.*

It's not healthy! Sometimes we'll bring a DVD over to put on after dinner, hoping to turn his parents on to something else besides the soap operas on TV—but unless it's from Hollywood, brainless and easy to follow, his parents don't show much interest.

I suppose my own parents are similar in a way. Although they do often socialize with their friends and go on outings a lot, rarely will they initiate deeper conversations. My dad likes to share articles with me from *The New Yorker* and both of them religiously consume *The Seattle Times* and *The Wall Street Journal* each day, but neither care to talk about spirituality or the meaning of life. Instead they'll happily spar about the latest news story or the stock market, but these conversations feel more like competitions of knowledge, as opposed to invitations into deeper meaning. My dad likes to quiz me, "Did you hear about (fill in the blank)?" and when I say no, which is often the case, he always acts surprised, "You haven't?!" I know he is trying to connect with me, but this pattern ends up triggering my sense of being judged.

Over the last few years, I *have* tried to share more of myself in my letters to my parents, and whenever I go home, I try to bring a greater sense of ritual to our family gatherings—requesting we take time to give thanks on Thanksgiving versus just digging in, or writing meaningful cards for Christmas or birthdays. But it takes so much effort to break out of old family patterns, that often it just is easier to go back to being quiet and appeasing, to go along with the usual, surface-chatter affair. At the very least, I try to say, "I love you" more often. "We love you too," my dad usually answers, the first person plural easier to own.

For the most part, Yizhong and I live our separate existence punctuated by our weekly visits. We talk about inviting his parents to our place more often, but rarely do we follow through. Even though it may seem to others like we have all the time in the world with our light teaching schedules and otherwise endless hours to write and paint, for some reason it's hard to surrender any given day. Our apartment is our sanctuary. Filled with soft colors, plants, paintings, incense and ambient world music, it is the only place in Chengdu where Yizhong and I feel free to be who we are together without other people's judgments or stares.

Years ago this place was Yizhong's parents' apartment, assigned to them by their work unit. But in the late eighties, as housing regulations started to ease and people were allowed to buy and sell their own flats, they moved down the street and gave this place to Yizhong. His parents met in 1962 as art students in college in Chengdu. In 1964, their schooling was interrupted for a year during the Cultural Revolution. His father was sent to work as a guard at a bank in Aba, a northwestern region in Sichuan dominated by Tibetans. They supplied him with a gun he wasn't instructed how to use. His mother was sent to work in a pig butchering plant in Chongqing. In 1966 they graduated, got married, and both began working for the Sichuan library in Chengdu, together making the equivalent of less than 60 yuan, or eight dollars a month. Yizhong was born in 1968 and spent most of his early childhood with his mother, or with the neighbor's mother. Yizhong's father was busy working and sometimes sent to do manual labor in the countryside northwest of Chengdu as part of the Cultural Revolution's re-education program for intellectuals. Sometimes he'd bring back frogs or crabs for Yizhong to play with.

During those years, many families were seperated and food was rationed, but since Yizhong's father is a Hui minority (China's Muslim group who are culturally and physically similar to the Han Chinese majority) they often got an extra portion of mutton or beef. Yizhong's father is not a practicing Muslim, but when he was a child, his grandmother forced him to recite the Koran each day. He couldn't read or understand the Arabic, but he could recite its sounds from memory.

Now, Yizhong's father often pressures him to get a regular nine-to-five job besides his occasional contract teaching positions, not unlike how my own mother often suggests I take courses in economics or computers to increase my chances of finding work. Yizhong's mother, on the other hand, never openly disapproves of her son's bohemian lifestyle. She often slides him hundred-yuan notes when she knows he's low on cash, and is not shy to sing her praise of his abstract paintings. Once, without telling him, she submitted one of his old oil paintings from his college days to a government-sponsored show. *My mother!* he complained. *She doesn't understand—those shows don't mean anything to me!* But how could he not be a tiny bit pleased when it was accepted?

Yizhong's father never asks or says much about his art. He did praise some of Yizhong's earlier portraits and landscapes from college, but I don't know what he makes of Yizhong's newer work— abstract self-portraits, mostly nude, faces tinged with melancholy or anguish. Too provocative perhaps, or too unskilled. In general, the older generation of traditional Chinese artists doesn't think much of the new kids on the block, the first wave of Chinese artists to adapt Western techniques and materials into a contemporary movement of their own.

It's hard for Yizhong's animosity towards his father not to rub off on me. Privately, we root for his mother to assert herself, and I make sure to give her paintings plenty of extra praise. I'll praise Yizhong's father's work too, but not so much, because he already has an ego. It's not like she's just some amateur hobbyist; she's a trained and reputed Sichuan painter as well, and a few of her pieces have even been exhibited in Paris and Australia. But as often happens to main-land artists with no English to negotiate proper contracts but who are eager for any opportunity to show their work abroad, her paint-ings were never returned to her and she was never compensated. Not long ago, we encouraged her to print a retrospective catalogue of her work, as Yizhong's father had. *Dui,* she nodded, I really should. But it took months of prodding reminders and Yizhong's father's grunting approval for her to actually begin the process. Then Yizhong's father decided he wanted a new updated catalogue as well. I volunteered my mother to translate their books into English and I proofread the final copy, grateful that I could finally offer something useful.

In recent months, I haven't thought much about someday leaving Yizhong. In fact, increasingly, I think about what it would be like for me to stay. What might it mean for me to let go of my doubt and give myself over to the love that is real between us? It is true, I do not feel the flashing heat of sexual and intellectual flirtation with Yizhong like I have with others, but it is also true that no other man has ever loved me so unconditionally and so tenderly. Maybe we don't always *fall* in love, but instead we choose to *let go* into it. What would it hurt for me to let someone care for me a little longer? I am so tired of being the one who leaves.

نۍ

Today, we have invited Yizhong's parents over for lunch, long overdue. It feels good to finally reciprocate. As much as his dad still makes me uncomfortable, I notice the small awkward gestures he makes toward conciliation, and I care for him, I care for them both. I wish I had more energy to give them than I do.

I stand bent over our tiny kitchen counter, slicing apples, pears, and bananas for a fruit salad I'll mix with fresh yogurt. I've already prepared a green salad with a homemade dressing of oil, vinegar, mustard, dried basil, and oregano. I'll also serve some gourmet goodies my parents sent me from the States like sun-dried tomatoes, olive-caper sauce, and smoked salmon. Yizhong likes this food, so I figure his parents might too, or at least they might find it interesting. I imagine laying out a delectable spread filled with new flavors and foreign delicacies.

But the bread Yizhong is able to find that morning is hard and stale, and then our toaster oven suddenly decides to stop working. I pour them tea and put the foods on our low square table.

"*Chi, ba.*" Eat, I encourage them. We've given them small plates and forks. I watch as they spoon some of the two salads onto their plates, and notice that the fruit already looks brown, the lettuce wilted. Too much dressing. They take small, polite bites.

"Here, try some of this." I hold out the salmon.

Yizhong's father takes a bite, then asks Yizhong, "Is it from a can?" His father rarely addresses me directly.

"No, it's smoked," Yizhong explains. His father swallows and nods, then reaches for a slice of bread. I watch as he puts a dab of the sun-dried tomato olive oil spread on top, then puts another slice of bread on top of that. I don't have the heart to tell him that he shouldn't eat the bread like a sandwich because it's too dry. Crumbs scatter across his lap as he takes his first bite. I cringe. "*Hen hao chi.*" Very good, Yizhong's mom says, and his dad tries his best to look pleased.

What was I thinking? I just offered them stale bread, raw vegetables, and strange smelling pastes for lunch. This isn't food fit for a special meal, and Chinese people aren't that fond of cold dishes in the first place. When it doesn't look like they plan on having more, even though I'm quite certain they have not *chi bao le*, eaten until they are full, I clear the dishes and fetch hot water to refill their tea. Yizhong lights a cigarette and his dad joins him. After a moment's hesitation, I light up too; it's too hard to resist while I'm in my own house, a place I don't usually feel self-conscious. Plus, I crave one to release all this tension. I try to enjoy each drag and disregard the fact that I am breaking protocol. It's not like they don't know I smoke, but I've done my best to avoid showing them. As they make small talk, I stare at the table and suppress the urge to cry.

Why is it so hard for me? Would the ease of a fluid tongue soothe the gaps in conversation, give me the missing key to social grace and protocol? In English, I know all the cues, the proper tones, the subtle openings, the timing involved in asking a question or telling a story or paying someone a compliment. But in Chinese, I am simplistic. My story is over in a sentence or two, my questions are premeditated yet still come out stuttered, my ears are strained to hear the answer, my head nodding if I get the drift, too shy to ask for clarification. Seeking the ease of smooth exchange, seeking to feel like an insider, I sacrifice total comprehension. It's an old trick, ask anyone. Just smile and nod and you will belong.

Having grown up amidst Chinese relatives, I *know* the role of a good Chinese girl, she who greets elders with deference, who never challenges or contradicts, who serves others before herself. But here, I feel like an irreverent, uncultured, bumbling, overweight American, not good enough, not polite enough, not Chinese enough. I am with their son day and night, I have taken over his world, yet who knows if I'll even stay in China? What if I decide to go back to America, leaving their son wife-less, leaving them grandchild-less, extending the possibility that he could be the end of their family line? What if I end up wasting their time?

I exhale and blow the smoke to the side, keeping my eye on their tea so at least I can make sure their cups stay full. Even though I have not contributed meaningfully to the conversation for over an hour now, I try to maintain a look of convivial good nature, wondering if it masks the disappointment weighing in my chest, the desire to go to the bedroom, shut the door, and cry.

When Yizhong's parents finally get up to leave, I tell them how happy I am that they came over and we speak of having dinner again at their place next week. When they are gone, I lie down on our bed and bury my head in my pillow. Yizhong lies next to me and strokes my arm.

Mei guanxi baobei. "Don't worry baby," he says. "They love you anyway, they really do."

14
Popo

When I was in middle school, after my grandmother no longer lived with us, my mother would call her every Sunday evening at nine. I remember listening to the one-sided drift of my mom's voice talking in Chinese, at some point rising in volume and agitation, sounds that in other families might signify a big fight, but that in our family were the sounds of a typical mother-daughter conversation. After they'd talk for almost an hour, my mother would search for my sister or me with the outstretched receiver. *Who will be first to say a couple of words to Popo?*

Feet dragging, weighted with anxiety, I would pull myself over to the phone. *Popo? Ni hao ma?* How are you? She'd say a few things. *Ni de shenti hao ma?* How's your health? She'd talk for a minute or so. *Hao, hao. Wo bu hui ganmao. Hao.* I love you, she'd call out to me at the end in English. *Wo ai ni,* I'd answer back in Chinese. It was always the same. Reminders from her to wear enough clothes and to not catch a cold. Me, struggling to remember how to say the most basic things in Chinese. It only made it worse when Popo would try and say a few words in broken English, signifying to me that my Chinese was really that bad.

I dreaded those Sunday night conversations, wished I could be excused for once. Afterwards, I'd often shut the door to my room, lie on my bed, and cry. I was ashamed that I could say so little in Chinese. Ever since my grandmother had moved to Los Angeles where most of my mom's family now lived, I spoke the language less and less. I envied the way my sister managed to remember more than I did and how when we visited Popo in LA she could dote on her in complimenting coos of Chinese. She was also the thinner one, the more feminine one, the one who wore cute dresses and eye shadow— the kind of girl old Chinese ladies would love to set up with their grandsons. I was the younger one, the chubbier one, the quiet one who sulked in the background. Only before we were about to leave would I finally sneak upstairs to try and say a few words to my grandmother, alone. To tell her I loved her and wished I could say more.

心

Now, my Chinese is a lot more fluent than it was when I was younger, especially after this last year that I have been living with Yizhong. The tones and rhythm of the language were already intuitive to me—it was the vocabulary I needed to pick up, words to bridge my adult intellect with my childhood language. When I call Popo from Chengdu, I am relieved at how easily the conversation flows, despite the static and an annoying delay. Finally, I can tell her more about my life and ask more questions about hers. Finally, I can speak confidently in Chinese. I've even passed the phone to Yizhong afterwards and listened as the two of them exchange warm greetings. I've also recently spent days drafting a long letter to my grandmother, knowing she'll be impressed by my new ability to write in Chinese.

Because I am now in China on a business visa, every six months I've needed to leave to renew it. This time, I've come back to the States for a month to visit my family and then to see my grandmother over the holidays. Staying with Popo by myself for the first time, I show her photos from China, thinking she'll be hungry to see how the country had changed. But Popo only glances at them quickly without pausing to study the details. None of them hold her interest except for the ones of Yizhong. These she inspects closely, asking about his family, his education, and whether or not he has money. Before long, she purses her lips and shakes her head, revealing her true feelings about my dating someone from the mainland, a place so "backwards and poor." Instead of expressing approval that I have returned to my roots, *her* roots, Popo asks why I am "wasting my time" in China. After all, she spent her life trying to get away from the mainland— why would anyone want to go back? The only other question she's ever asked about my life in China is when I am coming home for good. Then, putting down my photos, she sighs and says, "*Haishi Meiguo hao.*" America's still the best.

I want to ask Popo more questions about her life in China and Taiwan, but when I approach her directly, she doesn't want to talk about it. When I ask to interview her on tape, she puts me off for days. Finally I force her to sit down with me, but her answers are short and impatient, often implying my ignorance for asking the obvious. She refuses to digress into tangents or stories and gets mad when I jump around in chronology. I give up after half an hour.

心

From the little Popo and my mother have told me, I know that Popo was born in 1919 in Guangdong province, the daughter of well-to-do landowners. She met my grandfather when she was barely twenty. He was ten years her elder. At the time, Gong Gong was a psychology professor in a Guomindang (Nationalist) military academy in Guangxi province. Popo met him when she went there to study, and shortly thereafter, they married. Meanwhile, the Japanese army was rapidly advancing throughout eastern China. My grandparents migrated west with the Guomindang Party to Chongqing, the wartime capital, in Sichuan province. Here, in 1943, Popo gave birth to my mother, the first of five children she would bear over the next seven years. Popo's twenties were spent fleeing from one city to another. During most of this time she was pregnant and learning how to be a mother. She and Gong Gong left Chongqing shortly after my mom was born and migrated back east to Nanjing, the Guomindang's prewar capital. The Japanese surrendered in 1945, but meanwhile, the civil war between the Nationalists and the Communists intensified. In 1950, my grandparents left the mainland with their five small children, spent two years in Hong Kong, and then migrated to Taiwan where they settled in a rural area outside Taipei. Here, Popo taught elementary school and, later, worked as a student advisor in a school for overseas Chinese students, while Gong Gong commuted to teach college in Taipei, and later in Tainan.

This is the skeleton of Popo's story. It is only now as I piece together these dates and events that I realize that my mother, my aunt, and my three uncles were all conceived, born, and raised in the midst of war. I am beginning to suspect that the reason I know so little of my grandmother's and my mother's early life is because she does not want to remember.

"I've never been to China," she said to me once without realizing she was discounting the first third of her life. What she meant was, she'd never returned.

心

My grandmother lived with my family in Seattle when she first came to the States from Taiwan in 1975, the year I was born. But after my grandfather died when I was eight, Popo moved to LA where the rest of her kids had settled.

When I was young I used to dread our family visits to Los Angeles. The sprawl of intersecting highways, brown dusty hills, and slick shiny cars. The only exit whose name was familiar to me was Atlantic, which led the way to Monterey Park, then Chandler Street, and then my grandma's condo with its smudged white walls and oppressive barred windows. Generic Chinese paintings of peonies, birds, or calligraphy perched crookedly in cheap frames at mismatched levels, as if hung at different times by careless relatives stopping by and asked to do a favor. I'd sit on the spongy mauve couch and eye the crystal covered dish of stale candy while the dramatic tears and duels of some kung fu soap opera played in the background. Plunged back into the world of Chinese relatives asking me about school or making less than subtle comments about my weight, my response was shy and hesitant as I tried to remember how to speak in Chinese, before they'd relieve me by switching to English.

Popo was always excited with the house full of people, anxiously placing out food and raising her voice to argue with my aunt Helen. I'd sit with my feet pulled up on the couch next to my father, half watching TV, half conscious of the Chinese drifts of conversation in the background, mixed with the sound of a cleaver chopping and the crashing sizzle of vegetables dropping into the hot oil of the wok. We'd spend a week eating and visiting with relatives, taking an occasional day trip to Santa Monica or Venice Beach, courtesy of my father who would whisk us away with mutual relief. But mostly we sat around her condo, my mom scrubbing and vacuuming ferociously so that Popo's place was spotless by the time we left, my dad sneaking away in the mornings to buy coffee from Starbucks or to wander the neighborhood, where his presence as a white man was suddenly unusual. He'd go around the corner to the park where the old Chinese men and women practiced tai chi, ballroom dancing, or low-impact aerobics under a covered picnic shelter to the drill sergeant calls of a woman yelling through a megaphone: Yi, er, san, shi! Er, er, san, shi! One, two, three, four! Two, two, three, four!

Popo took tai chi for a while too, but later she told me it was too slow and she couldn't see the point of it—her own exercises were of more use. I remember when Popo used to live with us in Seattle, she would stand in her long underwear at night in front of the TV in the basement, swinging her arms in giant circles, the rest of her body stationary. By day, she'd study English, her tight cursive handwriting recording words and phrases in small notebooks, a dictionary and thick magnifying glass by her side. In the afternoon, when my sister and I came home from school, she'd feed us *cong you bing* and steamed *mantou*, and watch TV with us in the living room. Back then, she chose the name "Jane" for herself, but later changed it to "Julie." On my last visit, when I helped her schedule a doctor's appointment, I realized I didn't even know her name in Chinese. I've always just called her Popo, the name for your maternal grandmother.

心

Now, Popo doesn't get out much, except to buy the newspaper from the corner store for fifty cents. Even so, she must get ready. Since her arthritis makes her cold, she puts on long underwear beneath tight jeans and a thin wool sweater, even if it's eighty degrees out. After rubbing on lotion, she dabs her face with white powder, then ties a loudly patterned silk scarf around her neck. Finally comes the essential step: her thick wavy black wig. Ever since I was a baby Popo's worn a wig, which, in its "off" hours, sits on a stand on her vanity table next to a scattering of bobby pins and tubes of hot pink Revlon, a jar of Ponds cold cream, and stuffy old-lady Chanel. Even now, at 83, she won't go out of the house without it. Especially now.

Wig fastened in place, gold watch on her wrist, she is ready. She goes downstairs, finds her keys, purse, and sunglasses with the rhinestones (this is Los Angeles, after all), slips on her shoes, unlocks the two locks on the front door, unlocks the two locks on the second metal screen door, and steps outside.

It only takes her five minutes to walk to the store, which is good, because she doesn't like to be out in the sun. Here in Monterey Park, a mostly Chinese suburban community near East LA, she doesn't have to speak English to get by, since almost all of the restaurants, grocery stores, and banks are run by Chinese. When I visit, I feel like I'm in some odd hybrid world—too many Asians to be America, too clean and spacious to be China. Even the *Chinese World Daily* (which you can buy in Hong Kong and Taiwan) is printed here in Monterey Park.

The *Chinese World Daily* is my grandmother's gospel. This is how she knew that Clinton had an affair with Monica, and that Hillary is a good woman. This is how she learned she should stock up on bottled water after September 11th, and stay away from LAX around New Year's. And this is how she heard that too much Vitamin C might actually be bad for you, but eating large quantities of *mu'er* (a kind of fungus) helps the heart.

On her way back from the store, newspaper in hand, Popo checks her mail (usually junk) and inspects her potted plants on the front patio. Back inside her condo, she locks the four locks and moves to pick up the remote. Standing in front of the TV, she switches from channel to channel: *The Price Is Right*, a cooking show, one of the stations she gets in Chinese, back to *The Price Is Right*. Voices of exuberant strangers cheer and exclaim in the background as she sits at the foot of the long, glass-covered dining room table in a tall-backed wooden chair, its silvery satin cushion still covered in its original crinkly plastic.

Here, on the table, lie the small details of her life arranged in little stacks and haphazard piles: Social Security letters typed in English that she cannot understand; photographs of heavily powdered old ladies from her singing group; her favorite mug with a picture of two hands holding two mugs of beer and the saying "I've got a drinking problem: Two hands but just one mouth," yesterday's tea leaves thick and fully expanded inside; a lamp, the telephone, a jar with ballpoint pens, scissors, and magnifying glass; a small red tapedeck and a few dusty cassettes she hasn't listened to in years. She puts on her reading glasses and scans the front-page headlines, settling into her daily ritual.

In the background, the TV is always blaring. Popo gets eight channels in Chinese (and over a hundred in English), but she grumbles that there's never anything good to watch as she switches back and forth between Chinese soap operas, news, and variety shows from the mainland, Hong Kong, and Taiwan, in which ditzy young actresses are made to do tongue twisters, answer riddles, throw pies, or do otherwise silly things. Half the time, she is not even watching. She is in the kitchen cooking or upstairs getting dressed, but the television is on full blast all the same. It's company to her, familiar voices filling her condo with Chinese. When I'm around and Popo's not looking, I always turn it down.

心

Visiting Popo this time, without the presence of the rest of our family, I can observe her more closely, and try to imagine what it is like for her when none of us are here. When I first arrived a week ago, Popo was well-prepared with a fresh batch of soy sauce eggs and drumsticks she made the night before, and barbequed pork and sticky rice she bought from a nearby restaurant. "You love barbeque pork," she said, even though I'm not big on meat and can only handle eating a few of those fatty red slices. (Actually, she is the one who loves barbequed pork, but it goes against her low-salt diet.)

We spent the rest of the day in her apartment watching TV, reading, and eating, as would be the pattern for the next two weeks.

The next morning when I got up, Popo was cooking oatmeal with egg whites and sesame paste.

"*Chi mai pian,*" she invited me to have some.

I reminded her that I don't like to eat first thing when I get up. Instead, I made my coffee and went back upstairs to write in my journal. Before I knew it, Popo was calling me for lunch. *Ke Yi'an!* She called me by my Chinese name. *Lai chi!* "Come eat!" Back downstairs, I saw that she had heated up what seemed like every leftover in her fridge, in addition to making two new dishes. Popo always says that I don't eat enough, and I always explain that one person can only eat so much, and I *did* eat a lot, I am so full, and anyway, does she want me to get fat? I think she hears me, but the next day will be the same. Popo will prepare way too much food and then sigh at how many leftovers remain, shaking her head at my inability to do my part.

By that afternoon, I needed to get out of her place if only for a walk to the grocery store or park. I convinced Popo to come walk around the neighborhood with me, but she didn't want to go on the back residential streets—too quiet, she says, not enough people. Too dangerous.

"*Huai ren duo de hen!*" Bad people are everywhere! she insisted, scrunching her face in admonishment.

"Like who?" I asked.

"Like him," she pointed to a Latino teenager crossing Garvey Street.

"How do you know he's bad?"

"You can just tell."

Instead of walking outside, Popo does laps around her living room almost every day—two hundred if she's feeling good—around the coffee table, through the hallway to the corner of the next room, and back, around and around, resting occasionally for a moment when something catches her eye on TV.

Popo's other regular activities include eating $3.99 lunch specials with her friends from the Chinese evangelical church and singing with a group of old ladies (and a few men) from the Chinese-Taipei

Cultural Center. Last week, I got to see Popo perform on stage with two hundred of these Chinese *lao tai tais*, dressed in puffy white Cinderella gowns and gaudy red *qipaos* (the traditional tight-fitting, high-collared Chinese gowns), glittering rhinestones, and fake pearls. The host, a cheesy Chinese guy in his forties with a white tux and slicked-back hair, told bad jokes and gushed in the limelight. They opened with a high-pitch off-key version of "God Bless America," but the rest of the program was in Chinese. At one point, the host asked for those in the above-eighty bracket to step forward for the audience's applause, but Popo refused to implicate herself. (When I show her picture to my friends, they can't believe she's eighty-three; she looks more like she's sixty.)

Altogether, the show lasted two and a half hours with four costume changes. It was Popo's fifth year with the group, but she said I was the first in the family to ever see her perform. Her kids in LA are busy—commuting on backed-up highways, working to pay their kids' college tuitions, and going to church on their day of rest to somehow make peace with it all. They live about forty minutes away without traffic, or up to two hours away with traffic, and they don't have time for social visits.

ぃ

On my third to last day with her, Popo knocks on my door. *"Ke Yi'an! Women yao chuqu chi shengyu. Kuai zhunbei hao!"* We're going to go out and eat raw fish. Hurry and get ready!

I open the door, slightly annoyed since I've only just sat down with my morning coffee and journal.

"I invited my friends from church. They're coming to pick us up at eleven. Quick, get dressed," she orders.

I glance at the clock. It is 10:30. Raw fish is not my ideal way to start the day, but I obligingly gulp down my coffee and change, curious about who she's invited. Plus, it is one of the last days of my visit, and I know how much she likes to go out.

Mr. Yang turns out to be a Chinese man in his late sixties with warm eyes, grey hair, and a gentle demeanor. Popo tells me I should call him Yang Shushu, Uncle Yang.

"This is my granddaughter," Popo introduces me. "She can speak Chinese."

"*Ni hao.*" I nod.

"How nice that you came to see your grandmother."

"*Dangran, ah!*" Of course! Popo interjects, "She visits every year."

"Very good," he says.

I smile like a good Chinese girl.

As we walk to his silver Lexus, Uncle Yang explains his wife is not feeling well, so it will be just the three of us. Popo tells him she has something she needs to mail first. "A donation to the church. I give every month." She glances over to gauge his reaction. He nods and starts the engine.

Uncle Yang is friendly and soft spoken. As we drive on I-10 going west toward LA, he tells me that he came to the US over thirty years ago to study education in graduate school. Now he is a deacon with the church. We switch back and forth between English and Chinese, eventually settling on Chinese. He drives us to a popular spot in Little Tokyo where we join a long line of people waiting for the place to open at noon. When we are finally seated and sipping green tea, he asks me if I have a religion.

"She hasn't heard the Gospel before," Popo says before I have a chance to reply.

"I knew it." He beams. "When your grandma called me this morning and said her granddaughter was with her, I felt like this was an opportunity given to me to tell you about the Lord."

"Hmm," I respond in a tone I hope is neither skeptical nor encouraging.

"I knew you probably had not heard of Christ. When I came to this country, I didn't know him either. But my wife," he chuckles, "she helped me to see. You see," he leans closer, "it takes cultivation. You must go to church and study the Bible. It takes a long time; you must read it every day."

I nod.

"Before I was a Christian, I didn't know anything. Now, in my heart, I feel an Eternal Love. Before, I could not imagine a love like this. I can never lie again because my conscience will feel too bad. Now, I have Eternal Life; I can transcend this body, this flesh." He sits back for a moment and smiles. "Your grandma here, we called her out to the church."

Dui, Popo nods emphatically. "That's right. Normally, I never answer my door for strangers. But for some reason, I answered for you! What a coincidence!" *Hao qiao!*

He chuckles, "That's right. Our church outreach came to your grandma's door and we told her about the Lord." "Before, I didn't know," she says.

I grow edgy in my seat, considering how much I want to get into my spiritual beliefs with Uncle Yang. "Actually, I am very interested in religion, especially in finding the commonalities between religions," I finally say.

He frowns. "There are many false religions from Israel. You must be careful what you read."

I wonder what he'd think if I told him I read lots of books on Buddhism, but luckily, the waitress comes to take our order.

"I'll have the chicken teriyaki and sashimi combo," Uncle Yang orders. "It's good," he says to Popo and me. "You'll like it."

"Really, it's good? Okay, I'll try it," Popo says.

"I'll have the sushi combo," I say.

"What did you order?" Popo asks.

"She got the sushi. She chose well—more expensive than our combos!" Uncle Yang teases.

"More expensive? Why didn't *we* order it?"

I cringe.

"The chicken is good, you'll like it," says Uncle Yang.

Popo nods, the waitress leaves, and we sit and sip our tea.

When the food comes, Uncle Yang leads us in a prayer. I close my eyes and listen to what a Christian prayer sounds like in Chinese, before we reach the familiar part in English, "Amen."

The sushi is good; the wasabi shoots up my nose, a welcome break from greasy Chinese. As we eat, Uncle Yang continues to talk to me about God and all but ignores my grandmother. I do my best not to further the conversation, but he is on a roll. It is only polite for me to nod and listen—I can't very well debate theology in Chinese with the deacon from Popo's church! But Popo looks bored and I am relieved when she interrupts with questions about Uncle Yang's car and when they bought it, his home and how long they'd lived there, his age, and the age of his wife.

"A lot of people say I look like her, you know," she says.

"Yes, there is some resemblance," he agrees, then turns back to me, switching gears now into English . . . *The only true religion . . . dying for our sins . . .*. I nod, but the more dogmatic his words become, the more I tune him out.

Finally, when we finish eating, Uncle Yang pulls out a small religious pamphlet in Chinese. "I'm sorry. When your grandmother told me her granddaughter would be here, I did not know you weren't Chinese."

"It's okay, I like to practice reading in Chinese. I've been studying on my own while in China." I glance at the characters on the first page, of which I only recognize a few, and thank him, before tucking it away in my purse.

When we get home, Popo says nothing about Uncle Yang's attempts to convert me. She is not, how shall I say, the most zealous of evangelicals. In fact, when she first started going to the church a few years ago, she revealed to me her skepticism. *"Pian ren!"* she said, shaking her head with pursed lips. Fooling people! "Then why do you go?" I asked. *"Pengyou, ah!"* For friends, of course! As if it were the most obvious thing in the world.

儿

Now, after being with Popo for almost two weeks, I am more than ready to go home—first back to Seattle, and then to Yizhong and Chengdu. I've started to raise my voice to argue with Popo like my mom often does, frustrated by her repetitive admonitions to eat, sleep, and wear enough clothes. And the constant high-pitched chatter of the television and radio grates on my nerves, as does Popo's paranoia about locking doors or going out after dark.

Yet as I near the end of my stay, I also begin to feel guilty. Why is it that even in such a short visit, I still find it necessary to hide away in my room? If only we could listen to music or sit in silence together, then maybe I could find more moments to share my own stories or to seek out more of her memories. But now there is no time left; I am leaving the day after tomorrow. I put away my book and go downstairs.

"Lai, chi." Come eat, Popo says when she sees me, holding out a bowl of peeled pink grapefruit, the plump jeweled slices glistening with juice. I take the bowl and a fork and sit on the couch, watching as Popo's small wrinkled hands dig into another grapefruit and deposit the yellow peels onto an orange plastic tray in her lap. She sits in her soft gray chair, her eyes glued to her favorite Korean soap opera (dubbed into Chinese) about an orphan who cooks elaborate dishes and prepares medicinal treatments in a school full of girls who are training to be doctors. Every so often Popo's eyes flicker over to me. *"Chi, duo chi."* Eat, eat more, she says before returning to watch the show.

I take another bite, half watching TV, half watching my grandmother watch TV. This is Popo. Not the image she tries to project to her friends of an upper-class woman from Taiwan, with a family who regularly visits, and not the spunky Cantonese fireball persona of "my Chinese grandmother" whom I've proudly introduced to my American friends. This is a softer and older Popo, a Popo who looks more vulnerable, a little closer to her age. The one who is not wearing her wig.

When the program ends, Popo picks up the remote and begins switching between her eight Chinese channels. "Yuck," she says in English as she flips past a woman talking about the latest trend to shave the bikini line into a thin narrow strip. "Yuck." She makes a face at the actress giving a pitch for plastic surgery. "Yuck," she says as she flips past an advertisement for a Chinese funeral home. "*Dou shi* yuck!" It's all yuck! she says in Chinglish, scowling at her limited choices, before settling on the news. A Chinese anchorwoman is reporting on recent fighting in Palestine.

"Ke Yi'an, can you rub my shoulders?"

"Sure."

"Aunt Helen never gives me a massage." Popo sighs.

"Can you sit on this stool?"

She scoots over and I position myself behind her on a chair, digging my thumbs into her shoulders. On TV, images of exploding cars and soldiers flash in rapid succession.

"The right side," she instructs.

"Can we turn off the TV? You need to relax when you get a massage, relax and close your eyes."

Zhende ma? "Really? You shouldn't watch TV?" She reaches for the remote.

"Yes, you need to breathe." *Huxi . . . .* I try to breathe slowly and audibly myself to help her slow her rhythm.

She draws in a quick breath, deep yet shuddering, and exhales with force.

"Can you take off your shirt?"

She undoes the buttons on her blouse, revealing the straps of a beige bra. Her skin feels smooth and loose, but underneath lies a hardened mass of knotted muscles. Her body feels like her mind—braced in defense, as if on constant alert, waiting for an outside attack. When Popo gets something in her head, she can't let go of it. She'll think about it all night, barely able to sleep, needing to have some resolution. If she has to go to the doctor for a checkup, she'll worry for days, bringing on high blood pressure and colds. Otherwise, she is healthy. People have mistaken her for my mother, she looks that good.

"*Huxi.*" Breathe, I remind her, demonstrating a long, slow breath. She inhales and exhales two times with force. Then, a thought. "Last night I was so mad at Aunt Helen! So far to walk! Ridiculous! I almost lost my temper." The three of us had gone out to dinner and my Aunt Helen had insisted we walk the five blocks to the restaurant.

"Well, it was a nice walk . . ."

"*Aiya! Lei si le!*" Please! I was so tired. "That Aunt Helen is something else!" She shakes her head with disgust.

I can't blame Popo for being annoyed. Helen knew she didn't want to walk, but ignored her protests. "*Aiya*, Ma," she said, "you walk at home every day, right? This way you don't have to. Don't you think it's better than walking inside?"

Helen turned to me. "Don't you think it's nice to walk outside? There's a breeze, we get some exercise . . ."

"It's not that far to the restaurant, and it is nice outside," I conceded. None of us were that hungry, and I figured it was just Popo and Helen's usual bickering. I didn't think Popo would still be mad.

"Did you and Helen always fight a lot, even when she was a kid?" I ask now.

Popo pauses, then says, "I suppose we always butted heads."

Suddenly, she sits up. "*Hao le, hao le! Ni lei le.*" Okay, enough! You're tired.

"Really, I'm not tired. I just started. I'll let you know if I'm tired."

"Well, okay then." She leans forward. *"Ah,* right there, right there."
I dig in harder with the pad of my right thumb, then stand and press
my elbow into the spot.

"Ahh!" she winces, *"ohhh."* I lean all of my weight into that spot.
When I release the pressure, she straightens again.

"I didn't always have such a temper, you know. Gong Gong
brought it out in me. His temper was bad . . ." she frowns. "He'd kick
over a farmer's cart of oranges if he got angry."

"Really? He did that?"

Dangran, ah. "You bet! His temper was awful! Those days, people
were better, they wouldn't do anything in retaliation. But these days,
he'd probably get beat up for that kind of behavior."

I want to ask her if he ever hit her. Instead, I ask, "Were you ever
scared?"

Dangran, ah! "Of course!"

I'd heard about Gong Gong's temper before, but I'd never really
comprehended what it meant for the whole family. All of them had
"tempers," but why was this so? My mom rarely talks about her childhood. I wonder what she might have witnessed.

"I didn't know anything when I married him. I was so young,"
Popo sighs, "I didn't used to have a temper at all before I met Gong
Gong . . ."

"Maybe that's true," I say, "but you can't *just* blame Gong Gong . . ."

"I know, I know. We all are responsible for our actions. But really,
I used to be so much more easygoing. *Ah!*" she cries out as I find
another sore spot. I hold my thumb there and inhale, hoping Popo
will do the same.

When I release the pressure, she turns to me. "Do you ever cry?"

I am surprised by her question. "Well, sure, of course."

"Why do you cry?"

"I don't know, if I am feeling suffocated, or missing home. It's a release, it makes me feel better. Sometimes I also cry when I read about war or watch news. It can be so sad."

Aiya! Langfei! "What a waste! That doesn't have anything to do with you! You're sensitive," she says.

"Yes." I decide not to disagree this time.

"I often cry," she says. "My life is so sad."

"When do you cry?"

"Sometimes at night. Or when I'm sick, and here by myself; that's the worst. Like that time when I called your mother at three in the morning. So pitiful . . ." *Hao kelian.* She shakes her head. "I'm eighty-three now, you know. I'm old . . ." *Wo lao le.* she sighs, dropping her neck slightly with the pressure of my fingertips.

"But you don't look eighty-three."

"*Pai ma pi!*" Don't try and flatter me!

I laugh. "Really, you are so healthy. What do you think, you should look like you're forty or something?"

"Hmph," she chuckles, "I *am* quite healthy."

"No one would guess you are eighty-three!"

She nods, then sits up again, her body tensing, "My friend from church is in a nursing home now." She frowns. "She just sits there and doesn't recognize anyone. It's so sad . . ." *Hao kelian.*

"Do you go visit her?"

She grimaces and shakes her head quickly. "My friend told me. So pitiful." She sighs.

"Breathe," I remind her. She takes another quick breath, her body stiffening with the inhale, then slackening with the exhale. Her muscles are so incredibly tight, like a solid sheet of hardened rubber.

"*Hao le, hao le. Ni lei le.*" Okay, okay, that's enough. You're tired.

"I'm not tired. Really, I'm not tired, Popo"

I dig in even harder with my thumbs, using my other fingers to grab and pinch large folds of skin. She winces, her eyes squinting, "Ah, *ahh* . . ."

In a moment, she sits up again.

"Hao le, hao le. Gou le." Okay, okay. Enough now. "You can massage me again tomorrow. You should go to sleep, you're tired."

I finish with a finale of rapid karate chops on her shoulders. She moans in pleasure, then straightens. "Go to sleep now, you're tired. You can massage me again tomorrow."

"Okay." I lean down and gave her a hug goodnight. *"Wan an."*

"Goodnight," she answers me in English.

"Wo ai ni." I love you, I say in Chinese.

"I love you, too." She sighs and shakes her head. "I've held you since you were a little child, you know . . ." she reminds me, as she often does. *"Ni zhidao, ma?"* Do you know this?

I look at my grandmother's soft worn skin, her thin tufts of white and black hair, her compact frame, so frail yet so tough.

"Wo zhidao," I say. I know.

15

Walls

In Chengdu, my days are filled with the sounds of other people: radios droning, cleavers chopping, the vibrating thumps of a child hurtling herself across the room above. I've lived with Yizhong in this apartment for over a year now, but I've still never met any of my neighbors. I don't know their names or what they do, and they know just as little about me, the foreign girl living in their midst. Even the people with whom I cross paths in the stairwell are strangers to me, their faces obscured by dim lighting, shoulders turned, eyes averted, bodies avoiding contact in the narrow passage of space.

Now, an electric drill whines in continuous intervals from the apartment above. Across the street, the girls from the noodle shop yell out orders, "*Er liang niurou mian! Er liang paigu mian! Yi wan xifan! Yi long baozi!*" Beef noodles, sparerib noodles, rice gruel, steamed buns: it must be close to noon. I walk to the window, a large single-paned sheet of glass, and look five stories down. Shops line either side of the street, selling anything from DVDs to cigarettes to eyeglasses, and above the shops sit rows of cement apartment blocks like ours, their windows covered with blue and white striped plastic awnings that a government committee recently insisted everyone install for the "beautification" of the neighborhood. A vendor wheels a cart attached to the back of his bike, displaying mops, plastic buckets, and scrub brushes. Two middle-aged men huddle around a low table and play Chinese chess on the sidewalk, their game partially obscured from my vision by a tree, its leaves coated with thick dust.

I go back to the cushions where I sit on the floor before a low table to write and study Chinese. Usually, Yizhong is painting in his studio on the other side of the wall, but today he is teaching a figure-drawing class. He'll come home later this evening; we'll make dinner, then go rent a movie or two. The night is my favorite time here, when the metal shutters of shops come slamming down and only a few lingering sounds remain: a bottle shattering against the pavement; someone's rusty squeaking brakes; or the man who pedals his cart down our street around midnight calling, "*Y'erba, y'erba!*", the name of the steamed sticky rice balls with spiced meat wrapped in lotus leaves that he sells and keeps warm in stacks of bamboo steamers draped by a white cloth.

There's something lonely yet comforting about the singularity of his voice emerging out of the new silence each night. I wonder if he has another job during the day and is trying to help his family make ends meet. Or maybe he's zeroing in on some late-night customers, people like me who are still awake and can get their shoes on and run downstairs in time to call out in return, "*Y'erba!*" I bought them from him once. His wheels came to a screeching halt. He was young, maybe early thirties, although it's hard for me to tell with the Chinese. Five mao for one, about seven cents. I wonder how he can make a profit, but obviously he can or he wouldn't be out there. With a quick drop of his wrist he placed the *y'erba* into a light blue plastic bag in exchange for a small crumpled pink bill, and he was off. Calling out into the dark air again.

Now, I hear the feisty, nasal tones of Sichuan accents hurling insults in quickening pulses outside. I rise from the floor where I sit on a cushion writing at the low coffee table, and scan the street and find the culprits: a woman vegetable vendor threatening a man with a turnip. Around them, a crowd has gathered, quickly growing in numbers, making the center spectacle harder to see. People here love to watch a good fight or car accident, laughing or making comments from the side, but no one ever gets involved—that's other peoples' business. If you assist an injured person to the hospital, I hear you get stuck paying their bills.

From the window, I can see the fight clearly, but I'm unable to hear what the woman is cursing. My eyes drift across the street to find an old woman in her window, also watching the fight from her own perch. What was she doing before the noises called her to look? Was she in there alone all day? Perhaps sensing me, the woman looks up. Our eyes meet. I turn and walk away.

It unsettles me that people can see inside our apartment. When I go out, I can prepare myself for the stares of the public, but when I'm here, I expect to remain hidden. Plus, we're practically the only ones around here who don't have dark blue tinted glass or bars on our windows, so the view inside must be especially clear. Twice now, I've had the sense that someone was watching me as I changed in my bedroom, and when I looked up I was startled by the sight of a huge face: a glossy, larger-than-life poster of Chairman Mao, his round balding head and benevolent smile peeking out from behind my neighbors' red velvety curtains.

Our bedroom doesn't face the street but instead looks out on the back courtyard, which is surrounded by more concrete apartment buildings like ours, with rows upon rows of barred windows and laundry hanging out to dry. I'm too lazy now to close the curtains all the time, especially in this August heat, so I dash naked across the hall from the shower and stoop in low angles with my back turned to the window to slide on my bra and underwear, exposing as little flesh as possible. As much as I don't like to be watched, another part of me has started not to care; after all, I see the guys across from us walking around in their tighty whities all the time. Sometimes I think it would be proper to give a little wave of recognition when it's obvious that both sides are watching. But that would break the code of conduct: everyone looking, but not acknowledging what we see.

I get up from the table to look at the clock in our bedroom. It's almost three. Time to get dressed, I suppose. On weeks I'm not teaching, which is most, I try to force myself to get out at least once a day. There's usually some task I can accomplish, like mailing a letter or buying vegetables, to make my excursion seem purposeful. Some days, though, I can think of no good reason to leave the apartment. Yet I know I need to exercise—and the reward of returning home will make going out worth the effort.

Stepping into the stairwell, I shut and lock our two sets of metal doors. The apartment across from ours was empty for the longest time; the only sign of life was a mirror that hung on the front door to reflect bad spirits—which incidentally made Yizhong and me the receptors of the mirror's reflection. A few weeks ago, the door was open and I finally saw an older man sitting inside at a table, the place sparse, walls bare except for one scroll of calligraphy hanging near the entryway. I said nothing and passed by.

There are several stairwells in each building, accessing two units per floor. I make my way down the concrete steps, which are littered with cigarette butts and covered with thick dust. Weak light shines through the open cement squares that line the wall that faces outside. The other walls are streaked with dirt and footprints—don't ask me how they got there. On the fourth floor, I hear someone taking a shower; the steam rises out of their small vent into the stairwell. On the third floor, the people in one apartment have their door propped open. Inside, I see a black stuffed leather couch, imposing wood coffee table, and shiny linoleum floors. On the walls hang a glossy framed wedding portrait and a poster print of a lake with an artificially bright blue sky and glowing yellow autumn leaves. I'm always surprised at how clean and affluent the insides of people's homes are in contrast to the building's dreary exterior.

I keep going, past the door of the people on the second floor who sacrificed a chicken for *Chunjie*, Chinese New Year, and left dark red drops running from the courtyard, up the steps, to their front door. They're the same family that Yizhong tells me is always trying to lie about their electric bill—or ours. It's a ridiculous system, but each unit must take turns reading the meters, collecting money from each tenant, and delivering the total to the utilities department. The bill is sent for the whole building and a makeshift notebook is passed around from month to month, unit to unit, allowing the tenants to practice their skills of addition and subtraction by trying to make the numbers fit into the grand total, though they never do. This practice has been abolished in the newer buildings; it's just another one of those things in China that everyone knows doesn't work, but no one's gotten around to fixing. I suppose it facilitates neighborly communication, a monthly surprise knock on our door, "Collecting electric bill, water bill!" Our neighbors take long sideways glances into our living room as we search through our wallets for correct change.

Yizhong takes care of it when it's our turn, since there's no way I could navigate the system in Chinese, and technically, I don't even live here. As a foreigner, I was supposed to register with the police before I stayed in a local's home, but no one around here seems to care or know if the law is still in effect. Yizhong said the building supervisor asked him who I was when I first moved in, but since then hasn't breathed a word. Still, just knowing that I may be officially illegal here is enough to make me keep a low profile. Rules are constantly changing in China; even if things seem like they are liberalizing on the surface, you can never be sure. Yizhong swears his phone used to be tapped, since he was involved in student protests in Chengdu during the Tiananmen massacre of 1989 and since he's a long-haired painter with foreign friends. History has taught the Chinese people to be cautious about what they reveal to strangers. People freely criticize the government and crack Jiang Zemin jokes amongst friends, but in public, or in the private English classes I teach, topics like religion and politics are still off limits.

In the courtyard, I pass a group of young men and women who are gathered outside their ground floor unit, as they do each day. A few slap down cards on a makeshift table while the others lean back on empty bicycle carts and take long drags off cigarettes, watching the game. Some of the units in our building are now rented to the "floating population" from the countryside. Unable to find work and support their families in their rural villages, Chinese *nongmin*, or peasants, have been flocking to the cities in droves for the last two decades. Somewhere around 140 million people, ten percent of China's population, are now on the move in what's been called the largest migration in human history. And this number will double in fifteen years. Most stay in cities illegally; Chinese citizens are not allowed to change their residency unless they have paperwork from the company they work for, although some are allowed to relocate for a short period while they are contracted to dig ditches, move bricks, or climb scaffolding. I'm not sure how many are living in this particular unit, but inside I see several beds squeezed next to each other at odd angles and lined up in rows like at an orphanage. They cook on a small platform outdoors, as most of the ground-floor tenants do. The sound of metal spoons scraping woks and the smell of burning oil and hot peppers drift through the courtyard all day.

I glance over and catch a few watching me, but we don't smile or acknowledge one another. People in China don't smile or say hello to strangers, and these days, the last thing I want to do is draw attention to myself by breaking from the norm. Five years ago, in 1996, when I came here as a traveler the first time, I was happy to stop and chat with strangers, answer the same questions about where I was from and what I thought of China. I proudly revealed that I was connected to them by blood and could even speak decent Chinese. But after returning in 1999 and especially now that I live here and this is my daily routine, I am tired of playing the role of the walking cultural diplomat with endless patience to dispel stereotypes about foreigners.

A five-year-old child wobbles by me on his bike. A woman squats low to the ground scrubbing clothes in a plastic tub of water. I walk past a cart stacked with apples, and another with carrots, peppers, and greens, the cart owners nowhere to be seen. Yizhong says this courtyard used to have trees and places to sit, but now it's crowded with makeshift structures rented out as storage for the vendors who set up the night market on our street. Each day at four o'clock they roll out their heavy wooden trunks and line up. Then at five they burst out like a stampede of elephants towards their assigned spots on the street.

Slipping out the front gates, I pass the skinny guy in his white tank top who sits all day, begrudgingly opening the gate for cars to pass through. He looks up as I pass, his eyes bored and blank; he is used to my presence now, I am no longer a foreign surprise. Across the street, the girls from the noodle shop are dozing after the lunch rush, their heads resting on the tables. Their main business is between eleven and two. Afterwards they sweep the floor littered with tissues and bones, eat something themselves, then rest before the wave of evening customers. Yizhong and I are regulars there. When we walk in they ask, *Two bowls of beef noodle soup?* and we nod.

I walk past the place where I buy plastic bags of fresh soy milk, past the butcher who sells chopped spicy cold chicken or rabbit with peanuts, past the few Internet "bars" crowded with teens playing video games, smoking cigarettes, and chatting online. It costs up to two kuai, about one American quarter, an hour to use their grimy keyboards with stuck keys. In the last year, *wangba*s have sprung up everywhere; I've counted seven in our neighborhood alone, but that's probably because we live close to *Zhongyi Xueyuan*, a traditional medicine college. When I first arrived in Chengdu I stayed at a guest-house on the college grounds, recommended in my guidebook. Back then, I'd never have guessed that I'd later be living in this neighborhood, in an apartment with a local Chinese, walking and shopping these streets each day.

I cut through campus and spy another foreigner; more and more show up each year to study Chinese medicine for a month or two. When I see other foreigners in Chengdu I'm never sure if it is obvious that I am also from abroad or if to them I look Chinese. The same is true with the locals; I often hear them deliberating as I walk by, *Ta shi Zhongguoren haishi laowai?* Is she Chinese or a *laowai,* literally "old outsider." Knowing that I can and do sometimes pass as a local feeds my inclination to keep my eyes to the ground, my stride steady and purposeful, to not give people enough time to fully view and ingest me, digest me. I walk quickly for a burst of adrenaline, nothing slow and aware and leisurely, no air I care to take in deep.

I should be used to this by now, you'd think it would get easier, but sometimes I think it gets harder. The longer I'm here the more suffocated I feel by this eternally grey sky, the air thick with fumes, and the incessant stares forcing me into a heightened state of self-consciousness, never able to just relax, blend in. It's better when I'm walking with Yizhong, because together we form a protective bubble that allows me to walk with more confidence and pride—*yes, we are different, yes I am a foreigner, don't you wish you knew our story.* But alone, I am vulnerable, I have no one to talk to or direct my energy towards—it's either inward and closed off, or open and exposed to whatever energy comes my way.

Sometimes the stares are innocent and can give way to a smile of surprise—if you smile first; but other times they feel laced with resentment. More and more these days, as I approach each person on the street, their eyes taking me in, my body tenses and I look past them, to the side or to the ground. Each passing feels like a confrontation of sorts—do I defiantly meet their gaze, or do I pretend not to see or care? Sometimes when I stare back they get embarrassed and dart their eyes to the ground, and I can't help but feel some sense of triumph—*they looked away, I won.* Yet more and more, I don't have the energy for this game. Ideally, I try to strike a balance, keep my vision and senses open while still preserving my shield of aloof distance. I want to remain open to the possibility of a greeting, a hint of kindness behind a stranger's eyes. But the truth is, these days it's all I can do to keep the hard edge of a glare out of my eyes, a defensive snarl I never knew was in me.

心

When I return to the courtyard from my walk, the vendors are already setting up for the night market. Wheels rumble across rough concrete, poles clatter against the ground. First the vendors affix the metal scaffolding, from which they'll hang clothing and other goods. Then they spread out plastic, set up tables, and pull livelihoods out of duffle bags and boxes. Row upon row of stalls will soon be ready to sell you slippers, bras, vases, trousers, books, makeup, lamps, posters, fans, cactuses, shoes, toys, pillows, dishes, purses, batteries—almost every cheap made-in-China good you can imagine. When the sky grows dark, they plug in strings of hanging lights and groups of young teens wander hand-in-hand or huddle around *saokao* barbeque stands waiting for their chosen skewers of meat and vegetables to be grilled and layered with oil, cumin, salt and hot peppers. People sit at small tables on the sidewalk eating *huoguo* (spicy Sichuan hot pot) and swigging from tall bottles of sweet local beer. Occasionally, Yizhong and I will join them.

I walk back through the metal gate to my apartment. The old-timers who sit near the entrance in small bamboo chairs eye the plastic bags in my hands. I imagine them discussing what vegetables the foreign girl bought today, what she's doing here anyway, coming in and out of the apartment at odd hours each day. The woman with short, rough-edged hair who hangs out every day near the tiny room with the TV glances at me as I pass, but her eyes offer no flicker of greeting. She presides over the daily in-and-out flow of traffic, calling out to people when they have mail. Often if something comes written in English, she shows it to Yizhong, since he's the only one who ever gets foreign mail or visitors. In fact, ask any of the people around here, "Long hair, painter?" and most will nod and wave their hands towards the nest of units in back as if to say, *Yeah, he lives here somewhere, we know who you mean.*

If Yizhong and I lived in one of the new apartment high-rises sprouting up all over town we'd have a password, an elevator, a guard, a feeling of anonymity and independence. But here, in our complex, the old beehive hierarchy still exists. Each building has a supervisor who is a part of a "neighborhood unit" responsible for disseminating government propaganda, like the banners that ask residents to report any people practicing Falun Gong, a spiritual group that incorporates qi gong meditation techniques with elements of Buddhist and Taoist philosophy and claims seventy million members in China. The government fears any large, popular organization outside of itself and has branded Falun Gong a cult, its practice punishable by arrest or imprisonment. Our building supervisor will also blare messages over loudspeakers about how people from the countryside need to register with the police, about paying taxes, family planning, or my favorite, dental hygiene: *Wei. Wei! In the countryside, people are not used to brushing their teeth . . .* And so it goes, extolling the virtues of daily fluoride.

Every night they also play a prerecorded announcement of a woman's high-pitched voice telling the residents that it is now ten-thirty and we should all turn down our televisions and radios, close and lock our doors, and the people on floors two through six should refrain from throwing things out their windows. We are reminded to have morality and respect toward each other—and everything short of lights out, time for bed. Then it clicks off again and life goes on as usual, voices calling back and forth from open windows to the ground below, televisions arguing and firing guns at each other through muffled walls of privacy.

I climb up the five flights of stairs and step inside, relieved to be home. In the kitchen, I boil water, then go back to the living room. It's after five now and people are getting off work. Taxis force their way down our street through narrow openings between the market stalls, their horns acting as whips to herd bicycles and people out of their way. A woman plays a pounding techno bass to announce her DVD stall in front of our building. Every evening she blasts a mix of soaring love ballads, grating high-pitched children's songs, or mind-numbing techno. As always, a small crowd of *nongmin* crowd around, mouths agape, and watch the music videos. The night market is their daily free dose of distraction and entertainment, especially since they probably have nowhere to go besides a bunk bed in a dark crowded workers' hovel.

Underneath the techno I hear layers of whining ballads and synthesizer beats echoing from stalls and shops up and down the street. In the distance, I make out the sound of the bamboo flute seller playing tunes as he wanders amidst the crowds. And somewhere, the *di-di-di-di, di-di-di-di, di-di-di-di* of multiple mini alarm clocks going off from a display like some nightmare morning from hell. It doesn't make much difference if I close the windows; the noise still seeps in from all sides. Plus, the muggy heat is unbearable.

To the Chinese, this is *renao*, lively and enjoyable. Maybe if the night market didn't happen every day beneath my window I would appreciate it more, but I also know I could never have the same affection for noise and crowds as the Chinese do. Some of Yizhong's Chinese friends who have moved to Germany have complained how quiet and lonely the streets are abroad. But as an American, I prefer to have ample space around my body as I walk; I am fond of silence, solitude, and natural landscapes, none of which exist in Chengdu.

I make myself a cup of tea, then turn on music, hoping to drown out the commotion outside. Yizhong won't be home for at least another hour, so I open a book and turn a few pages, before realizing I have not absorbed a word. I don't feel like reading, I don't feel like writing, and my own music feels like just one more layer of noise.

Standing up, I push back the table and chairs to the walls, flip through our CDs, and choose a raucous, staccato, electronic one, normally too grating for me to listen to. Blasting it, I jump up and down, fling my head back and forth, kick up my legs, twist my torso—part aerobics class, part ecstatic rave, part thrasher metal concert—I let fly in this small padded cell called my living room.

As I dance, from the corner of my eye I spy a boy across the street leaning out his window, watching me. He's maybe seven or eight. I move closer to the window and flail my arms and body with more gusto. *Yes, that's right little boy, I see you.* His mouth drops open and he smiles, then he flails his body in imitation. I lean my head out and growl like a tiger. He growls back with a roar. Raar!! *Raaar!!* Raaar!! *Raaar!!!* Back and forth it goes. A few people appear at their windows across the street to check out the new commotion. *You want something to look at?* I lean out and roar even fiercer.

Soon, the boy's mother or some adult figure approaches from the background, probably telling him to get away from the window. He disappears, but then he's back. I silently cheer his resolve to play, and roar again. Yet after a few more rounds of exchange, I step away from the window, tired of our little game. Sitting back in a chair, out of sight of the boy, I feel the urge both to laugh and to cry. Outside, I hear him roar again.

16

Refuge

At the living room window, I pull up the bamboo shade, then light a coil of sandalwood and place it on the sill. Here also rests a white silk *khata*, dried red rose petals, a small cactus, a postcard of a Buddhist fresco from the caves of Dunhuang, and a photo of Yizhong and me, smiling, happy. I've never called it an altar to Yizhong before, I'm not even sure how to say altar in Chinese, but this is what I want it to be—a place that announces my deeper intentions, my longing for peace, in the world, in myself. My longing to give with my life.

The problem is I don't feel any reverence these days. I don't feel it in my body, I don't feel like bowing, I'm no longer sure what this act means. Plus, it doesn't feel right the way the altar sits underneath the giant single-paned window that lets in so much noise and dust, smack dab in the middle of our most public room. It is just a token, a nod toward a distant way of being. For ever since arriving in Chengdu, I've gradually withdrawn from the intensity of my old spiritual yearning. I think back to who I was before I came to China: how I used to spend so much time alone, in nature, practicing tai chi or dancing Butoh, hoping to be a bridge builder between cultures, or at least a beloved teacher of English. But now all I do is hide away in our apartment, teach an occasional class, and write in my journal about my growing homesickness and unhappiness.

More and more I am starting to wonder again, what am I doing here? How long can I bear to stay? For something like two years, I haven't gotten down on my hands and knees and prayed, nor danced from a place that is open and naked. I'm too self-conscious now to rekindle these acts in front of another, even someone as accepting of me as Yizhong. How can I explain my longing in Chinese, if I can barely explain it to myself in English? Yet my body still speaks what I am slow to acknowledge— my tears come more frequently, my cramps come more heavily, and my upper back aches, a sore spot in between my shoulders that I sometimes ask Yizhong to rub.

My body reminds me that all is not well here. All is not forgotten.

心

Yizhong sits in his studio on the other side of these cement walls. I picture him at his desk, smoking a cigarette and staring out the window, maybe thinking about what he might paint today. After a while, he gets out his journal or maybe flips through the rest of yesterday's newspaper. Eventually he'll stare at his paintings.

Yizhong's favorite medium is watercolor with pen and ink, but recently he's been experimenting with acrylics and bold colors, and also painting bigger, too big to use a table or easel. I know he wants to break out of the same old thing, but his studio is too small, he says, he doesn't have enough space. His latest painting is another one of me, this time from a photo he took on our trip to Cambodia last fall. My dark brown hair is in a short bob, tied back with my mustard silk scarf. I'm leaning across a table at an outdoor café in Siam Reap, smiling, happy, my chin propped under my hand. This was the only time we ever left the country together, Germany aside. We ended up in Cambodia because I helped Yizhong secure an art show at a gallery in Hong Kong, his first big solo show, but it was hard for him to get a visa to attend. The only option was for him to go to another country first, a place where it's easy for Chinese people to visit. Then as long as Yizhong could prove that he had a ticket to fly on to somewhere else, he was allowed to pass through Hong Kong. We were both excited to travel in Southeast Asia together. I'd been to Thailand, Vietnam, and Laos, but never Cambodia. So we spent a day in transit in Hong Kong, before flying on, and in another two weeks we returned to launch Yizhong's show.

In Phnom Penh, we wandered the potholed streets, eating at food stalls, taking photos, and visiting genocide museums with mass burial sites. No longer on Yizhong's turf, I took the lead again when seeking out hostels or buying tickets, reminded of what it felt like when I visited him in Germany. Only now, I got the sense that everyone assumed we were Japanese—the only Asian people you often encounter in the backpacking circuit. No one ever guessed that I was American, or that Yizhong and I came from different countries, and it was liberating to pretend for a while that we were someone else. To imagine a life together where we both could travel freely between borders as we pleased.

The day we arrived in Siam Reap we had just checked into our hotel room when we turned on the TV and saw images of the twin towers falling, the same footage over and over, while a Chinese anchorwoman on CCTV relayed the limited few facts that were known in a tone that felt a note too chipper. It felt unreal, America so far away. The next day, we hired two motorcycle guides and entered the temples of Angkor Wat. It was off-season and often we were the only ones in sight, zipping down the rural roads with thatched huts and banana trees, or walking through the ancient sites of worship overgrown with vines and exploding roots of giant trees. It felt like we'd escaped—escaped China and some bottled-up version of ourselves—and now we were children, playing, free. Exploring the most magical place I'd ever been, an awe-inspiring human feat of accomplishment, now being reclaimed by time and nature. Together, we scrambled over fallen stones, climbed up crumbling steps, and pointed out corners where the light fell so perfectly it seemed meant for our eyes alone.

When we returned to Hong Kong and held Yizhong's show, hardly anyone attended the opening. 9/11= poor timing. Yizhong sold one painting to a young German man (who had an artist boyfriend from Hong Kong), and the rest we left with the gallery. His collection was mostly watercolors and pen and ink, a continuation of the series he started in Germany. I'd helped to translate Yizhong's artist statement, although the gallery named the show, *Abstract Self-Portraits*. Accurate, but boring. The painting that sold (one of my favorites) was of a skinny man, naked and kneeling, with a bird squawking above him in the corner, all in shades of greys and blues. When I asked Yizhong what the bird represented, he said he didn't know; a bird just always appeared in his paintings whether he planned for it to or not. It was a part of him, yet outside of him, something like the soul.

To me, the bird in Yizhong's painting feels like a trickster—always there, watching, goading, teasing, mocking, hinting at what he both knows and doesn't know. Sometimes the bird hovers above the man, other times it flies at his side. Sometimes, only a feather remains, and once there was no man at all, only a bird. To me, the bird represents the deepest part of Yizhong, his witness, the part of him that watches and sees himself clearly, even when the rest of him is blind to its cries. If my Chinese were better, I might ask him if this rings true.

Soul. *Linghun*. 靈魂. This was one of my "spiritual" words, one of the words I wrote down on the list I kept when I first moved into my teacher's apartment, back when I still felt all of the anticipation that went into this journey, its trajectory newly unfolding. Back then I trusted that the arc of my journey was spiritual, maybe tied to Tibet, and definitely connected to my greater work in this life. I looked up all kinds of words in my dictionary, anticipating long talks about art, religion, creativity, life's purpose. Yizhong taught me words like spirit: *jingshen* 精神; imagination: *xiangxiangli* 想像力; and inspiration: *linggan* 靈感—soul feeling. But now, I am no longer sure what these abstract words even mean.

Yizhong, more and more, is the reason I am still here. I never would have lasted here this long without him. As an artist, he gets me, and I get him. We give each other plenty of space to do our work. But how long can I sit in this apartment, writing in my journal? How am I helping anyone by being here? What am I even learning anymore, besides seeing more and more of my weakness? I still feel certain that my life is tied to China. I still have dreams of writing books or translating between cultures. Yet most days now my spirit is heavy, my confidence low. In Chinese, the phrase "I'm not inspired" translates into "I don't have any soul-feeling." Maybe this describes me. I've found refuge in this apartment with Yizhong, but my heart feels more and more weak.

At some point after I returned to Chengdu, I stopped going by Ani and switched simply to An—a true hybrid between my given Chinese and English names. The name, Ani, now felt tied to a younger me, a more naïve me. A me that still placed too much importance in titles and names.

A part of me does still wonder where my old fervent seeking related to Buddhism and Tibet has gone, and whether my old resistance to taking refuge in Buddhist vows somehow made my connection to the teachings less potent. Mostly I didn't want to have to explain myself to others—to represent myself "as a Buddhist" when I still wasn't sure about so much. I also never felt comfortable joining the communities of mostly white, middle-aged strangers who populated American Buddhist sanghas. I attended a few meditations and dharma talks, but I was always turned off by the chanting in another language, by anything that hinted of appropriation. Now, I'm trying to trust that so-called Buddhism already lives inside of me, inside of my own awareness—watching my mind, thoughts, judgments, feelings, body, and breath—and this awareness helps me to be more compassionate towards myself and towards others. But none of this feels like enough. Why am I so unhappy?

Here, in China, I have even fewer people to talk to about my inner world. And although I feel loved by Yizhong in such sweet ways, I've lost my old solitary practices. Here, there is so little space to be alone, so little nature to disappear in, so few spaces that feel holy. Although there has been a resurgence of faith over the last decade in China—courtyards thick with incense, people buying and offering tall red joss sticks, placing them into giant bowls of sand—here, at Buddhist or Taoist temples, these ancient philosophies I first learned about while reading alone in my college dorm feel more like feudal religions with everyone just praying to statues for their own family's good health or fortune. I've never felt in these places the presence of the sacred. And I've lost touch with how to access this place in myself.

These days I just cry more and more. I retreat to our bedroom after another evening of hanging out with Yizhong's friends, listening to the familiar sound of his voice as he gets more buzzed and excited about whatever they're speaking of, usually ranting against some aspect of the government. These conversations are interesting to me and I wish I could join in—tell them about how my friends have been writing passionate e-mails, telling me about the W.T.O. protests, about the way they barricaded the streets in Seattle to halt the meetings, the way the police used tear gas. But as usual I stay quiet, for even if I follow most of what's being said, I can't keep up or speak fast enough to easily participate. This is an old feeling of mine, in any language. I grow silent, and eventually so distant that I might as well not be there. Afterward, I go to our bed, bury my head in the pillows, and cry. Yizhong comes and sits next to me, stroking my arm. *"Oh, baobei . . ."* He asks, "What's wrong?" But I can't explain because I'm not even sure myself.

Is it me? Is it him? Is it China? Am I done here? I miss my family, my friends, and my identity lived through English. And I miss my home near salt water and tall evergreen trees, long solitary walks breathing fresh air into my body. I never realized before just how much I depended on wild spaces, or how I once took clean air for granted. In China, everything is coated with thick dust. And everywhere, there are people. On sunny days, flocks of people gather in the city parks, by the river, in the teahouses, on the sidewalks, perched against railings, sitting on benches, squatting beneath any lingering tree, every spot of shade. The rivers stink—dead stagnant water, shorelines draped with blue plastic bags and rubbish, and the water tastes like chemicals no matter how long you boil it. New slogans painted on the temporarily erected white walls that border construction sites proclaim in English and Chinese, "Blue sky, green grass, clean streets, friendly people!" Or, "Let's do everything possible to maintain Chengdu's image as a clean, modern, and civilized city!" The government wants to "Develop the West," its latest campaign, and Chengdu is its shining headquarter; every corner shows the progress. In one week, a street is torn up and made over. Empty buildings are stacked in rows with fancy faux European-style pillars, cheap tiles, and tinted blue glass; real estate billboards proclaiming in English "Wonderful Space" or "Roman Holiday" with pictures of smiling white couples—the ultimate in status.

I try to imagine the old courtyard that Yizhong grew up in, his tales of swimming in the Fu river and eating from peach trees, a mere couple decades ago. Now, only a few patches of the old city remain, a lane or two we occasionally stumble upon like entering another era, sunlight streaming in, old impressive doorframes, arched rooftops, quiet, dreamlike—before the street spits you back out into traffic on the other side.

Maybe if I go back to America, I can find my old center of gratitude and prayer again. Maybe I just need a break. Maybe I've stayed too long. Grown too dependent on cigarettes and alcohol for stimulation and release, too dependent on one person to fill my emotional needs. Maybe I'm too sensitive to live here for long, too permeable, too weak. If there is an inner peace that I can cultivate wherever I am, I have not yet figured out how. I still have so much to learn about how to take care of myself. How to trust in what my body tells me I need.

In the morning, Yizhong and I wake late, snuggling in close like nesting rabbits, the air cold on our cheeks. I burrow in deep and breathe in his smell, a smell that somehow reminds me of my mother, something like peas. Maybe it's a Chinese smell, or just skin and hot breath, the smell of someone else's body.

I love Yizhong like I've loved no other—his easy good nature, his intellectual curiosity, his artistic vision. I love to watch him mix paints or chop vegetables as he prepares for a meal, carefully planned and methodically executed, filling rows of small bowls with ingredients. And I love the way he takes care of me, helps speak for me in public, cooks for me, holds me tightly at night. When I stare into his eyes, I see gentleness and adoration, eyes like a child, wide, kind, and accepting. And I've longed to be loved like this for so long. Yizhong has given me this gift, this refuge that not everyone has the privilege to receive.

It breaks my heart that I cannot give this back to him fully. For there is still a place I fear that I cannot go with Yizhong, a place I can't find in his eyes, no matter how openly we stare. Sometimes Yizhong will rub his finger against the furrowed spot between my eyebrows, and ask me, "What are you thinking?" *Ni xiang shenme?* Nothing, I'll shake my head, but I know that he knows I'm withholding something.

Is it possible to live a happy and wonderful life with another, to choose someone based on friendship and loving connection, even if you sense something is missing? How much of what I can't share with Yizhong has to do with language and how much goes beyond words? I know that I could eventually learn to express more in Chinese. And for the most part, I don't even mind that he cannot read my writing, for this way I never have to worry that he'll see my private fears or unhappiness. Writing has been my lifeline wherever I am, but especially while in China. Writing has been my way to always feel witnessed. Writing has kept me honest, even when I'm tempted to evade the truth. Notebooks upon notebooks, a steady voice, a daily practice: one continuous thread of longing.

Maybe this is the path I have chosen all along.

心

Now, I stand in the living room at the windowsill and light incense, my small nod to something greater than the confines of my heavy heart and mind. I clear the low square coffee table of the previous night's debris—ashtray, wine glasses, chocolate wrapper—and turn on our little space heater, before carefully arranging two cushions on the floor. Sitting down, I cover my lap with a small white fleece blanket, open my journal, and uncap my pen. At the top of the page, I write down the date, and *Good morning*.

This is the way I begin again.

PART THREE

PILGRIM'S PATH

17

You Have to Do What You Have to Do

"What is going on, Anne? This isn't like you." My mother tries to talk to me as she stands in the doorway, but I brush her off as I get ready to go out again, annoyed that she is judging me, annoyed that I am staying again in my parents' basement. Her questions tap into my own guilt and doubt.

What *am* I doing? It is the spring of 2002 and I've come home for a six-month visit, taking a break from life in China. I also see this separation as a test of my love for Yizhong. How much will I miss him? How soon might I forget him? I want to gain clarity, to see if I can imagine bringing my two worlds together—to see if I can imagine marrying Yizhong, the only way we can live together in the States. Before I left China, we started collecting paperwork for him to come visit by early fall, but we also avoided talking directly about marriage.

But now I finally know that I must face the doubt that has plagued me, the tiny hints of dissatisfaction barely confessed in my journal. I know that I must leave Yizhong, because I am cheating on him with not just one man, but possibly two.

い

When I arrived back in the States, I spent my first couple months indulging in everything I'd missed: old friends, weekend road trips, the coast, the woods, old college haunts. So many choices and so much freedom! Hungrily, I scanned the weekly alternative newspaper for music or art shows, wrote in coffee shops, researched grants and grad school programs, salivated over all the possibilities for today and for my future. After living in Chengdu, Seattle now felt more like a small town than a big city, a town filled with wide spacious streets where nobody stared with mouths agape nor whispered as I passed. Here, I could be up close and intimate with friends, yet I could also once again be anonymous, free, and unobserved. Here, too, I began to notice how many more men were looking at me. And I liked this. Maybe it was because I was thinner now, and back to wearing more feminine, fitted clothes. Or maybe it was a new confidence I projected. Or maybe, too, the fact that I knew I was "taken" gave me a boost of nonchalance, relieved me of any concern whether a passing interest could lead to more, allowing me to indulge in flirtation without real stakes.

Over the summer I started teaching English to a group of ten high school students from the former Soviet Union, here on a program sponsored by the State Department. Teaching teenagers for seven hours a day was a challenge for me, and at the end of each day I was exhausted—drinking a beer, having a smoke, and planning the next day's lessons from the comfort of the couch underneath my parents' deck. I did enjoy this role, however, and knew it would bring in the money for me to buy a ticket for Yizhong. We'd finally made progress on the paperwork front and were now aiming for him to come to the States in early fall.

I had been talking to Yizhong about once a week. I missed him and over the phone we spoke with the soft baby-talk we were accustomed to. He told me how he called out for me in the morning, which made me think of his mom and how she calls out for her mom the first thing each morning, ever since her mom died when she was young. He told me about dinners with our friends He Yi and Xie Ping, and it was easy for me to picture his days. He also updated me about his recent English lessons, as he was now attending classes at a school where I'd previously taught. I was proud of his progress. But it was much harder, of course, for Yizhong to imagine my life here, filled with tales of new places and people, none of which he'd ever seen. His e-mail subject headings were full of exclamation points: *Ai ni baobao! Wo de baobei! Wo ai ni!!!* (Love you, baby! My precious! I love you!!!). I loved him too, but I couldn't deny that the longer we were apart and the busier I became, the more distant I felt from the cloistered bubble of our old life.

As the summer progressed, I kept working long days and bonding with the other teachers. Most of us were women, except for Mark. Mark was guarded at first, often hiding behind sarcasm and jokes, but during our last couple outings, when we escorted the kids to Seattle's waterfront and to Mt. Rainier, I started looking forward to our exchanges.

In mid-August, after the program ended, four of us chaperoned the students at a hotel near the airport before their flights the next day. In between checking in on them, we shared a bottle of wine, staying up late and feeding off of their giddy "last hurrah" energy. Finally, near 3 a.m., we decided we should sleep a couple hours. Mark and I lay next to each other on one bed, our bodies close, aware of each other's proximity but not touching. Our attraction was obvious, but the others in the room held us back. Finally, when it was time to get up, I rose to go to the bathroom, and when I walked out, he was waiting by the door. Our bodies suctioned together in a kiss, electric.

A hunger shot through me. I wanted to kiss him again, but instead I spent the next few hours in a daze, carrying a secret guilt and excitement. After shepherding all the students to their gates, Mark and I took the shuttle together back to the hotel. He suggested having breakfast, and I hesitated, but agreed. On some level I knew what was happening, what I was already choosing, but until I followed him home later in my car, I could pretend I had not yet crossed the line. Not just a kiss, a momentary slip, but something I had clearly chosen.

I slept with him that afternoon, and it felt reckless, yet good. This was not like me, as my mom would later remind me—spontaneous sex with someone I barely knew, without even the excuse or filter of alcohol. I knew now that I had to break up with Yizhong. I also knew that I was not going to fall in love with Mark; he was just a catalyst to move on. But since I'd already cheated, I figured I might as well enjoy sleeping with him some more.

心

I tell my mother not to worry about me, that I know what I am doing, but beyond this, I don't know what else to say to her. We've never talked about romantic relationships, much less sex, with the exception of the letters that she translated between me and Yizhong. She'd felt strange about that too, but at least on some level I felt I was pleasing her then because he was Chinese. Now, I am sleeping with a guy that I know I'm not falling in love with. And I don't care what she thinks or says.

With Yizhong I was always the dominant one, always on top, always calling the shots. With Mark, I feel ravished. Out of control. He tears into me with this hungry look in his eye, flings me into positions with suggestive force, goes down on me until my face tingles—and one time, my hand even goes numb, nerve endings sparking everywhere. We have that kind of chemistry. He talks dirty to me, and I love it. No one has ever turned me on so much just by whispering a few words. He asks, "What do you want?" and cajoles me into answering. I am perpetually wet around him, breathless from the moment we start kissing.

Since neither of us are working now, and he lives a mere couple miles from my parents', we've started seeing each other almost every day. Sometimes I do want to take a break and process all that is happening, but I can't resist going back the very next day and having sex again, trying out my body, my desire, with this new person, on the bed, against the wall, in the park, out in the open. Remembering how to flirt, tease, and fuck in English. Breaking open and doing what I want, regardless of the consequences.

Over the phone now, Yizhong can tell I am distant. At first I am not sure when I will tell him, but then, after a week or so, I can't wait any longer. *I need to break up with you. I still love you, but my spirit needs more*, I say in Chinese, unable to express myself better.

"I don't understand. You've only been gone five months. It's so sudden. Is there something else you're not telling me?"

"No," I lie. I can't bring myself to tell him, at least not like this, over the phone, even if some part of him probably already knows. It feels too hurtful, especially when I know I am not falling in love with this new person. I will still go back to China in September, I tell Yizhong, for I can't bear to not say goodbye in person. I owe him this. And I need it too, for myself. But I am also clear that this time it will be a real goodbye.

じ

My mother knows I've been seeing Mark and obviously disapproves, but what I can't even fathom how to explain to her now is how I am also interested in another person. More than interested. Maybe falling in love. It is too much to expect anyone to understand.

A few weeks after I got involved with Mark, I ran into an old acquaintance from Olympia at a music festival in Seattle. Matthew wore a suede cowboy hat, with his long hair tied back in a ponytail. "Well, hey there," he greeted me, his energy the same as I remembered—open and down-to-earth, yet also mysterious and slightly unsettling. I first met Matthew five years before when I moved to Olympia and we both were working at a Middle Eastern restaurant, he as a baker and I as a prep cook/hostess/server. I remember seeing him for the first time, a handsome, sturdy white man with long brown hair pulled back in a braid, sitting at a table writing in his journal during his break. "Don't forget to breathe," he said as I spun about frazzled on my first busy day. Eventually I learned that he was in a long-term relationship, so as our paths crisscrossed over the next few years, I didn't give him much thought. I did dream about him once, however, or rather dreamed of finding a lover who was somehow like him—earthy, confident, and centered. And another time, after running into him in the street, I wrote in my journal, *I wonder if we'll be together one day.*

We exchanged numbers at the festival and a week later, Matthew called. He was in town again because his grandmother was in a hospital north of Seattle, dying. I invited him out to hear music with me and my sister that night, and told him he could crash at her place afterward so as to avoid a long drive. That same night Mark wanted to see me, but I didn't return his calls. There was something between Matthew and me, but I wasn't sure what it was. Whatever it was, I knew that I didn't want to see both of them at the same time. I needed to step back from Mark and reclaim my autonomy, to resist the sense that I was getting pulled into the orbit of another, no matter how exhilarating sex with him could be. He was not my boyfriend, I didn't owe him anything, and I didn't fully trust our fling.

After the show, I lent Matthew a sleeping bag and we lay next to each other on the carpeted floor of my sister's living room. I'd taken my contacts out, so my vision was blurred, but we were close enough that I could still see his gaze. We began to stare, without looking away, in a penetrating way I'd only ever shared with my one of my closest friends. Eventually I scooted closer so I could see his eyes more clearly, and neither of us broke the gaze. I am not sure how long we stayed like that; it felt like a whole hour. At one point, we smiled, but still we didn't speak to interrupt what was happening. Finally, I reached for his hand and we squeezed in acknowledgement, then closed our eyes to go to sleep.

The next day I felt elated, yet slightly crazy. *What just happened?* No one had ever looked at me so deeply before for so long. We didn't say much about it, although we both knew that something had opened between us, something was beginning.

When Matthew visited the next weekend, however, I felt awkward. Whereas I was used to being the quiet one, being with Matthew made me feel downright chatty, uncomfortable with his long pervading silences. He was so quiet and we'd still barely spoken about what happened, besides saying it was "intense." We went on a walk to Lake Washington, and only before he was about to leave did we finally embrace. A vastness radiated from his chest. Just like when I stared into his eyes, it was as if there was no wall of separation to hit, if only we could let ourselves stay in this place of connection. In some strange yet true way, I felt I could already tell him I loved him, even though we barely knew each other.

۲

"Your face has so many expressions. Has anyone ever told you that before?" Matthew asks.

It is my last day in Seattle, and we stand facing each other in a wooded park. He drove up here to meet me and say goodbye. When we hug, I can feel his heart beating and hear his long, deep breaths. His wide, barrel chest feels cavernous, like I can get pulled inside him completely.

"No, like what?"

"I don't know, it just changes a lot. I noticed that the night we first stared at each other. I saw all these different faces flash through."

"Do you remember what they were?"

"I don't know, it's hard to put in words. I saw a child's face, and an old woman." He pauses, then takes a breath. "And, I hope I don't freak you out by saying this, but I also thought I saw my wife."

心

When I arrive in Chengdu a day later, the sky is grey, everything is grey. Yizhong stands waiting for me outside the airport terminal. He looks skinnier than I remember, dressed in a blue denim jacket and black jeans. His long, dark hair hangs loose around his olive skin. It feels almost as it did when he came to greet me at the airport in Germany. Only then, everything was just beginning. Now, everything is coming to an end.

He pulls me in close and I breathe in his sadness. We ride the bus into the city, holding hands, exchanging few words. I have not yet decided what I will tell him. That I slept with my co-worker, but don't plan to stay with him? Or that there is this other man who could quite possibly be my future husband, for when he said those words, "I think I saw my wife," I know where they hit me, a shock of surprise incomprehensible to my mind, too much to accept, yet somehow ringing true. *What should I tell Yizhong? What version of truth?* I don't know. Right now, I just need to wait to see if it feels right to explain the full story, or if some details are better left unsaid.

For the next couple of weeks, we do our usual thing: walking to our favorite teahouses, going shopping for pirated CDs, watching DVDs at night. We don't have sex at first, although we still share a bed. In moments, it almost feels as if nothing has changed between us. Except for this new layer of sadness. I am thankful that Yizhong doesn't hurl angry words at me, nor push me for more explanations beyond my scant abstract elaborations: *our love is not balanced, I'm not happy here, I still love you but my spirit needs more.*

Yizhong has yet to tell his parents that we are breaking up. I asked him to explain to them first, since I can't imagine breaking the news to them myself. Then, after he tells them, I can try to further explain, thank them, and say goodbye. My plan is to travel solo once more, to revisit Xiahe, a Tibetan town and monastery that made a huge impression on me on my first trip, and to take some time to say goodbye to this phase of my life and to this country. But Yizhong isn't able to tell his parents; he says he will soon, when he is ready. And every day that we keep my departure a secret makes it harder to bring it up. Meanwhile, his parents are moving into a new condo in the suburbs—a huge space compared to where they live now, with a big studio on the upper floor for his dad, a small studio for his mom, and a rooftop garden. They invite us to come and stay a few days. When we arrive, Yizhong's mom excitedly gives us a tour, showing us "our bedroom" and "our slippers" that she bought for us to keep there. The four of us sit on their brand-new plush purple couches and watch *Black Hawk Down* on their brand-new glare-resistant TV. Each day I wait for Yizhong to explain what is going on, and each day he doesn't have the heart. *How can I tell them when they're so happy? I'll tell them. I will. But I don't want to deal with their questions right now. I know they won't understand,* he says. And how can I fault him when I am having such a hard time explaining to Yizhong why I am leaving myself?

I only planned to spend two weeks in Chengdu before moving on to travel on my own, but I keep waiting, waiting for more closure with Yizhong and his family. We decide to take one last trip together, to visit a Taoist mountain in Sichuan. Here, as we hike the well-tread forested paths by day and keep each other warm under layers of thick quilts at night, our imminent parting sinks in on another level. Although our time together is cloaked in sadness, I am relieved that we can say goodbye in this way, appreciating each other and the love we share instead of withdrawing into distance or anger.

And then, finally, I have to leave. I cannot bear to draw this out any longer. And so, in the end, I leave Chengdu without explaining to Yizhong anything more about what happened in Seattle, and without saying goodbye to his parents. Carrying on my inherited legacy of secrecy and silence.

I divide up our CDs and our photos, giving him the albums and taking home the negatives. I pack up my journals and a few other important things to send home. The rest I leave behind.

During our last days together, we cry and hold each other tightly as we sleep, our awareness of our love heightened by our knowledge of my coming departure. *You have to do what you have to do*, Yizhong says, his willingness to let me go his parting gift.

18

Pilgrim's Path

I walk the *kora*, left to right. I turn the prayer wheels clockwise, one after another. Some turn smoothly, spinning fast, with a gentle push. Others must be pulled with force, calling out with squeaky groans, as if begging to be oiled. I walk the *kora*, left to right, touch each well-worn wooden handle, each radiating spoke. I watch the turning, blurring motion, panels of color: red, blue, yellow, white, violet, green. I walk with Tibetan pilgrims, in front of me, behind me. They never stop moving their lips, saying mantras, rushing past me on a mission, no time to pause and stare for long, too many circumambulations to complete.

My day's objective: get up, drink tea, eat, walk the *kora*. Even if I just circle once, I need to honor, need to pray. Need to welcome back this place: Xiahe, Labrang Monastery, Gansu Province, a poor and rugged, desolate part of northwestern China. Xiahe is a dusty town in a river valley nestled between brown barren hills, mounds of dry, cracking dirt erupting from the earth like the rippled feet of elephants. This was the last place I visited in China on my first trip; the place where I vowed I would come back.

I stay close to the Tibetan part of town, near the monastery and the *kora*, the path that circles its exterior with a steady stream of pilgrims. The *kora* is lined with prayer wheels and *chotens*, small white temples that represent the cosmology of the universe. The path is dirt, the sun is bright. I wear two shirts, one sweater, one fleece, and one down vest, but the cold still cuts to my core. It's late September and I'm leaving China, this time for who knows how long.

Two days ago I said goodbye to Yizhong. We kept each other warm off and on for three years, but now it is time for me to go. I've been living too long in a city of nine million, congested with smoke, traffic, angry people. I've been living too long with no space to breathe in, no nature to retreat to, no rituals but writing to help me remember how to pray. Now, I walk alone, as I did when I first arrived in this country. Alone, I walk and pray.

Six years ago, I discovered Xiahe. Back then I arrived here from even more isolated lands, so coming to Xiahe had felt like returning to civilization, or rather returning to a popular stop on the *Lonely Planet* route. But this time, I took a fifteen-hour train from Chengdu to Lanzhou, and then an all-day bus. This time, I've arrived here not after weeks of backpacking, but after years in a place that I still think of as home, home in China anyway, home with the one person to whom, despite our parting, I still feel closest.

A part of me wonders if I really needed to come here. And yet, I also want to trust my heart that said that before I flew home, I needed to revisit Tibetan land, to confront my old yearning and ask what I still feel. To come back to this culture in which a nun's pursuits are not viewed as a frivolous departure, but as an essential occupation. I want to ingest these mountains again, these monks and nuns, these country people: Tibetans. This other face of China.

My first time here, I wanted to walk the *kora*, I even turned a few wheels, but I felt too self-conscious. Now, today, I'm back on this path, this path I have always been walking.

Outside of Lhasa, Xiahe is the leading Tibetan monastery town, says my *Lonely Planet* guidebook. At its peak, 4,000 monks studied here; now there are around 1,700. Labrang is one of six major monasteries of the Gelupga or Yellow Hat Sect of Tibetan Buddhism. This means little to me except that it is the sect of the Dalai Lama. His picture is not allowed in temples, but I've seen it in the homes of monks and villagers. The religious controls are not as stringent here as in Lhasa, though Tibetans have told me that the monastery is still highly monitored by Chinese authorities. Religious freedom looks good for tourists. See? We allow the people to turn their prayer wheels, bow to statues, carry forth their superstitions. The temples are being restored, the natives are content.

Labrang monastery was built in 1709. Like most temples, it was all but destroyed during the Cultural Revolution of the late 1960s and 1970s. Teachers were killed or fled to the hills, monks beaten, books burned, treasures looted. Finally, in the eighties, after Mao died and the Cultural Revolution was denounced as a mistake, the slow work of restoration began. Brick temple walls were resurrected, painted white or warm terracotta with a strip of dark blue on top dotted with white circles, and above the blue, a wide swath of brown. Now, rows of narrow rectangular windows are also painted with dark blue trim; above each one hangs a white rippled cloth awning. New wooden doorways are intricately carved with dragons, flowers, and Tibetan Buddhist symbols; other doorways are draped with billowing cloth, bright canary yellow or simple white adorned with more Buddhist symbols—wheels, conch shells, fish, lotus blossoms.

But I am no longer interested in the temples. I've been inside my share already, sat in darkened corners of musty halls that smelled like burning yak butter, trying to be inconspicuous as I listened to young whispering monks, distracted by my presence. I've cringed when other tourists entered the halls in the middle of a prayer session—a Chinese woman talking loudly to her companion, high heels clicking behind her, or two gangly Europeans, cameras slung around their necks, hovering in the shadows. I know I am an outsider just like them, but I cannot help but see their foreignness from a distance, feel annoyed by their gawking pleasure, their awe of what they see as exotic.

I don't want to observe, I want to participate. Today, I walk the *kora*. Shadowed under wooden awnings, the prayer wheels come in rows, one after another. Each one is the size of a big conga drum, some are shaped like hexagons. Each is painted with bright colors, symbols, mantras, probably *om mani padme hum,* the mantra of compassion. Inside the temples, the walls are painted with wheels of life, hungry ghosts stuck in hell, human meat devoured by vultures, gods with gnashing teeth and necklaces made of skulls. Tibetans are not Zen Buddhists. Intricate blueprints for the soul, rituals, cosmology, scores of gods and goddesses—they are interesting, but I find them distracting. I prefer my Buddhism clean and simple: awareness of each moment, compassion for all beings.

Compassion for myself, compassion for Yizhong, compassion for the Tibetans *and* the Chinese. We are all suffering, going through our own versions of pain, yet most of us don't know how to sit with this. Tears are seen as weakness, not a source of strength. Retreat is seen as defeat, not a gathering of resources. How can we help others heal, if we don't tend to what is inside? Acknowledge all we feel, or all we don't let ourselves feel. Yes, I've felt like a failure each time I've left to start over again, realizing I could not stay. And yet this is what my heart has needed. I cannot deny myself my truth.

A small alcove appears before me, and I step inside the darkened room. Two wheels frame each side of the entrance, and a giant wheel, perhaps eight feet tall, rests in the middle. A circular handle runs around its base, one continuous metal grip. I grab hold and lean my body into the spin, walking, left to right. With each rotation a bell rings at the top. I wonder if this is a particularly auspicious prayer wheel, if size makes a difference. Perhaps there's an especially powerful prayer written on a rolled scroll tucked inside.

I step back out into daylight, cross the dirt road that runs through town and divides the monastery in half, then continue to walk the *kora* on the other side. There are no wheels along this part, only temple walls and tall wooden doorways. Beneath my feet, the path is littered with garbage: plastic bags, wrappers, bits of string. To the north, across the icy river, a road heads out of town, and behind the road are more barren hills. Near the base of one hill lies a narrow patch of green, the only trees for miles it seems—new growth, probably juniper, which is burned in vats around the temples. Breathing in, I taste its sweet smoky scent; soothing, like campfire smoke or incense, forest and church all mixed in one.

I slow to let a trail of pilgrims pass. I try not to stare too hard, but neither do I look away. An old woman walks in a green knit cap and a long black *chuba*, a thick traditional Tibetan robe; two young men in dirty sports coats and baseball caps saunter by; a young woman, her neck loaded with chunks of turquoise, coral, and amber, pulls the hand of a child behind her. They walk faster than I do, speed past holding strands of prayer beads, their dry cracked lips mouthing *om mani padme hum* as they rub each bead. I wonder if they have committed to a certain number of circumambulations in one day or week, and are in quest of a specific answer to a prayer. Or maybe this is an annual pilgrimage, demonstration of devotion. I try to not get in their way.

Left to right, left to right, I don't know why left to right, I just know my right arm is working overtime, wheel after wheel. I spy two foreigners taking pictures of the *kora*, and I wonder if they think I'm stupid for walking in these circles. Maybe they are whispering and pointing at me as I pass, *Look at that American girl, who does she think she is, pretending she's a Tibetan Buddhist . . .*

Now, here comes the giant *choten* with its blackened spots where

Tibetan pilgrims touch their heads in devotion. I circle the *choten*, but I don't lean over to touch my head, because I don't know what exactly it signifies. I just skip this part; my ritual is not the same as theirs, even though I am turning their wheels.

Still, I worry that I appear less devout. I worry that others by my side will see straight through my purple vest and denim jeans to my mind full of contradiction. Contradiction between the part of me that wants to honor my Buddhist path, this lineage I am a part of, and the part of me that resists all attempts at classification. God is too big for one religion, one name, much less one sex, a He or She. God is even too big for my darling Buddhist concepts, like impermanence, interdependence, and the practice of living in the here and now. There are times when all concepts lose their meaning, times when writing or reading words in a book does not satisfy my desire to call out, sing, dance, pray—to honor this life and all of its Mystery in a way that is expressive. *I am in your hands, oh sweet One. I know You are listening. I am listening. We are listening. We are listening to each other's prayers.*

To my right is the wall behind the monastery, to my left is the edge of a mountain. Another empty part of the *kora*, which we walk until the next set of wheels appears. I take it all in: air, mountain, footsteps, body moving forward, squeezing gently past the slower walkers, trying to give elders their due space. A woman with long greying braids smiles as I approach her side. She wears a dusty olive green *chuba* lined with wool and trimmed with colorful striped cloth. A pink sash is tied around her waist; on her feet, worn canvas sneakers, dirty white with a stripe of red. Taking my arm, she nods and smiles a toothy grin, giving me a thumbs up. We walk together, nodding, smiling. I'm not sure if she knows I'm a foreigner; it's possible she thinks I'm Chinese. But what does it matter, she is welcoming me, nodding, telling me it's good that I am here.

We walk behind the monastery in silence. Up ahead, a young

woman lies stretched across the ground, prostrating. Wooden blocks are tied to her knees and to the palms of her hands with strips of white tattered cloth. We step around her. I turn my head to look closer. A spot on her forehead has been rubbed bloody and raw. Now it is scabbing, this place where she touches her head to the earth, over and over, head to earth. She seems unaware of our presence, immersed in her prostrations, an expression of fervent anguish on her face—or is it devotion? Every step, she rises, brings her palms together, raises them to her head, her throat, her heart, knees dropping to the ground, body stretching out, and up again: one prostration. How many did it take her to get here? I've seen people walking like that in Tibet, on a road in the middle of nowhere. Who would choose to go that route? Only the most faithful, or the most desperate and afraid? Desperate for some kind of healing, desperate for a miracle?

I cannot imagine prostrating like she does, yet I am drawn to her devotion. I long to offer my life, my being, this walk, this day, to something greater than my own tired story. I inhale into the place in my chest from where I've cried so many tears. Tears of sorrow and of joy, tears of love—and the ache of letting go. I breathe in and feel my senses ripen; I exhale, grateful to be alive. Alive, *alive*, I am alive. I trust that I am guided, and I know I guide myself. Gravel presses indents into the soles of my shoes. Air brushes tiny secrets across the surface of my cheeks.

Kan! Yi ge laowai! "Look! A foreigner!" From the edge of my vision, I see two Chinese men standing on the hillside to my left, cameras slung around their necks, pointing my way. I don't acknowledge that I understand them. One cries to his companion with a slight tone of mockery, "The *laowai* has come to turn the prayer wheels! Hahlow! *Haah*-low!" he calls with exaggeration. I pretend I do not hear. Can't they see I'm praying? Or trying to, learning to. Join mind, body, breath—heart source, heart prayer. But now they are disturbing me, calling me out of my reverie, questioning my place here, just when I have finally been able to explain it to myself.

I keep walking. They drift into the distance. Yes, I am turning the prayer wheels today. I am joining the pilgrims at Labrang who cannot imagine the world I come from: the Westerners who flock in droves to see the Dalai Lama, the concepts of God I hold in my head, the loneliness of our people, the wealth of our homes. *I know my reasons for being here are so different from your own, and yet, I long to walk by your side. To look into your eyes without shield or guard, to smile at you with unembarrassed love, to know that beyond all thought and language there is a shared space we understand.*

I touch these wooden handles, the ones that so many have touched before. *Hand breath heart wheel body spinning:* one continuous motion.

19
Jiu Jiu

He doesn't recognize me until I call out, "Jiu Jiu!" Weaving through the crowded train station, I spot my uncle right away. He wears a thick puffy beige parka and a black knit stocking cap, and he peers anxiously through the crowd, his neck stretching out like a turtle. I wave and give him a hug. Here he is, in the flesh. The "black sheep" of our family.

"Ke Yi'an." He smiles and pats me on my back. The first time that anyone in China has called me by my Chinese given name. He looks older than I expected, something like my grandfather. "Jiu Ma is at school," he speaks to me in English. "We'll go pick her up and then go out to eat." He grabs my backpack and beckons me to follow as he hails a white minivan taxi. I nod, relieved not to have to navigate transportation by myself for a change, happy to follow someone's lead.

My uncle climbs in front next to the young driver, and I take my place in back. "This is my niece," he announces enthusiastically in Chinese, "visiting from America." The driver glances at me cautiously in the rearview mirror and nods. As we drive through the congested grey streets of Tianjin, my uncle rambles on to the driver about the traffic and the weather in a booming voice. He turns to me every so often to point out some landmark, then returns to further engage the driver. I stare out the window and listen as Jiu Jiu gives his opinion on everything without being asked. *This* is my Uncle Ted? He seems jovial and outgoing, if not a bit overbearing. No one I know in China ever talks this much to strangers.

Growing up, all I ever heard about Uncle Ted was that he was paranoid. I remember hearing that he had several locks on the door to his and Aunt Vicki's apartment in Iowa and that he kept a gun. Later, after he'd lived and studied in the States for many years, like the rest of his siblings, he and Vicki moved back to China and cut off contact with the family, leaving no forwarding address, and the adults more or less ceased to mention him. I think he and my grandmother had some kind of falling out, but I never understood the details. Something to do with him listening in on her phone conversations when he was living with her, maybe even threatening her with a knife. Something to do with money.

I'd never tried to contact Ted and Vicki before, even though they're my only relatives in China. No one, with the exception of my uncle David, who recently started doing business in Tianjin, had seen or talked to them in years—and it was my impression that this is the way Ted wanted it. Uncle David gave me their number and told me that my Aunt Vicki was now a professor at a prestigious university. He said they were doing well, yet I was still hesitant to call. David was a relative by marriage, not blood, I reasoned, so maybe it was easier for Ted to see him. I, on the other hand, am the daughter of Ted's older sister, a sister he hasn't spoken to in years. Would he want to hear from me?

I didn't call my aunt and uncle until after I reached Beijing (after visiting Xiahe, I went to Xi'an, and then headed east to the capitol). I wanted to wait until I was close enough that it wouldn't seem like I'd come all this way just to see them. But in a way, I had. Although I'd wanted to explore Beijing to see if it was a place I might want to come back to live and work someday, more than this, I'd hoped to visit my family. When I finally worked up the nerve to call, I spoke to my Aunt Vicki and she welcomed me warmly. My uncle would pick me up from the train station.

I wondered if I would recognize him. The last time I saw my uncle I was thirteen, visiting my grandmother in LA along with my family. It was a rare occasion when our entire family was present; the rest of them barely all got together except for when my mother came to town. All that I really remember of my Uncle Ted from that visit is his image in the family portrait that was taken. He stood in the back in a beige suit, the tallest person in the picture. His eyes were sad, his face long and sallow, his hair dark and greasy. Today, I wasn't sure what to expect from him; perhaps he'd still wear a somber expression. But when he calls out my name, Ke Yi'an!, he exudes warmth and enthusiasm.

心

After a fifteen-minute cab ride, we arrive on campus and go find my aunt in the science building.

"Ke Yi'an." She smiles and gives me a hug, then looks me up and down. "Welcome!" she says in English.

"*Xie xie, Jiu Ma. Hao jiu bu jian.*" Thank you, Auntie. It's been so long, I answer in Chinese. On one hand, I feel like I'm hugging strangers, especially since I rarely spent time with them as a child, but on the other hand, some body memory in me is being triggered with a childhood sense of the familiar. My aunt's face is round, her short hair dark and wavy. She is small and sturdy, dressed in a long sensible black skirt and a white lab coat, a flash of a red and green scarf underneath. Her students, also dressed in white lab coats, wander in and out of her office asking questions, greeting my uncle, and turning to greet me curiously, this surprise niece from America.

My uncle moves around Jiu Ma's office with familiarity, sitting at her computer to check e-mail, picking up papers from her desk, chatting with her students.

After my aunt finishes up her work, we head to a restaurant on campus. It's not even five o'clock and the large round banquet tables are almost empty. After ordering a large spread, we begin to talk, mostly in Chinese, liberally sprinkled with English. My aunt and uncle are pretty fluent, but I can tell they are rusty, and I'm happy to show them how much I can hold my own in Chinese. It is, after all, the language I've been living in for the last three years. I fill them in on what I've been doing, tell them about teaching and writing and Yizhong, tell them I want a break from China, but I may still come back here to work in the future. Their eyes light in surprise at the mention of my Chinese boyfriend, yet neither asks me any questions, perhaps out of politeness, when I tell them we've just broken up.

"Where would you live if you came back?" my aunt asks.

"I don't know, maybe Beijing or Shanghai, somewhere more international. I'm not sure, though."

"What would you do there?"

"Probably teach English, and write. Maybe be involved with art somehow." I have an idea about writing a book about Chinese artists and writers, but I don't feel like getting into this with them. Dish by dish, the food starts to arrive.

"With your language skills, you should go into business," my uncle says. "You should get a law degree, and then you could go into business with me and your aunt."

"Hmm." I try to act interested. "What kind of business are you in?"

"Pharmaceuticals." My aunt switches to English, spooning a couple of spareribs into my bowl.

"We're developing and testing a new drug right now," my uncle says, handing me their card. "I designed the logo." He goes on to talk about the need to set goals, have a plan, climb ladders, knock on doors. "You, with your mixed race, your fluency in Chinese, and with a law degree, you could throw bricks at the doors of any big corporation! You could make a lot of money. All you need is to know China and find a niche in the world market. Find a place here to make it, then become the exclusive representative to sell it . . . to Walmart, Costco, you name it. China is the place, anything is possible here. Money talks in this world, money talks."

My uncle continues to speak about America's declining economy, all the layoffs and downsizing. The way he goes on and on without waiting to hear my reaction, it's hard for me to imagine him calmly negotiating with business clients. I nod and listen, trying to disguise the fact that I have absolutely no interest in going into business, with or without them. My aunt, meanwhile, is quiet and collected. Beneath her silence, I sense a discerning judgment, taking everything in. If she is embarrassed by my uncle's rambling, she doesn't show it.

Finally, I find a pause to say something. "Actually, I'm not really interested in doing business. Maybe I'd like to be involved with cultural exchanges, like between artists and writers in America and China, but not business." In truth, even the prospect of coming back to start any kind of new life in China without Yizhong seems overwhelming right now, but I also can't imagine just walking away from this country, or from the progress I've made with speaking Chinese.

"You can do both," my uncle insists, jabbing at the air with his chopsticks. "You can work by day and write at night. You need to have a plan, a safety net. Few writers make their living writing, anyway. And most who have any talent are usually crazy." He breaks into cackling laughter, before his voice turns serious again. "Really, you should think about going into business with your aunt and me." My aunt nods in agreement. It's almost as if they've discussed this already.

I am growing annoyed, but I don't want to contradict them too strongly since they are my elders. Mostly, I hope that if I say little, my uncle will grow tired and change the subject.

After dinner, we go back to their apartment. They live in the teachers' accommodations on campus, on the sixth floor of a typical grey cement building block with run-down units. Inside, the floor is slick white linoleum tile, the couch and chairs a shiny dark wood, and the white walls bare except for a few framed Chinese watercolors. In the corner sits a tall white vase filled with bamboo stems and a small rock sculpture. Heat rushes through the vents in loud, rumbling whooshes. I am tired, and grateful for the warmth. In Chengdu, we didn't have central heating, so even though it didn't get as cold outside as it does here, we were always shivering and wearing hats and coats indoors.

"We don't have much room," my aunt apologizes, as she shows me to the guest room.

"It doesn't matter," I say. *Mei guanxi.*

The room is cluttered yet tidy, crowded with a bed, desk, dresser, wardrobe, and a few chairs and boxes tucked into the corners. It feels luxurious to spread out in bed that night, to have a whole room to myself, after spending the last month on the road. While traveling, people kept asking me what I was doing in China, and I still found myself saying, "I teach English and live with my Chinese boyfriend in Chengdu," rather than divulging my whole story to strangers. In part, this old persona still feels true; I no longer know another version of myself while in China, and I'm certainly no longer just a traveler. I miss Yizhong now more than ever, the reality of our parting finally sinking in.

Yet now, lying in the comfort of a private room, in a matter of hours I've been transported from the role of a lonely American traveler into a good Chinese niece visiting her aunt and uncle. I am surprised at how familiar they feel, how quickly we've fallen into these roles. Tonight, I am warm. I am safe. I am a guest in a relative's home.

心

In the morning I hear my aunt and uncle shuffling around the kitchen, then the sound of the door shutting. I sneak out of my room to make myself a cup of Nescafé, then climb back in bed to savor this time alone and write in my journal. A while later, I hear my uncle return and know that I should get dressed and join him. He is in their tiny kitchen scrambling eggs and frying sausage, which he wraps in a flour tortilla-like Chinese pancake with melted cheese. I wonder if this is his typical morning breakfast—after all, he'd lived in the States long enough to pick up Western habits—or if this is special, for me. He hands me a plate and we sit in the living room, switching between English and Chinese.

"Aunt Vicki is busy with her classes today, so we can walk around for a while, then visit her for lunch, then go out and tour Tianjin."

"Sure." I take a bite of my eggs. "Have you been up long?"

"Several hours. Every morning, I walk your aunt to her office, then come home, read some magazines. Then go back and bring her lunch."

I nod. I wasn't sure before, but it seems that only Jiu Ma works, and Jiu Jiu must help her with their pharmaceutical business on the side. As a teaching scientist, she's probably developing the drugs in her lab, while he goes around and networks. Jiu Jiu gets up and grabs a few magazines off the bookshelf to show me. They are American science magazines and he's been taking notes from them, he says. He talks about how he likes to watch travel videos, then starts rattling off statistics about population growth and world migration patterns, which somehow leads to a conversation about China's superiority, a topic I've grown used to while living in China.

"But do you ever miss living in the States?" I ask.

He shakes his head emphatically. "Too much crime. I gave up my

US passport. Jiu Ma still has hers. One of us needed to get a Chinese one for convenience. Anyway, I never want to go back to the US. China is going to become the number one power soon. Japan also in decline. No good." Then Jiu Jiu's eyes light up with mischief. "There's an episode of *Gilligan's Island* where a man said something about Japanese water torture and the other man said, *I don't know anything about Japanese water torture, only Chinese water torture. Japanese copy!*" He breaks into his cackling laughter as he delivers the punch line to his joke.

I smile and shake my head, wondering when the last time was he watched *Gilligan's Island.*

"Well, surely there are *some* things about America that are nice," I venture.

"Like what?"

"Like . . . the scenery, the natural landscape . . ."

"Scenery! Huh! You have to drive so far to get anywhere."

"Well, and the pollution here is bad . . ."

"Pollution! Do you know that 1.3 billion people live in China? That's one fifth of the world's population! America accounts for only four percent of the world's population but do you know how much of its resources it uses?"

"I know it's a lot."

"Thirty-three percent! If you want to talk about consumption and pollution . . ."

I don't have the energy to argue or match facts with him. I was just stating that the pollution here is bad; no one can deny this.

"So, if you *had* to say, what was your favorite part about America?"

He thinks for a moment. "When we lived in a college town in Missouri, we'd go out a lot, on drives, picnics . . . there was a place we'd go and gather pecans. That was nice."

"I didn't know you lived in Missouri."

"Oh, we lived all over America—Indiana, Missouri, Iowa, San

Francisco, Hawaii . . . mostly for Vicki to go to school. We went all over." He shakes his head. "Nothing so great."

"So when did you move to China?"

"In 1984 we came to Beijing. Then after Tiananmen, we went back to America and stayed in Los Angeles for a while. We came back here to Tianjin in 1994, when your aunt accepted her position at Nankai." He reaches over and absentmindedly brushes a piece of lint off my sweater.

"So what was your *least* favorite part about living in the US?"

A pause, then decisively, "Chicago. The black people. Gangs, people avenging deaths." He shakes his head in distaste. I try to imagine him as a young college student from Taiwan going to Northwestern.

Then he turns to face me, a wide serious expression in his eyes. "You have to be careful. If you are ever stranded in a car on the highway, don't get out or open the door for anyone. If someone comes up to the window, don't roll it down. Write on the window with lipstick, 'Call the police if you want to help me,' but don't get out. Do you understand?" I nod, though inside I am rolling my eyes. His paranoia reminds me all too much of my parents' constant admonishments ever since I was old enough to come and go on my own: "Call us when you get there!" "Did you wear your helmet?" And "Did you double-lock?" the moment I got home from anywhere, as if I could possibly forget what they'd long made sure was also my second nature.

I listen to my uncle as he continues to talk about America, about the Midwesterners who are so dumb they can't fry an egg on both sides without breaking the yolk, about the Mexicans with their six or seven kids per family, the Uni-bomber who lived naked in a cave yet kept his PhD diploma from Michigan, how Hainan is better than Hawaii, how all the Hong Kongers want to come build houses in Qingdao, how he has a signed copy of Deng Xiaoping's first collection of works.

I barely get a word in, but it doesn't matter. Jiu Jiu does not pause to see if I am following, or care about having a two-way conversation. I can understand why they might be drawn to stay in China if Jiu Ma has a good position with a university here and they are doing well in business. Here, they are advantaged because they speak English and have lived abroad, whereas in the US, no matter how good their English, they would always be immigrants experiencing racism, and living in a second tongue. But something about his extreme defensiveness of China and criticism of the US seems overcompensating. I can't help but feel that Jiu Jiu is trying to prove to me, or rather to himself, that he is happy here.

"Do you want to see my coin collection?" He gets up suddenly and stands on a stool, pulling down several albums from the top shelf of a large bookcase that also houses their TV. He has coins from all over the world—American silver dollars, European francs and marks, Japanese yen, but most of the coins are Chinese. Some go back to the Qin and Song Dynasties, he says.

"It's not age that determines their worth, though, it's how many were issued. My most valuable is from the Nationalist regime."

"Here." He pulls out a small gold coin on a gold-colored string and hands it to me. "You can have this."

"Really? Are you sure?"

He nods.

"Thanks." I turn it over in my hand.

"It's from the Han dynasty. See how it's so shiny? That's because the metal has oxidized. It's from 25 AD."

My mind can barely comprehend that date. I surely would've thought it was fake if I'd seen it in a store, yet I trust that my uncle knows his coins. I thank him again and hang it carefully around my neck. Every so often, as we continue to talk, I look down and admire the brilliance of the gold against my black turtleneck.

He keeps turning the pages, showing me his favorites.

"Here." He hands me two coins. "Give one to Ke Yi'ling," he says, referring to my sister. They are a dark tarnished metal, an inch and a half in diameter, grooved with characters and tinged turquoise, with a square hole in the middle.

"Are you sure? It's too much."

Again he waves his hand in dismissal.

"Thanks. When are these from?"

"From the Qing dynasty. But these are not as valuable. The really valuable ones I keep locked in a safe. Everything's locked in the bank. Here, what's to steal? Nothing. But still," he pauses, "I keep a machete just in case. Lots of burglars in China. You never know."

He looks at his watch. "We should go soon. I'll take you to the park, then we can meet Jiu Ma for lunch."

From their apartment, we walk across a busy road to a nearby park, where we take pictures with Jiu Jiu's old Polaroid. I smile and pose before the sparse vegetation, the rundown pagodas and protruding rock sculptures, then Jiu Jiu poses solemnly with a straight back and no smile. He eagerly waits for each photo to develop. The photos come out faded and tinted pink, looking aged before they've even dried. Jiu Jiu can't understand why; maybe the camera's fluid is too old, he ponders.

Afterwards, we meet Jiu Ma at a noodle and dumpling place on campus. She smiles and listens quietly as Jiu Jiu talks of this and that. Before we leave, she hands him a wad of cash, then Jiu Jiu and I head off in a cab to a tourist area that sells all kinds of Chinese knick-knacks—clothes, figurines, calligraphy, toys, vases, fake antiques. Jiu Jiu wants to buy me a chop—my Chinese name carved into a piece of stone. I protest at first, as I've been taught to do, but I like the idea. I've always wanted to get my own chop. We find a stand and I write my name. Jiu Jiu asks the man to carve it in an older-style script, then we walk around and shop while waiting for the man to finish. Jiu Jiu buys a bunch of slippers in different colors, on sale, and eight bags of beef jerky. I buy some beaded purses that he helps me bargain down

to five dollars apiece, chatting jovially with the salesgirl as if he knows
her, telling her I'm his niece from America. I've noticed already that
when we're around others, he'll make a point of speaking to me only
in English, his chance to show off his skills. I've also noticed how the
shopkeepers or waitresses call him "Lao Xiansheng," which is a term
of address usually reserved for old men. He does in a way seem like a
doddering old man, bumbling along, telling people things they probably don't care about, endearing in his lack of self-consciousness.

When an hour has passed, we go back to retrieve the chop. It
doesn't stamp very clearly; the cuts are too thin or maybe not deep
enough. But I like it all the same, the smoothness of the translucent
beige rectangular piece of stone, the soft pad of red ink that comes
with it, the square print that contains the curved elongated lines, the
image of my name. It feels right to finally have one before I leave
China, this signature of Chinese identity, this gift from a long-lost
uncle.

心

When I was a teenager, China was a mystery to me. I'd heard that
Ted and Vicki were living in Beijing when the Tiananmen protests
started in 1989, and the image of my aunt and uncle witnessing tanks
and bloodshed from some "third-world" apartment only confirmed
to me that they were strange. *Who would* choose *to live there if they
could live in America*, I wondered. I thought it must be related to Ted's
paranoia and desire to get as far away from our family as he could.
The names Ted and Vicki began to take on an ominous association.
Everything I knew about them was clouded in vagueness, cryptic
explanations offered to satisfy a child's passing curiosity. China was
not real to me then, and neither were they. But now, despite his oddi-
ties, I realize I have things in common with my uncle. Like him, I am
the only one in my generation to have come to live in China. And,

despite our other reasons for wanting to be here, we also both came here to break from our past roles or lives, to escape a more claustrophobic version of ourselves.

I've spent two days with them now, and I will spend just one more. It is a short visit, and in some ways I'd like to stay longer; after all, I am finding that I like my aunt and uncle, and that I can relate to Jiu Jiu's inquisitive spirit, his fondness of details, history, science, and old coins. He seems mentally more alive and youthful than many of my relatives back home. But I also don't want to overburden them, especially since they won't let me pay for anything or touch the dishes. And although we haven't talked much about our family, my visit must bring up old feelings in ways I can only guess.

After breakfast, my aunt and uncle announce that they want to buy me a new winter coat. My aunt hints not so subtly, "It's time you gave up some of your schoolgirl habits and started dressing more your age." The only coat I have with me is a moss green fleece jacket, my traveling clothes, but it's also true that my style has changed since I first arrived in China, and my wardrobe has not yet caught up with it. My uncle had already commented that he didn't understand why I was wearing that ugly thing, but I didn't take offense.

We spend a whole day shopping. Normally, I hate shopping in China—especially in the malls where the salesgirls swoop in like hawks if you let your eyes linger on an item. But my aunt shops with an authority and determination I don't possess. She knows what she wants, and the salespeople can be used, if necessary, but just as easily dismissed. I trail after her from display to display, floor to floor, mall to mall. I try on black wool coats of all lengths and styles, some knee length, some that come to just below the hips and tie with a sash, some cheap, some pricey; my aunt says cost is not an issue. She discourages me from one pea coat that is more masculine in style, and I shake my head at the more matronly or ultra-feminine ones that she holds up for inspection.

My uncle follows in the background, picking out his own contributions, commenting on stylish collars or cuts, nodding or shaking his head, every bit as opinionated about what a young lady should wear. Occasionally, he bursts abruptly into stores, asking the salesgirls what they think would look good on me, and I turn away, embarrassed. Finally, we end up in a semi-covered outdoor market filled with cheaper goods and shopkeepers who expect to haggle over their prices. When I try on my coat—long, fitted, and black with two rows of buttons and a narrow triangular collar—we all know it is the one. My aunt quickly bargains it down from 120 to 80 yuan—the equivalent of $10. I wear it home, feeling trendy and chic. We are all pleased.

That night, Jiu Jiu digs out some photos of my sister and me from when we were little. I barely remember his presence as a child, and yet, as I look at these photos, a part of me thinks I do. He tells me a story from when I was three years old. I was in my room playing with some rings. When he turned around, I went to hide them. He guessed where they were from the direction I'd gone, and found them easily under a pile of clothes. He brought them back to show me he'd found them, and my eyes grew wide with surprise. "*Yanjing da da.* This shows you are smarter than your sister," he says. "*Ke Yi'ling,* she would've just shouted, *Don't look at my rings!* Whereas you went and hid them."

I don't know if that makes me smarter, but more secretive perhaps. We continue to talk. Jiu Ma contributes an anecdote here and there, but mostly she just listens. When I mention that my parents now live in a house with a view of Lake Washington, Jiu Jiu's eyes grow wide, a look of surprise—or is it envy? Later, he complains about his siblings, how one is too argumentative, another too much in pursuit of luxury, another too conservative. He complains how my grandmother smoked when she was pregnant and that's why he and his brother have such bad skin. This is the first time he has mentioned her.

Slowly, I gather the courage to bring out the one photo I have with me of our extended family. It was taken in LA a year and a half ago at my grandmother's 82nd birthday celebration in a Chinese restaurant. Jiu Jiu puts his glasses on and holds it between two hands, staring intently. My aunt stands and peers over his shoulder. "They all look old," he says, referring to his siblings. "Is that Stephen?" he asks, pointing to the bulky teenager in back. Yes, I nod. Stephen, my youngest cousin, was a baby the last time he saw him, and is now a sophomore in high school.

In the middle of the photo is my grandmother. I've been afraid to bring her up, afraid to ask the questions I most want to ask.

Finally, I take a breath and ask, "What happened between you two?"

He shakes his head vehemently. "I *hate* her. To me she is already dead."

"But *why* do you hate her?"

Jiu Jiu's voice gets bitter and he leans forward in his chair. He tells me how selfish she was as a mother, how she'd rather go play mahjong than take care of her kids. His voice softens ever so slightly as he tells me how he was once my grandmother's favored child. How Gong Gong, my grandfather, used to hit my grandmother, and how he used to try and protect her. How he used to be loyal to her, and she to him.

Then he tells me how when he and Jiu Ma were living with her in LA, he'd go pick up Jiu Ma late at night from her school and they'd stay up late, talking and watching TV. My grandmother would come downstairs and see them laughing and having a good time and she'd get mad. "She doesn't like to see other people happy. It makes her happy when other people are unhappy like she is." Then one day he picked up the phone and heard his mother complaining about them. Something about how they hadn't paid their share of rent money. Later, he says, she told him, "I love the child best who has the most money."

My aunt and I sit silently, listening. I know my aunt must have heard this rant many times before, but I suspect it has not been triggered in a long time. Knowing my grandmother, I can almost imagine her saying such callous things in some moment of fury. But I also know the stories from my parents. How Ted would spy on, or even threaten her. How the same story is told by different people in different ways.

After a silence, I say, "But don't you think, after all this time, things could be different?"

"No," he says firmly, then stands and begins pacing the room. "There is no love in my heart for her, my heart is dead to her. If she were to come here looking for me, I'd move to Africa. I'd move across the world to get away from her!"

I choose my words carefully. "But you are obviously still so upset. Wouldn't it be better to try and talk to her? Or at least to talk to some of your siblings?"

"Your mom is okay. But the rest of them." He shakes his head with disgust.

"Why is the family like this?" I think of my mother and her siblings, the way they can all be so argumentative and easily stressed out. How little they all get together or talk. My mom occasionally talks on the phone to her sister, but rarely to her two brothers in Los Angeles and Taipei—and never to Ted in China.

"Why do all of you have such hot tempers? Why are you all so disconnected?" I ask.

"Why? Because *she's* at the center," my uncle spits, pointing at my grandmother's picture. "*That's* why."

A heavy silence follows before my aunt speaks up. "I think all of the children were probably emotionally disturbed."

I suspect she is right, that my mother and her siblings all experienced trauma as children, much more than anyone has ever shared with me, and maybe more than anyone even remembers.

"I think we could all use some sleep," my aunt suggests.

Getting ready for bed, I sit on the small plastic red stool in their bathtub and sponge myself with a washcloth and bucket of warm water. I started bleeding yesterday, and now my body aches and cramps in the way that it has begun to here in China, in a way that it never did before. Afterward, as I lie in bed, I begin to cry. I cry for my uncle and aunt, who are cut off from our family; I cry for my grandmother, estranged from her children; I cry for my mother and her siblings, who no doubt experienced violence and neglect; and I cry for my family, who does not know how to speak together openly of our love and our pain. I also cry for Yizhong, whose heart I have broken; I cry for his mother and father, who I never said goodbye to in person; and I cry for the scattering of friends I made in China—friends whom I may never see again, friends who didn't even know me that well, but friends whom I cherish all the same. I cry for these last couple of months of renewed loneliness, and I cry for all of the love that I carry and seek. Most of all, I cry for the silences, for all of our silences, and for all that I still have not yet learned how to say.

心

The morning of my departure, my aunt takes me aside in the hallway while my uncle is in the bathroom. "Ke Yi'an," she says, "I also used to think like you do. I used to think that he should try and make peace with the family. I tried for many years to get him to see things differently. But now, a lot of time has passed, and your uncle, he is doing better. I have a good job, we have our business, he has projects that keep him busy." Her voice begins to crack and she pauses and takes a breath. "He has some mental problems, so he can't work. I think this is the best way it can be."

Tears well in her eyes. She looks to see if I understand.

"He can be very cruel and forceful with his words but he doesn't mean them. He can't control himself. They come out all at once, out of nowhere, like spitting needles—*pa, pa, pa, pa, pa.*" Her lips mimic the sound of rapidly exploding gunfire. I nod. We are both crying now. I hug her.

Maybe she is right—maybe it is too late for reconciliation. After all, she is the one who's lived closest to this story; she would know. Perhaps the best thing for Jiu Jiu is to forget, to keep the wound buried, medicated, far away. To live out his life in relative ease and peace. To pretend that this chapter is closed and dead to his heart.

If I had more time, I might ask my aunt what she means by "mental problems." Does Jiu Jiu's illness have a name: is he bipolar, manic depressive, paranoid? I don't know how to say these things in Chinese, but my aunt surely would know how to in English. I'm not sure how long I would have had to stay with them for me to feel comfortable asking her such questions. Or maybe it would never feel okay, maybe these silences now belong solely to the private world of a husband and wife.

All I know is, as I stayed in their small humble apartment, I hoped that I could serve my family in some small way. My whole time in China I've struggled to prove that I am a part of this culture, but mostly I've felt my displacement, reminded each day of all the ways I do not belong. Yet now, unexpectedly, it is my aunt and uncle, the outsiders of our family, who have made me feel welcomed, have fed and given me shelter, no questions asked, because I am family. Not some abstract "one big family" of the Chinese race, but immediate family, nuclear family, a group of people who are handed the same cellular legacy from generation to generation, the same trail of silences to ignore or to embrace.

20

How to Learn Chinese

Maybe I started too late. I should have learned as a child, should have listened to my mother when she sat me down with my sister on Sunday afternoons and made me copy a grid of characters, should have known I later would be thankful. Or at least, I should have studied more in college, but instead I first wasted my time with Russian, a language I've never used since, except to impress friends with a few phrases, like *Hello, my name is Anya, I love to drink vodka.*

In China, I thought I could learn on my own; no formal classes for me. Since I could speak some Chinese, but couldn't read or write, who knew at what level I'd belong. Now I think maybe I should've just forked over the money and become a foreign student. Instead, I made flashcards and copied characters over and over while sitting in cafés or at my desk. I practiced speaking with friends at bars, and most of all with Yizhong, all the while hungrily writing down new vocabulary in my notebook.

At first, this method of acquiring language was fruitful. Characters began to jump out at me on the streets, symbols that carried meaning amidst a sea of otherwise indistinguishable dashes and strokes. Soon I could even write a short letter to my grandmother in Chinese, making up for all those times on the phone when I could barely say more than I love you, *wo ai ni.* At this rate, I thought I could perhaps read a newspaper in a few years, which requires about 3,000 characters. Eventually, I could even interpret, translate, infiltrate—enter Chinese society on a level that was still restricted to me; I could join the domain of the educated and elite, bypass the official barriers and statements, and break through and make my way to the backrooms where the goods of true value are stored. I would prove I was here for the long haul, not like those expats who stay a few years and have their grand China adventure, yet never return. I wanted to get inside the *heart* of these people. To do this, I needed more words.

The dictionary was my bible. I carried it at all times, looking up words that popped into my head or that I heard spoken on TV or with friends. Language was a game, an elaborate puzzle of meaning, and each day I was winning, acquiring new expressions and passageways of connection. Mostly I copied characters, imprinting particular successions of strokes in my mind. But occasionally I stumbled upon gifts of surprise. Like the day I realized that the word for things, *dongxi*, was made up of the two characters for east and west, *dong* and *xi*. 東西 East + West = Things! And then there was *xin*, the word for heart in Chinese that I've known since I was a child. But now in the dictionary, I saw how *xin* could also mean mind, feeling, or intention, as well as center, middle, or core. Mind, heart, and center held together in one word. *Xin:* 心. To learn this was to know everything.

The problem was, I kept getting sidetracked. Quitting my job, getting caught up in relationships, and moving between cities and homes; I should have realized earlier how hard it is to make progress without a teacher. And then once I was settled in Chengdu with Yizhong, I mostly just focused on spoken Chinese, listening closely to conversations around me, writing down words I'd heard enough times to recognize but still didn't know their exact meaning. Later, I would look them up in my dictionary, and find the ones I was looking for out of context. But actually studying the writing of characters? This was too time-consuming. And the longer I was removed from the world of English, the more my time sitting down with pen and paper needed to be reserved for staying connected to *its* rhythms, devoting whole, uninterrupted days to documenting my life in China in a vocabulary that knew no restraint. And so, I abandoned learning characters for months at a time, then came back for brief periods of renewed discipline. Over three years passed in China starting and stopping like this, forgetting characters as quickly as I learned them. How did I expect to go deeper into this culture if I remained illiterate? I would forever be handicapped, one layer removed, relying on others for translations.

心

Ever since I've left China and returned to the States, I've vowed to be more fluent the next time I go back. I still want my life to be tied to China, for all these running starts not to be for nothing. To commit to Chinese is my promise to myself, to this country, to my friends, and most of all to Yizhong: *I will not forget you and all that you taught me.*

There were others I met who made great impressions, but it was only Yizhong I let myself be vulnerable with, Yizhong who honored me in a way that allowed me to better honor myself, and Yizhong whom I've stayed in touch with and still consider a dear friend, no matter how long it has been since we've spoken.

I never felt judged by Yizhong. I always trusted that he got the gist of my meaning, and more importantly, that he got the gist of *me*. Within the privacy of our relationship, Yizhong helped me to reclaim this language, to make it belong to me again, only this time as an adult. He allowed me to flounder and make mistakes without making me feel stupid or foreign. And he helped me to discover the part of me that had been cut off when I was young, alienated yet not extinguished. Yizhong helped me to bridge the child in me who knew and felt the Chinese language intimately, with the adult who now spoke hesitantly as a *hunxue*, as I tried to create a home for myself in China.

Now, in Seattle, I've found a teacher who is letting me audit her class at the university for free. Chinese 202 is held every morning at ten, Monday through Friday. Several hours of homework are assigned each night, and each week we are tested on a new list of characters. My spoken Chinese is better than that of most of my classmates—only a couple of them having Chinese blood or having spent time in China—but my characters are rusty. I have to study hard to catch up.

With relief I quickly discover that many characters are still familiar to me, stored in my memory, my fingertips moving from one stroke to the next. Every night I sit at my desk in my studio apartment with a cup of tea and copy down the week's list from the book, then test myself with note cards to make sure I can write them from memory. Studying characters can be tedious, but also meditative. It means hours of repetition, none of which requires too much thought. I can listen to music, even daydream, as long as my fingers are still moving, filling every inch of each notebook page, not bothering to stay in the lines. I imagine what it would look like to plaster my walls with these pages filled with the same words written over and over, in all directions. To an American, they might look exotic and intriguing; to a Chinese, I'm sure my characters would look crude.

Regardless of the quality of my penmanship, in America it is easier to accept without judgment my stunted, seesaw history of progress in this language, because here my yearning to communicate fluently is not tied up with the daily struggle to make a home. Removed from the context in which I most wanted to use this language, I can apply myself now with patience and discipline, and trust that my detours have all been part of the plan.

Every weekend, my mother helps me with my homework—a minimum of 500 words about anything, but I rarely stop at 500. I write about my life in China, my new neighborhood in Seattle, my grandmother in LA, the war in Iraq, meditation, friendships, the meaning of work, George Bush's reelection. Even though the ideas I express are simplistic, already I can say so much more than I could while I was living with Yizhong. Writing allows me to articulate my thoughts in a way that speaking can not. I can take my time to look up characters, string out sentences, rework and revise. A part of me feels redeemed for all those times in China when I settled for fragmented approximations, wild stabs at meaning supported by quick searches through dictionaries, hoping I'd chosen the right word. From America, I've e-mailed a few of these essays to Yizhong so he can see how much my Chinese has improved—and so that he can know more of me, more of everything I didn't know how to say. Yizhong, of all people, should have known that I was not as simplistic as my words in Chinese implied, and yet, how could he? How could anyone truly know the workings of my mind and my heart without the full capacity of my language?

In class, we are expected to learn both the traditional and the simplified characters, but we can choose to write in either. I choose simplified, since this is what they now use in mainland China, and what I studied while I was there. I choose simplified, even though I think it is stupid the way they've removed the heart radical from the word love. I write each piece by hand, composing most of my sentences in *Pinyin*, the romanization system for Chinese, so I can quickly transcribe the flow of my thoughts in Chinese before looking up each character in the dictionary. After several drafts, I hand my work to my mother to mark up with circles and arrows, questions, cross-outs, suggested revisions. When she is finished, I sit by her side at our old dining room table and we go over my mistakes.

My mother often curses the way the Communists butchered the Chinese language. *What's that character?* she asks. *What?! That's hui? How stupid!* Some of the simplifications she can understand; they make sense linguistically or are abbreviations that people have informally used for years. But some make no sense at all, she says. Some characters that were already relatively simple were further simplified, whereas other characters that were complex were left untouched. There is no obvious logic involved.

My mother also complains that my sentences are too long. *You can't write like that in Chinese*, she says. The problem is, I am still thinking in English, translating in my head as I write. When I argue with her about a phrase, she grows frustrated and insistent. I know she is proud that I am finally studying Chinese seriously, but since I am her daughter, she doesn't have to be patient or nice. *Don't yell*, I complain, my chest growing tight. *I'm not yelling*, she says, *I'm just trying to tell you, it doesn't make sense in Chinese. If you don't want my help, I have better things to do!* Of course, I can not afford for her to walk away; my teacher would wonder what happened to her star student. *Okay, okay. Let's finish*, I say. Taking a deep breath, my mother and I return to the troubling passage until we come up with a version we can both live with. It may be my writing, but it's still my mother's language.

I cannot expect her to understand exactly what I am trying to say, but she tries her best to come up with her own closest equivalent in meaning. As I bite my tongue and nod, feeling slightly defeated, I remember that long before I ever wanted to leave home and create a life for myself in China, it was my mother to whom I most wanted to belong, my mother I most wanted to please.

21

Learning to Speak

I.

As an infant, the first tones I heard were Chinese. The voice of my mother. The voice of my grandmother. The soft murmurs of the women who held me and rocked me and sang me to sleep. Soothed by their voices, I drifted in a world without language, and yet I was already learning the sounds of Chinese. The voices of my ancestors—passing again from mother to child—rising and falling, imprinting their memory in my cells.

English, the language of my father, was also familiar to me, but it was less prominent, somewhere on the periphery, connected to the world outside the intimacy of my home. In preschool I understood the language that floated around me, but I had little experience asserting myself within its midst. This world I was a part of and yet removed from. At first, my teachers were worried because I was so quiet. Then slowly I learned how to play and talk in English. One day my teacher happily reported to my parents that I had been caught with the other girls peeking into the boys' bathroom. It was a sign of progress. But I never stopped being quiet.

II.

After three years in China and living in America again for two, I finally attend my first overnight meditation retreat. When we break silence at the end of the weekend, I am surprised by the sounds of others' voices. How the pitch and inflections of the woman who sat next to me do not match the person I imagined when all I knew was her presence, the way she entered the room, took off her shoes, and settled onto a cushion to sit. Her speech feels too human, somehow intrusive, and I wonder if mine will sound this way too.

Once words are allowed, we feel pressured to speak. Nervous laughter, bristled edges of defense, or notes one octave too cheerful creep slowly back into conversations as we recall the task to assert who we are, to announce our individual selves, to form unique narratives and opinions. We return to old patterns, imitations of self, because words are worth more than quiet, or so we've been taught. Because too many in this world have stayed silent.

ル

But through silence I've learned how to listen. Through silence I can gauge when to speak. Through silence I can sense when a channel to exchange meaning is open, or when I am caught in a volley of empty rounds. In silence, I remember how to give and receive, let go of the need to have something to say, the urge to cast myself in relation.

Of course silence can also suffocate, settling in my chest like layers of silt, a sign that I have waited too long. I want to speak now more than anything. I want to share my voice, my heart, my deepest self with my family, with the world. I want to let myself love and be loved with my whole being—but it still feels more comfortable to stay hidden. A web of gauze winds circles around my face, even as heart song trembles through my body.

For years I've gone on, restraining, withholding. Yet the more I've learned to reveal, the less I can bear to hide. I am tired of being the quiet one, the one who bites her tongue to preserve the peace, to avoid the discomfort of confrontation. Slowly, steadily, a line has been drawn—a desire stretched taut across my throat, an old and tired seam splitting open.

III.

Mama, I know you have worried about what I am writing in this book. And trust me, I tried to leave you out. But how could I write a book about returning to China without writing, at least a little, about you?

Now, I have so many questions I want to ask you—about your childhood, about your parents, about your longing. Why didn't you ever tell me that Gong Gong used to hit Popo? Is it because you don't want to remember? I think you once told me about how you huddled in a cave while bombs dropped in Chongqing, but I am not sure now if I invented these details. It is always so hard to get the details from you. Maybe it was not you, but Popo who huddled in a cave, with you in her womb. Maybe in the end this is the same.

What other memories have you withheld or locked away from retrieval?

What other traumas informed you and your siblings' lives?

As I begin to conceive of the untold stories that you and Popo and so many generations of Chinese women have inherited and continue to pass on, it helps me to better understand my own sorrow. I used to wonder if the pain I felt came from a memory of past lives—which is possible, I still believe, however impossible to prove. But now I also see how this pain has come from my family, my bloodline, my ancestors. No, I've never suffered from abuse. But silence can be its own form of neglect. And like you, I have absorbed our family's history—whether fleeing a country in the midst of war, or going back further into China's long scrolls of famine, secrecy, denouncements, and betrayals.

Each of us have absorbed our mother's pain.

心

Mama, I want you to know that I have always known how much you love me. Despite what I may have missed from you, I recognize the tenderness of your gaze when we greet or say goodbye. Even if I still wish we could speak more intimately, I accept our relationship for what it is—your boundaries, my boundaries, and the small efforts we take to push beyond. I want you to know that I understand you, to the degree that I can, and I admire you and how far you've come. The first in your family to move to the States, the effort it took to earn a Masters and Phd and then to work for the city, all as an immigrant woman of color, writing in your second language.

Mama, you are my childhood idol: a smart, analytical, professional woman. Your closet lined with dresses, suit jackets, and heels. Your face painted on each morning—foundation, eyeliner, shadow, blush, and lipstick. Your high cheek bones, your confident banter. Your place at the front of the room in every exercise class. Your friendly, opinionated, not easily intimidated nature. So unlike my own introverted distaste for conflict; me, who would never yell at a customer service rep, but instead ask nicely and accept what I am told. I have always admired how unlike me you are. But I know, too, that there is a softer you, a weaker you, a tired you. A you who loves being out in nature, who loves to write calligraphy, to dance, to paint—whole other lives you might have imagined if you had been born into another time and place.

Maybe someday soon I can begin to ask you more about *all* of you. Not just the you whom I've imprinted or imagined.

ぃ

Mama, do you know what my dream is, most of all now? I want to present my true face to this world. I want to listen to people's stories, to help them find their voices and be able to sit with their feelings. I want to write my own stories and hold my own feelings. I want to be present and aware in my body, so I can learn to better witness other people's pain, to not become overwhelmed and turn away. I'm not sure what goals I will ultimately accomplish, what outward markers of success, but I do know, in my core, that this path I've chosen is vital. And as I think about my past, and your past, and Popo's past and beyond, I know I am carrying on our family's legacy, living out an unarticulated dream of being willing to witness and name what is.

22

Full Circle

Matthew had an intimacy with the land that I admired, an intimacy I craved for myself. The Pacific Northwest had always been a part of me—the yellow-orange maple leaves carpeting the ground in October; the smell of wet moss and cedar; the comforting presence of saltwater, never too far away. And yet, it wasn't until I left Seattle— first for those couple years in Minnesota, and later in China—that I realized how much I missed my home. Not just my family and friends, and not just speaking English again, but this physical landscape that was a part of me too.

Through Matthew, I began to imprint the names of native plants and trees, vegetation I'd grown up seeing but never studied closely, with names I could now rattle off, like salal, Oregon grape, and Indian plum. On our walks, he'd snap off stems of "pickle weed" (sea asparagus) from amidst the wetland grasses, or wild ginger root from the woods for me to taste. He also knew the calls of the birds that dwelled on or returned each year to the fifty acres on which he lived, whether winter wrens, great horned owls, or the melodic Swainson's thrushes whose song ushered in the lush spring of May. And Matthew knew how to watch the patterns of wind and water, whether out on the canoe or kayak that he kept on the bank near his cabin in the woods, or on his sailboat moored a couple miles away.

But more than anything, I loved how Matthew could hold my gaze and not turn away. How it felt like we could just keep going deeper.

I never told Yizhong the full story of what happened the summer I went back to Seattle. Mostly, I feared that my words could not do my love for him justice. I didn't want to reduce our break-up to a sexual transgression, yet I didn't know the word for catalyst. How could I possibly explain, in my awkward Chinese, that yes, I'd cheated on him with one person, but actually it was another with whom I might already be in love?

No, it was much easier, and kinder, I thought, to just explain the things about our own relationship that I had realized (or had always known) were incompatible. How our love or need for each other was imbalanced. How "my spirit needed more." As inadequate as these words were, it was the best I could do, and Yizhong accepted my explanations. I think he knew there was more I was not telling him, but he chose not to press me. And as time went on it became that much harder—or perhaps unnecessary, even cruel—to bring it up again and reopen the wound.

And yet, I always felt bad for not sharing the truth. He'd given me so much; why couldn't I offer him this decency? Because it was too hard, I told myself, to find the right words in Chinese, especially since I could barely find them for myself in English. Yes, I'd had an affair that summer with my co-worker Mark, and my body had come alive with a new hunger. But what was harder to explain was how I'd then run into Matthew, and how two men were waiting for me to choose between them upon my return from China. How would I have explained to Yizhong how I felt a future before me with Matthew, even though we had yet to kiss or spend more than a few days together? How would I have explained how I *was* sleeping with

Mark, but I didn't plan on dating him for long? I didn't want Yizhong to feel he could be replaced so easily by a fling, but I wasn't able to articulate what I sensed Matthew and I would eventually become. It was easier to say nothing.

I also never could have predicted that it'd end up taking several years before Matthew and I would finally be together. I'd thought that the thing with Mark would be over quickly once I came back from China, but he was persistent and our connection was heated; our bodies could not get enough of each other. Meanwhile, Matthew lived in Olympia, so it was harder to see him regularly. In his presence, I felt how guarded and jittery the last few years of urban, cloistered living had left me. His gaze rendered me naked as if there was no language to prop myself up behind; I tasted a new level of silence with him, a silence so rich that I feared to break its spell with any half-truths or unnecessary chatter. But Matthew could be so quiet and he asked me so few questions that our conversations could be awkward, especially over the phone. Although I too sensed the inevitability of our coupling, another part of me resisted its heaviness.

I didn't want to end things with Matthew, but it seemed he was done with me if I couldn't make up my mind, and a part of me was also relieved to let go of this big, heavy thing, laden with all of its unspoken expectations—like how he'd told me that night that he saw his wife in me. I spent the next few years in Seattle, living for the first time in my own apartment, studying Chinese, teaching ESL to Chinese immigrants, working as a nanny, and otherwise forging a new identity back at home in both English and Chinese. Throughout this time, I also kept dating Mark, even though I knew deep down I'd never marry him, just like in the beginning I'd known with Yizhong. The difference was, I never fooled myself this time into thinking that maybe it could work in the long run. In part this is because I couldn't forget Matthew. How he'd said to me, "You're shaking in your boots at being seen." And how my heart had hurt, literally hurt, for months after our break-up. How I'd massage my chest with the palm of my hand, pushing gently and rubbing slowly in circles.

I finally broke up with Mark two and a half years later, during the winter of 2005, right before I turned thirty. We had things we needed to learn with one another, but I was done betraying my intuition. Now, I could finally tell Matthew how I'd felt this whole time. We'd spoken maybe twice over the last two years, although we'd never really addressed what had happened. And yet, I had always hung on to the idea that maybe, just maybe, we could still be together someday.

When I called Matthew to tell him I was available again—and had never stopped feeling heartbroken over our breakup—he was surprised but didn't react with much telling emotion. About a week later, he told me he broke it off with his girlfriend; he'd felt for a while like they were nearing their end. We made plans to see each other the next week in Seattle. Although we couldn't speak yet about what had happened—and what was happening now—we both knew it was finally our time. Wherever this choice might lead me, I knew it was the next right thing to do.

ا۟ى

Throughout this period, Yizhong remained an important friend. We talked less and less, but still called each other once every couple of months, or at least e-mailed. He knew about Matthew, but not about our earlier saga. It felt okay now to acknowledge I was with someone new, for he himself was married to an English woman and they had a two-year-old daughter. I wanted Yizhong and Matthew to meet each other someday, to know these other parts of my life, and thus these other parts of me. I also wanted to know what Yizhong's new life was like. So a year after I moved into the cabin with Matthew, the summer that we got engaged, I invited Matthew to fly to England with me for two weeks in July.

I imagined that I might finally confess more to Yizhong while on the trip, get a chance to talk to him about what had really happened when I'd returned to Seattle that summer. But their house was small, he was a tired parent, and it proved hard to get more than a few minutes with him alone. Not to mention the fact that it was weird, because when all of us were together, he now spoke to me in English, something we had never done before, save for a few casual lessons. I could tell he was nervous, and since Matthew and his wife couldn't speak Chinese, Yizhong was probably speaking English out of courtesy to them, but it still felt odd and made me sad for this new layer of distance between us.

My last chance to talk to Yizhong came during our last few days together when we all drove to WOMAD, an annual world music festival held out in the countryside. But with his two-year-old in tow, I barely ended up seeing him, so Matthew and I mostly roamed on our own. On the final night, Yizhong was outside their tent smoking a cigarette when we got back to ours, and I knew this was my last chance to speak with him. "I'll come in in a few minutes," I said to Matthew and he nodded and crawled inside our tent, while I sat down next to Yizhong.

"Can I bum a drag of your smoke?" I asked him in Chinese, unwilling to speak to him in English when it was just us.

"*Dangran.*" Of course, he said, handing it over. We passed the cigarette back and forth a few times, before I worked up my rusty vocabulary.

"There's so much I want to say to you, but our time together has been so short. And my Chinese is so bad."

"*Meiyou! Wo de yingwen bu hao.*" No, my English is so bad! "*Duibuqi.*" I'm sorry, he apologized. "I'm so busy with raising a kid. It takes a lot of time. I'm so tired all the time."

"You don't need to apologize." I shook my head. "But . . . I want to tell you, I'll always be thankful for you and your friendship. I will always love and care for you." My voice cracked. Tears ran down my face.

"I, too, will always love you, Anne. You mean so much to me."

I leaned forward and took his hand.

"When we were in Chengdu, you were so good to me. I'll never forget our time together, all you taught me. Thank you." *Xie xie ni.*

"It was you who taught me things, Anne. You don't need to thank me."

"No matter where our lives take us, I hope we can always be friends," I said.

"I hope so, too."

I felt hopeful for Yizhong, even though life was hard right now as he was learning to raise a child, struggling to learn English, and to fit in to a new culture. Nevertheless, he had set up a studio, and although he couldn't yet paint anywhere near as much as he wanted to, his work was evolving with a new freedom and intensity—darker colors, more layers and raw brushstrokes, and more nudes with provocative poses or expressions. I had faith that someday his paintings would receive the acclaim they deserved, and I was grateful that he, too, was no longer living in Chengdu. That he could experience life somewhere where government censorship and a tight moral code of social relations were not so ingrained into the daily fabric of his existence, and where the sky was not so grey and oppressive.

It was late. I'd shared the most important thing I'd come here wanting to express: my love for him, my gratitude. And I'd also reminded him that I was working on my book again, my book about the time that I spent in China. I asked once again if it was okay for me to write sensitive details about him, about us, and he gave me his blessing. He didn't even ask me what I meant by sensitive; he trusted me. I hope that my words will not let him down. Maybe they will illuminate some silence that he too always knew but couldn't name.

Now, all those details of what happened during the summer I left

China felt like old news, a past life, maybe no longer even relevant. He had a wife and child; I was engaged. We were both forging new lives, loving new people. They said they wanted to come visit, but tickets are expensive, and lives are busy. I was grateful he could at least meet Matthew, and hear a taste of who I was in English. And I got to witness Yizhong as a loving father, as a Chinese man in England, and as a husband to a woman who was warm and accepting of our presence. Finally, I also got to meet their beautiful Chinese and English daughter. A girl whose mixed-race *hunxue* story of growing up between cultures and languages will no doubt carry traces of my experiences, but also be entirely her own.

Afterword
To Be Radical

When you hear the word radical, you may think I mean something extreme, on the fringe, demanding a complete overhaul or extraordinary change.

But the original Latin meaning of radical is: *of, relating to, or proceeding from the root.*

To be radical is to be rooted in your essential nature.

To be radical is to know your origins.

To be radical is to listen for what each moment reveals.

To be radical is to know when to withhold, and when you must finally speak.

Acknowledgments

This book has been such a long time coming, going through so many stages of gestation, hibernation, revision, and rebirth. Part of the long journey toward publishing a book involves becoming a braver person. I wish I could thank every one of you who has come across my path over the last twenty years, offering me courage, kindness, and grace.

I especially want to thank "Yizhong" for being my opening into living inside of Chinese again, for remaining my friend for all of these years, and for your love.

The first seeds of *Heart Radical* were planted when I discovered freewriting and learned to call myself a writer, in large part thanks to Natalie Goldberg's books. Her guidance from afar helped me to trust in my path as a writer, and to embrace writing as a practice that I could always claim and know.

I also want to thank my many teachers—too many to list—from Ms. Pruzan in 2nd grade, to Ms. Tegenfelt in 4th, to Mr. Levinson in 9th: you nurtured my seeds of creativity and called forth the writer in me before I could name her myself. Thank you, too, to my professors at Evergreen: Bill Arney, Olivia Archibald, and the late Doranne Crable. And to my mentors from Antioch: Hope Edelman, David Ulin, and especially Sharman Apt Russell and Brenda Miller, thank you so much for your guidance and feedback. Chunman Gissing, thank you x1000 for welcoming me into your Chinese class and home, helping me to feel even more connected to my other mother tongue. And thank you to Ani-la, to the Dalai Lama, Thich Nhat Hanh, and to my grandma, the late Florence Kellor.

To those who took me in while I was in China and Tibet—my Uncle Ted and my late Aunt Vicki, Uncle James, Tamara, Xie Ping, Yizhong's parents, Rongjie, Xinmin, and so many more who showed me kindness, thank you for welcoming me as kin. And to those who gave me a space to housesit and write when I came home, especially Carrie Kalina, thank you so much as well.

I am forever grateful to the late Frank and Els, who were instrumental in making my journey possible, through their financial support and their legacy of travel, writing, and seeking that was modeled to me since I was young. And I am indebted to the Duwamish and Coast Salish people, upon whose stolen land this book was mostly written.

This book would also not be what it is today without the help of Anne Geissman Canright. Thank you so much for being my most dedicated reader. I am incredibly grateful for the time you put into skillfully editing so many drafts. Thank you too to others from Antioch; if we are still in touch, I am grateful. I am especially grateful to Susan Southard, Christin Taylor, and Khadijah Queen: thank you so much for all of your generous love and support.

Writing a book takes a village, and each small success or support I encountered gave me the confidence to keep going, even when I wanted to give up. Thank you to Angela Jane Fountas for publishing one of my first pieces in the anthology *Waking Up American: Coming of Age Biculturally*. Thank you to Nancy Canyon for your feedback on an early draft. To Samar Abulhassan, thank you for your encouragement. To J.T. Stewart and the Jack Straw residency, thank you for the push to write "Searching for the Heart Radical" and a version of

"How to Learn Chinese," and for giving me a mic and a stage. Thank you to the editors at *Fourth Genre* for publishing "Popo"; to the *Los Angeles Review* for publishing "Walls"; to *Blue Lyra Review* for publishing "Sky Burial"; to *Raven Chronicles* for publishing "Merging"; to *Stone Table Review* for publishing "Pilgrim's Path"; to *Duende* and *Out of Many: Multiplicity and Division in America Today* for publishing "Learning to Speak". And an enormous thanks to everyone at Hedgebrook, 4Culture, and to Carolyn Maddux and the board at Hypatia-in-the-Woods for the invaluable time, space, and moral support that your awards gave me to keep on, keeping on.

In this final leg of my book's journey, I want to thank Cheryl Strayed: to receive your words of praise buoyed me in a way I needed more than I knew. And thank you to Lisa Bowden and Kore Press for making this connection possible. Thank you Jill Rothenberg for your help with my synopsis. Thank you to E.J. Koh, Joyce Chen, Nikkita Cohoon, Kristen Millares Young, and Stacy Scheel Hirsch for your time and support. And a huge thank you to Brooke Warner, Lauren Wise, and everyone at She Writes for empowering women writers. And to Sharon Ho Chang, for your books and inspiration. To Grace Loh Prasad, Grace Hwang Lynch, and Jen Soong, thank you for our memoir sisterhood. To Kelly Martineau, Mary Pan, Jenne Hsien Patrick, and Jill Currie, thank you for being my finest readers and sisters in writing. To Heather Jacobs, thank you so much for your gentle listening and keen editing eye, and for helping me to get to the finish line! To Rosalie Morales Kearns, thank you for all of your help. To Dave, thank you for your support and love. And to Carol, thank you for guiding and witnessing me.

I also must thank my oldest and dearest. To my sister, Shelley, thank you for being one of my early readers, and for holding me up for so long. To my dear Amy Selena, thank you for all of the years of spiritual friendship and love. To lovely Jess, thank you for always being there for me. To beautiful Heidi, thank you for the witnessing, support, and for your home in the woods. To Kristin, thank you for the many years of friendship. To sweet sister Ellen, thank you for the intimacy of all we share. To Matthew, thank you for the many years of partnership, love, and growth. To Cedar, thank you for being born; I love you always! To Popo, my family, and all of my ancestors, thank you for trusting me with our story, even if you didn't choose for me to tell it. And to my parents, I am forever grateful for all of your love, support, and belief in me.

Finally, thank you so much to my Seattle and online communities, to the Hugo House, to the Binders and the Booketeers, to my fellow Shapeshifters, and to the many wonderful students and friends who have helped me grow as a teacher, writer, and human being—you are too many to name here, but please know you are each precious to me. In your presence and partnership in truth-telling, vulnerability, and courage, I have strengthened my voice in a vital way. Here's to speaking our truth in whatever timeline it takes for us to arrive at the version we need to hear.

May you all know how loved and cherished you are.

谢谢你

About the Author

Anne Liu Kellor was born and raised in Seattle. Her essays have appeared in *Longreads, New England Review, Seventh Wave, Witness, Fourth Genre, Entropy, The Normal School, Vela Magazine, Literary Mama,* and many more. She earned her MFA from Antioch University Los Angeles, and is the recipient of fellowships from Hedgebrook, Seventh Wave, Jack Straw Writers Program, 4Culture, and Hypatia-in-the-Woods. Anne works as an editor and coach, facilitates writing retreats, and teaches creative nonfiction workshops at the Hugo House and beyond.

SELECTED TITLES FROM SHE WRITES PRESS

She Writes Press is an independent publishing company founded to serve women writers everywhere. Visit us at www.shewritespress.com.

How Sweet the Bitter Soup: A Memoir by Lori Qian
$16.95, 978-1-63152-614-5
After accepting an exciting job offer—teaching at a prestigious school in China—Lori found herself in Guangzhou, China, where she fell in love with the culture and with a man from a tiny town in Hubei province. What followed was a transformative adventure—one that will inspire readers to use the bitter to make life even sweeter.

At the Narrow Waist of the World: A Memoir by Marlena Maduro Baraf
$16.95, 978-1-63152-588-9
In this lush and vivid coming-of-age memoir about a mother's mental illness and the healing power of a loving Jewish and Hispanic extended family, young Marlena must pull away from her mother, leave her Panama home, and navigate the transition to an American world.

Accidental Soldier: A Memoir of Service and Sacrifice in the Israel Defense Forces by Dorit Sasson $17.95, 978-1-63152-035-8
When nineteen-year-old Dorit Sasson realized she had no choice but to distance herself from her neurotic, worrywart of a mother in order to become her own person, she volunteered for the Israel Defense Forces—and found her path to freedom.

Learning to Eat Along the Way by Margaret Bendet
$16.95, 978-1-63152-997-9
After interviewing an Indian holy man, newspaper reporter Margaret Bendet follows him in pursuit of enlightenment and ends up facing demons that were inside her all along.

Nothing But Blue by Diane Lowman $16.95, 978-1-63152-402-8
In the summer of 1979, Diane Meyer Lowman, a nineteen-year-old Middlebury College student, embarked on a ten-week working trip aboard a German container ship with a mostly male crew. The voyage would forever change her perspective on the world—and her place in it.